# FROM FARMYARD TO CITY SQUARE? THE ELECTORAL ADAPTATION OF THE NORDIC AGRARIAN PARTIES

# From Farmyard to City Square? The Electoral Adaptation of the Nordic Agrarian Parties

*Edited by*
DAVID ARTER
*Nordic Policy Studies Centre*
*University of Aberdeen*

LONDON AND NEW YORK

First published 2001 by Ashgate Publishing

Published 2017 by Routledge
2 Park Square, Milton Park, Abingdon, Oxfordshire OX14 4RN
711 Third Avenue, New York, NY 10017, USA

First issued in paperback 2017

*Routledge is an imprint of the Taylor & Francis Group, an informa business*

Copyright © David Arter 2001

All rights reserved. No part of this book may be reprinted or reproduced or utilised in any form or by any electronic, mechanical, or other means, now known or hereafter invented, including photocopying and recording, or in any information storage or retrieval system, without permission in writing from the publishers.

Notice:
Product or corporate names may be trademarks or registered trademarks, and are used only for identification and explanation without intent to infringe.

**British Library Cataloguing in Publication Data**
From farmyard to city square? : the electoral adaptation of
    the Nordic agrarian parties
    1.Political parties - Scandinavia 2.Scandinavia - Politics
    and government - 1945-
    I.Arter, David, 1944-
    324.2'48'087

**Library of Congress Control Number:** 2001089131

ISBN 13: 978-1-138-25829-7 (pbk)
ISBN 13: 978-0-7546-2084-6 (hbk)

# Contents

*List of Figures* vi
*List of Tables* vii
*Notes on Contributors* xi
*Preface* xiii

1  The Swedish Centre Party: The Poor Relation of the Family?
   *Anders Widfeldt* 1

2  The Norwegian Agrarian-Centre Party: Class, Rural or Catchall Party?
   *Dag Arne Christensen* 31

3  The Finnish Centre Party: A Case of Successful Transformation?
   *David Arter* 59

4  The Danish Venstre: Liberal, Agrarian or Centrist?
   *Jørgen Goul Andersen and Jan Bendix Jensen* 96

5  The Icelandic Progressive Party: Trawling for the Town Vote?
   *Gunnar Helgi Kristinsson* 132

Conclusion
*David Arter* 162

# List of Figures

| | | |
|---|---|---|
| 2.1 | Employment in Agriculture and the Population in Urban Areas in Norway, 1950-1990 | 32 |
| 2.2 | The Norwegian Centre Party's Electoral Support, 1936-1997 (%) | 42 |
| 2.3 | The Amount of Space in the Agrarian-Centre's Manifestos Devoted to Regional Policy, Environment and Agriculture, 1945-1989 (%) | 45 |
| 2.4 | The Norwegian Centre Party's Support in Rural and Urban Communes | 50 |
| 3.1 | The Finnish Centre Party Organisation in 2000 | 82 |
| 4.1 | Class Cleavages in Denmark around 1900 | 102 |
| 4.2 | Party Membership of Venstre and the Social Democrats, 1947-1999. Number of Members | 114 |

# List of Tables

| | | |
|---|---|---|
| 1.1 | Swedish Agrarian/Centre Party Participation in Governments, 1936-1994 | 5 |
| 1.2 | Swedish Agrarian/Centre Party Election Results, Parliamentary Elections 1921-1998 | 8 |
| 1.3 | Swedish Agrarian/Centre Party Membership, Selected Years, 1930-1998 | 13 |
| 1.4 | The Social Composition of the Swedish Centre Party Vote, 1960-1998 | 14 |
| 1.5 | Party Vote of the Swedish Farmers, 1960-1998 | 15 |
| 2.1 | Space Devoted to Agriculture Relative to Industry in the Manifestos of the Norwegian Agrarian/Centre, 1957-1985 | 46 |
| 2.2 | Income from Sales and State Subsidies as part of Net Farm Income, 1959-1985 (%) | 47 |
| 2.3 | The Norwegian Centre Party's Voter by Occupation, 1957-1997 (%) | 49 |
| 2.4 | The Primary Sector Vote by Party, 1965-1997 | 51 |
| 2.5 | Norwegian Centre Party Membership, 1961-1997 | 52 |
| 3.1 | The Average Agrarian Poll in Norwegian, Swedish and Finnish General Elections, 1919-1962 | 62 |
| 3.2 | The Economically Active Finnish Population by Industry, 1950-1970 | 66 |

| | | |
|---|---|---|
| 3.3 | The Economically Active Finnish Population by Occupation in 1990 | 70 |
| 3.4 | The Finnish Centre Party's Performance in General Elections, 1966-1999 | 71 |
| 3.5 | The Finnish Centre Party's Participation in Government, 1966-2000 | 73 |
| 3.6 | Membership of the Main Finnish Parties, 1945-1995 | 84 |
| 3.7 | The Changing Nature of the Finnish Centre Party's Support Base, 1948-1991 | 87 |
| 3.8 | Party Support by Economic Activity in Finland in June 2000 | 87 |
| 3.9 | Support for the Three Main Finnish Parties by Region at the 1999 General Election | 89 |
| 3.10 | The Finnish Centre Vote by Types of Commune in 1999 | 90 |
| 4.1 | Danish MPs by Profession, 1850-1876 | 99 |
| 4.2 | Estimation of the Danish Parties' Share of Votes in Urban Areas, 1903-1926 | 105 |
| 4.3 | The Distribution of Votes at Danish Parliamentary Elections, 1920-1998 | 106 |
| 4.4 | Venstre's Electoral Support in Three Regions (%) | 109 |
| 4.5 | Venstre's Participation in Government, 1950-2000 | 112 |

| | | |
|---|---|---|
| 4.6 | Party Choice Among Danish Farmers, Selected Years 1964-1998 | 115 |
| 4.7 | The Occupational Composition of Support for Venstre, 1964-1998 | 117 |
| 4.8 | Family Background and the Composition of the Venstre Vote in 1994 | 118 |
| 4.9 | Support for Venstre by Occupation, 1964-1998 and for the Conservatives in 1984 | 119 |
| 4.10 | Support for Venstre and the Conservatives in Selected Occupations, 1964-1998 | 120 |
| 4.11 | Support for Venstre within Selected Groups. Deviance from Election Result, in Percentage Points | 122 |
| 4.12 | Self-Placement on a Left-Right Scale from 1 (left) to 10 (right) | 123 |
| 4.13 | Images of the Parties' Placement on a Left-Right Scale from 1 (left) to 10 (right) | 125 |
| 4.14 | Policy Image of Parties: Location on a Scale from -100 (right/new right) to +100 (left/new left), on Various Dimensions, 1998 | 126 |
| 5.1 | Possibilities for Forming Two-Way Coalitions without the Progressive Party in 1946-1999 and Seats in Excess of Effective Majority | 149 |
| 5.2 | Icelandic Progressive Party Share of Votes and Seats, 1916-1999 | 151 |
| 5.3 | The Progressive Party's Vote by Socio-Economic Group, 1983-1999 (% of total group vote) | 153 |

| | | |
|---|---|---|
| 5.4 | Urban and Regional Components in the Progressive Party's Vote, 1959-1999 (%) | 154 |
| 5.5 | Support for the Progressive Party according to the Composition of the Government in the Foregoing Electoral Term, 1953-1995 (% of valid votes) | 155 |
| 5.6 | Mean Issue Positions in 1999 by Respondents' Party (1=strongly agree, through 5= strongly disagree) | 156 |
| 6.1 | The Proportion of the Economically Active Population Employed in Agriculture in the Nordic Countries in 1920 (%) | 165 |

# Notes on Contributors

**Jørgen Goul Andersen** is Professor of Political Sociology in the Department of Economics, Politics and Public Administration at the University of Aalborg. In recent years he has written widely on voting behaviour and political attitudes in Denmark, along with the challenges facing the welfare state. His research interests include electoral behaviour, political participation and citizenship.

**David Arter** is Professor of Nordic Politics and Director of the Nordic Policy Studies Centre at the University of Aberdeen. He has written extensively on various aspects of Scandinavian and European politics. His recent published research has examined the regionalisation process in Northern Europe, perceptions of parliamentary change in the region and a study of the Finnish Committee for the Future.

**Dag Arne Christensen** presently holds a post in the Ministry of Local Government and Regional Development in Oslo. His doctoral thesis from the University of Bergen, published in 1998, analyses the EU policies of the left-socialist parties in Scandinavia. He has published several comparative articles on Scandinavian party politics

**Jan Bendix Jensen** completed his undergraduate studies in the Department of Politics at the University of Aarhus and is presently engaged in doctoral research at the University of Aalborg. His main interests lie in the fields of electoral studies and the welfare state in comparative perspective.

**Gunnar Helgi Kristinsson** is Professor of Government at the University of Iceland. He completed his doctoral thesis at the University of Essex on the farmers' parties of Iceland, Norway and Sweden. He has published on many facets of Icelandic politics, particularly in the area of public administration. He is presently undertaking a study of local government performance in Iceland.

**Anders Widfeldt** gained his doctorate in 1997 from the University of Göteborg for a thesis examining party membership in Sweden since 1960.

He is presently lecturer in Nordic politics at the University of Aberdeen. His recent published work has dealt with the representativeness of Swedish parties, the populist Right in Scandinavia and the public funding of political parties.

# Preface

In his path-breaking work on the catchall 'people's party' in the mid-1960s, Otto Kirchheimer made it clear that because of their defence of a specific clientele, agrarian parties could not become catchall parties. But could the distinctive family of Agrarian Parties in Sweden, Norway and Finland, re-designated Centre Parties in the 1950s and 1960s, be expected to do any better? And what of those parties – *Venstre* in Denmark and the Progressive Party in Iceland – that emerged primarily to promote agricultural interests, even if they were not class parties by name? Accordingly, the basic research question in this volume is: 'How successful have the Nordic agrarian parties been in their attempt to transform themselves from class parties to broad catchall parties drawing significant support from voters engaged in the non-primary sectors of the economy?' The study therefore focuses on *electoral adaptation* – that is, the redefinition of party identity – and *institutional modernisation* – that is, the development of new policies, programmes and strategies. It aims to provide a detailed profile – presently not available in any language – of an historic group of parties, with distinctive strength in the Nordic region, as well as to attempt an assessment of the process of *party change*. Edited volumes have covered social democratic parties (extensively), liberal parties and conservative parties but, curiously, not agrarian-centre parties. It is hoped that the present collection will remedy this omission and provide a text of interest to Scandinavians, comparativists more generally, as well as the increasing body of scholars specialising in political parties.

The individual chapters, covering the agrarian parties in all five Nordic states, are structured in four main parts. The first focuses on the process of the emergence of the parties. There is an examination of the political and socio-economic conditions at the time of their inception, the particular party's links, if any, with agricultural producers' organisations, the nature and regional distribution of its support base (whether based on independent family-sized farms, larger farmers, crofters etc) and fluctuations in its support. How relevant was the Lipset and Rokkan model for the emergence of strong agrarian parties to the particular country in question? Moreover, did the individual party advocate measures of agricultural protection or free trade? Then there is the interesting issue of *persistence*. Indeed, it might be argued that it was not so much the emergence of farm-specific parties in the Nordic region that was distinctive – peasant parties arose across central and eastern Europe in the period before and after the first world war. Rather, it was the fact that they persisted until the late 1950s in Sweden and Norway and until 1965 in Finland. Why? (Agrarian-peasant parties have re-emerged across post-communist Europe, *inter alia* in Poland, Hungary and Croatia, but that is another story.) In this first section there is also a discussion of the 'relevance' (in Sartori's terms) of the farmers' parties – their involvement in government and in strategic legislative coalitions. Finally, there is an assessment of the role of agrarian parties in relation to such key issues as state-building, land reform, welfare development, constitutional change and, of course, war.

The second section in each chapter involves a detailed analysis of the process of programmatic renewal and/or change of name (Denmark emerges as a deviant case). What were the root causes of modernisation and when did it happen? In the Finnish case, for example, the change of name was first mooted in 1950, but took a decade and a half, and a change in the leadership, to be realised. What was the time-scale elsewhere and to what extent did accelerated industrialisation, urbanisation and rural depopulation prompt an internal party debate about a suitable response? Was there unanimity on the way forward or did modernisation divide the party? Who were the personalities on both sides of the argument? And what were the objectives it was hoped would be achieved?

The third section in the country chapters considers the evolution of the modernised parties from their change of name/strategy to the present. It covers the main development points including electoral performance, governmental participation (with whom and with what results?) and the organisational strength/weakness of the party. When were the significant turning points in the recent history of the party? Moreover, how far has the modernised party been a 'genuine pivot party' in the sense of meeting the three necessary conditions for such parties set out by Hans Keman: that they occupy the centre space in the party system; possess centrality in terms of programmatic identity distinct from left and right; and play a dominant role with regard to government formation and the policy-making process. In short, they are able to bargain with parties of both left and right.

The final part of each chapter may be regarded as the crucial section. It involves a presentation of electoral data and an in-depth analysis of a) the social composition of the former agrarian party vote, b) the political cohesion of the main social classes – farmers, workers, salaried employees etc, c) the regional distribution of party support. The focus here is very much on the last decade, especially given the extensive volatility affecting the electorates of the former agrarian parties and their wildly contrasting fortunes at the polls. Why, for instance, has electoral adaptation appeared to be more successful in Finland when compared with Norway and Sweden? And what of Iceland and Denmark? There is also an analysis of the new party programmes and a consideration of the extent to which parties have become (too) closely associated with particular controversial questions. What has been the strategy for expanding their electoral appeal? According to Kirchheimer, 'National societal goals transcending group interests offer the best sales prospect for the party intent on establishing or enlarging an appeal previously limited to specific sections of the population'. What sort of national goals have been emphasised? Furthermore, what has been the attitude of the respective parties to European integration? Above all, are they still class parties or have they transformed themselves into catchall parties with a secure future into the new millennium?

The volume brings together a group of notable country experts. The first three chapters, which are presented in the order in which the parties changed their names, concentrate on the Agrarian-Centre Parties in Sweden, Norway and Finland respectively. My colleague, Anders Widfeldt, has contributed the Swedish chapter, Dag Arne Christensen the Norwegian, whilst I have written on the Finnish case. Jørgen Goul Andersen and Jan Bendix Jensen combined forces in analysing the Danish *Venstre* and last, but not least, Gunnar Helgi Kristinsson has profiled the Icelandic Progressive Party. My conclusion attempts to draw the threads together and to make some general observations regarding the electoral adaptation of the Nordic agrarian parties.

I am hugely grateful to all the contributors. Electronic communication both facilitated and expedited the editorial process, but my 'nit-picking' queries were doubtless enough to try the patience of Job. Happily, we are all still on cordial e-mail terms, something which is clearly testimony to the tenacity of Scottish-Nordic academic co-operation! I should also like to add my thanks to Janet Michaelsen for doing the formatting work on the book in her usual, efficient way. The Americans are reputed to insist 'Never trust a thin chef'! The average weight of the contributors to this volume must, of course, remain a closely guarded secret, but they have combined to produce a highly 'trustworthy' analysis of a neglected family of agrarian-centre parties. To stretch the pun to breaking point, the book should provide food for thought for all those with an appetite for studies of party change.

David Arter
Kinneff, Aberdeenshire

September 2000

# 1 The Swedish Centre Party: The Poor Relation of the Family?

ANDERS WIDFELDT

**Introduction**

If this book had been written twenty years earlier, around 1980, the story of the Swedish Centre Party would have been one of success. In response to urbanisation, the party successfully changed its strategy and broadened its electoral appeal. Having been formed as an agrarian interest party, it changed into a mainstream right-of-centre party. The transformation began around 1960 and was successful for two decades. The success peaked in the mid-1970s when the party led the non-socialist attack on the governmental dominance of the Social Democratic Party. The Centre Party held the post of Prime Minister between 1976 and 1978, and 1979 to 1982.

The past two decades, however, has been a different story. Electoral setbacks in 1979 and 1982, which at the time were largely regarded as temporary, turned out to be the start of a long-term decline. At the 1998 general election, the party received 5.1 per cent of the vote, compared with its best-ever performance of 25.1 per cent in 1973. Opinion polls in the first months of 2000 indicated that it is in real danger of falling below the 4 per cent representational threshold in the next election, scheduled for September 2002. The party has not experienced such a low level of support since its embryonic days around the time of the first world war.

In this chapter, it will be argued that the history of the Centre Party can be divided into three phases. For the first four decades after its formation, it was a party with its ambition limited to representing the rural parts of the country. In the 1950s, the strategy was modified with a view to broadening its appeal. During the second phase, from the late 1950s until the late 1970s, this adaptation was successful. The third phase, which is still continuing, has been characterised by decline, almost to the brink of extinction as a parliamentary party. This chapter will examine all three phases. In addition, the three critical junctures which heralded the start of a new phase will be identified. These junctures or watersheds involved one or more events which catalysed a significant measure of change in the party or its environment.

So far, the amount of scholarly work on the Swedish Agrarian-Centre Party has been fairly limited. The bulk of the available literature has been published by the party itself or written by its sympathisers. Much of it is useful, in that it contains valuable documentation of events and personalities, although inevitably perhaps it is rather tendentious. In several cases, this literature is part of the party's own official history writing and, accordingly, has to be treated with some care, even when written by academics. This 'official output' includes work on the party's ideological development, various phases in the party's history and accounts of its affiliated organisations. There are also a number of personal biographies.[1] The academic literature is more limited. Much of it has focused on the transformation from a Farmers' League to the Centre Party. Jonasson deals with the party during the final year of the coalition with the Social Democrats in 1956-1957, the period in which the party transformation began to be implemented. Larsson also deals with the modernisation of the party, but extends his time frame to between 1945 and 1960. Forsberg focuses on developments from the change of name in the late 1950s until 1973. Mohlin has provided the only substantial scholarly piece of work so far that deals with the first twenty years of the party's history. The most recent addition to the scholarly literature on the Centre Party is provided by Lundgren Rydén, who deals with its European policy between 1957 and 1994.[2] Literature in English is scarce. Micheletti analyses the attempts of the Swedish farmers' movement to influence government agricultural policy, while Christensen compares the modernisation and adaptation efforts of the Norwegian and Swedish Centre parties.[3]

Thus, there are many important aspects and phases of the Swedish Centre Party that remain under-researched. The best-researched areas are the early years of the party, and the period surrounding its modernisation in the 1950s. This chapter does not claim to fill these gaps. Rather, it will seek to tie together existing research findings. The account is divided into four main parts. First, there is a chronological account of the party's history and an identification of the three distinct phases in its evolution. Second, there is a discussion of its organisational structure. Third, there is a consideration of its electoral appeal. Finally, the ideological development of the party is assessed. The evidence amassed will then be used to analyse the nature of the party, in an attempt to ascertain whether it has developed into a catchall party. In addition, its policy on Europe will be discussed to illustrate the electoral and organisational dilemma the party has faced during its decline from around 1980.

## The Origins of the Swedish Agrarian-Centre Party

The exact date of the foundation of the Centre Party is a matter of some dispute. The party itself usually claims to have been formed in 1910, when a farmer, Carl Berglund, from the county of Skaraborg in southwest Sweden, launched the weekly newspaper *Landsbygden*. Its first issue contained an appeal to smallholding farmers and the rural population to unite into a political movement. A proposal for a party programme was published a few months later. It is, however, questionable whether this really can be regarded as the formation of an actual party. True, the first local party branches were formed in 1911, but they were not conjoined as part of a fully-fledged party organisation under national leadership. Larsson dates the party formation to early 1914, when Berglund and his followers formed *Bondeförbundet* (Farmers' League). However, the early years were quite chaotic with splits, mergers and a number of independent organisational initiatives.[4] Between 1915 and 1921, two rival farmers' parties co-existed. Besides *Bondeförbundet* (BF) there was *Jordbrukarnas Riksförbund* (The Agrarian League - JR) which was formed on 6 February 1915. This was the first anniversary of the so-called 'Farmers' March', when 30,000 farmers from all over the country converged on Stockholm to pledge their support for the king and express their concern about the state of Swedish defence. Several of the initiators of JR had been involved in this march.[5] In the Centre Party's 75th anniversary volume, Fiskesjö claims that the social and programmatic differences between JR and BF were small.[6] Mohlin, however, argues that JR was politically further to the right, and represented the interests of large-scale landowners, while BF was mostly based around smallholding farmers.[7]

The formation of BF and JR can be seen as a response to a perceived vacuum in the party system. In the late nineteenth century, before voting rights were extended to the majority of the male population, the agricultural sector was represented by the *Lantmannapartiet* (Country Party). This was to all intents and purposes a conservative party, which represented the larger landowners. *Lantmannapartiet* split into two separate parties on the issue of protectionism in 1888. Remnants of this split were part of the coalition behind the formation of the Conservative (now

Moderate) Party in 1904. Before 1917, the nearest thing to a parliamentary mouthpiece of the rural population was the so-called 'free-minded' faction of the Liberal Party. Indeed, several of the leading lights in BF had a liberal background. There developed, however, a widespread feeling among smallholding farmers, and the rural population in general, that they lacked adequate political representation. The contrast to the industrial working class was striking. The latter boasted well-organised unions and a Social Democratic Party that had seats in the second (lower) chamber of the *Riksdag* from 1896 onwards. According to the Centre Party's own historiography, the rural population rejected socialism, but also believed that conservatism and liberalism could not provide any solution to the widespread poverty.[8]

After various teething troubles, BF and JR grew in strength. There was in fact an intense rivalry between them, and it appears both sides initially thought themselves capable of coming out on top. After the 1917 election to the second chamber of the Riksdag, when BF gained nine seats and JR five, it was apparent that neither of them was capable of defeating the other. Moves to merge the two parties emanated from JR in 1917. They were initially met with scepticism in BF, but the merger was eventually concluded in 1921 and ratified a year later. The merged party kept the name of one of the former rivals, *Bondeförbundet*.[9] As indicated by the name, the merger did not signify any attempt to broaden the electoral and organisational base of the two farmers' parties. Until the late 1950s, BF exclusively represented the rural population. No serious attempts were made to contest city constituencies, and the party's membership was confined to rural areas. The party was also very reluctant to commit itself to either of the two main ideological 'blocs'.

These limitations did not prevent it exerting real political influence. In fact, the party's 'non-aligned' position proved strategically advantageous. In 1933, BF took part in the so-called 'cow trade' deal with the Social Democrats, which facilitated parliamentary stability as well as helping to lay the foundations for stable economic development. The deal involved the BF giving its support to a neo-Keynesian Social Democratic programme designed to combat unemployment in return for measures of agricultural protection.[10] Although it did not immediately lead to a government coalition, the 'cow trade' established the BF as an influential political actor. This was confirmed in 1936, when the party took over from the Social Democrats as a one-party caretaker government, albeit for only three months. After the election that same year, BF joined the Social Democrats as the junior partner in a 'red-green' coalition that had parallels across the Nordic region. BF subsequently participated in the four-party government between 1939 and 1945 and in a second coalition with the Social Democrats between 1951 and 1957 (see Table 1.1).

**Table 1.1 Swedish Agrarian/Centre Party Participation in Governments, 1936-1994**

| Years | Prime Minister | Status | Other parties |
|---|---|---|---|
| 1936 | Pehrsson-Brahmstorp (Agrarian) | Minority (caretaker) | None |
| 1936-1939 | Hansson (Social Democrats) | Majority | Social Democrats |
| 1939-1945 | Hansson (Social Democrats) | Majority (wartime coalition) | Social Democrats, Liberals, Conservatives |
| 1951-1957 | Erlander (Social Democrats) | Majority | Social Democrats |
| 1976-1978 | Fälldin (Centre) | Majority | Moderates, Liberals |
| 1979-1981 | Fälldin (Centre) | Majority | Moderates, Liberals |
| 1981-1982 | Fälldin (Centre) | Minority | Liberals |
| 1991-1994 | Bildt (Moderate) | Minority | Moderates, Liberals, Christian Democrats |

*From Farmers' League to Centre Party*

In the years after the Second World War, it became apparent that the party's electoral and organisational bases were eroding at an alarming rate. Industrialisation and urbanisation had begun in the nineteenth century. The proportion of the workforce in the agricultural sector first began to drop around 1880, but it was still more than 50 per cent of the economically active population in 1900. The decline continued into the twentieth century and accelerated in the 1940s.[11] Clearly, a party whose *raison d'être* was the promotion of agricultural and rural interests would have to broaden its appeal in an attempt to staunch the electoral decline. In the 1930s the party had been supported by 12-14 per cent of the electorate, but there was a continuous decline after the end of the war and a nadir of 9.4 per cent was reached in 1956. This was partly attributed to the increasing unpopularity of the coalition with the Social Democrats, but already in the 1940s there was awareness in the party that something had to be done to meet the decline of its support base. The affiliated Youth Organisation was particularly active in this discussion.[12]

Against the backdrop of rapid socio-economic change, it was obvious that a party name like the 'Farmers' League' was becoming an increasing liability. In fact, it had been refurbished in 1943, when a prefix was added to the original *Bondeförbundet* so that the party became *Landsbygdspartiet Bondeförbundet* (the Rural Party Farmers' League). This was to emphasise that it was not narrowly a class party for farmers, but represented the entire rural population. It was not enough, however. For one thing, it was a cumbersome name, and the party was still often referred to as simply BF. Something, moreover, had to be done to attract new groups of voters. From the late 1940s, the question of changing its name was on the party agenda at regular intervals. In 1947, an internal party commission suggested that the name should incorporate the words 'Centre Party', but this was rejected at the party conference in 1948. In 1955, an internal ballot of members was held on the name issue when a majority voted in favour of retaining the existing name.[13]

The party name remained a current matter, however. After the disastrous election of 1956, an internal commission was launched with the task of investigating possible ways of broadening the party's appeal. In its report, the commission argued that a name change was imperative and suggested two alternatives, the Centre Party and the Coalition Party. There was, however, some resistance among the rank and file to abandoning the party's historic designation. The opponents argued that a change of name would risk attenuating the links with the party's core group, the farmers and the rural population. The party leader, Gunnar Hedlund, was a strong advocate of a change, arguing that the decline in the number of farmers made a modernised name a matter of urgency. 'The house is on fire', as he put it. The decision taken at the 1957 party conference was a compromise, however. In an attempt to accommodate the sceptics, the name was amended to *Centerpartiet Bondeförbundet* (The Centre Party Farmers' League).[14]

This solution turned out to be short-lived. In a motion to the 1958 party conference, it was argued that the name 'Centre Party' had established itself in the press and among the general public. It was claimed, moreover, that it epitomised the party's ambition to extend its appeal to attract new groups, such as salaried employees and small-scale business owners. Since the previous conference, the prospect of a complete name change had gained support, not least because the political situation had changed and the party had grown in confidence. In a national referendum on the pensions system held in October 1957, the party presented its own alternative and this, significantly, had received 15.8 per cent of the vote, a substantially higher proportion of the vote than support for the party at the time. Shortly afterwards, the Centre Party left the coalition with the Social Democrats. In June 1958, the party polled 12.7 per cent in an extraordinary election to the lower chamber of the Riksdag, which was its best result for over ten years. Thus, it could be argued that the partial name change had been a success, and that it was relatively natural to go all the way and adopt the more straightforward name 'Centre Party'.[15]

*From 'Hothouse Growth' to Electoral Decline*

The party's change of name was part of a conscious modernisation effort. Soon after leaving the coalition with the Social Democrats, the Centre Party declared its allegiance to the non-socialist, 'bourgeois' bloc. This coincided with a concern to make electoral and organisational inroads into urban areas of the country. There had been attempts to contest urban constituencies in southern Sweden before the Second World War, but without success. The party fought its first parliamentary campaign in Stockholm in 1948 and in Göteborg in 1952. However, these efforts were not immediately auspicious. It was 1964 before a Centre Party MP was elected in the capital city of Stockholm. Two years later, the party entered the local councils of Sweden's three biggest cities Stockholm, Göteborg and Malmö for the first time. Yet it was not until 1970 that it had at least one MP elected from every parliamentary constituency. The development of the party's electoral support is traced in Table 1.2.

Although the breakthrough in the biggest cities took time, the attempt to broaden the party's support base was on the whole successful and led to a significant increase in electoral support. With minor interruptions, there was a continuous increase in the share of the vote between 1958 and 1973. Between 1968 and 1979, the Centre Party was the second largest party in the country and it headed three different coalition governments between 1976 and 1982. The 1976 election none the less marked the start of an electoral decline, which has been almost continuous and increasingly rapid. Whilst the 1988 election reversed the downward spiral, the party's poll in 1991 fell below 10 per cent of the vote for the first time in 35 years. In 1998, moreover, the Centre was a mere 0.8 percentage

8 *From Farmyard to City Square?*

point from failing to make the Riksdag. The prospects for the next scheduled election in 2002 look highly uncertain.[16]

**Table 1.2 Swedish Agrarian/Centre Party Election Results, Parliamentary Elections 1921-1998**

| Year | per cent votes | Seats | Year | per cent votes | Seats |
|---|---|---|---|---|---|
| 1921 | 11.1 | 21 (230) | 1964 | 13.4 | 35 (233) |
| 1924 | 10.8 | 23 (230) | 1968 | 15.7 | 39 (233) |
| 1928 | 11.2 | 27 (230) | 1970 | 19.9 | 71 (350) |
| 1932 | 14.1 | 36 (230) | 1973 | 25.1 | 90 (350) |
| 1936 | 14.3 | 36 (230) | 1976 | 24.1 | 86 (349) |
| 1940 | 12.0 | 28 (230) | 1979 | 18.1 | 64 (349) |
| 1944 | 13.6 | 35 (230) | 1982 | 15.5 | 56 (349) |
| 1948 | 12.4 | 30 (230) | 1985* | 12.4 | 44 (349) |
| 1952 | 10.7 | 26 (230) | 1988 | 11.3 | 42 (349) |
| 1956 | 9.4 | 19 (231) | 1991 | 8.5 | 31 (349) |
| 1958 | 12.7 | 32 (231) | 1994 | 7.7 | 27 (349) |
| 1960 | 13.6 | 34 (232) | 1998 | 5.1 | 18 (349) |

*Comment:* 1921-1968: Elections to the lower chamber of the Riksdag. 1970-1998: elections to unicameral Riksdag. Figures in brackets indicate total number of seats. * In 1985, the Centre Party formed an electoral alliance with the Christian Democrats (CD). The result includes 8.8 per cent votes for Centre Party lists, 2.3 per cent for CD lists and 1.3 per cent for joint Centre/CD lists. One CD representative was elected, but officially sat as a Centre Party MP.

Precisely what factors contributed to the downward electoral gradient are difficult to pinpoint. Two episodes, however, appear to have been particularly relevant. The first took place in autumn 1973, when there were advanced plans for the Centre to merge with the Liberal Party. This represented an important development in Swedish political history that remains under-researched. So far, the best treatment is provided by Möller in his general study of non-socialist party co-operation between 1957 and 1976. The backdrop to the proposed merger was the formation of joint Liberal-Centre lists in the 1964 and 1968 elections to the lower chamber. Indeed, it needs emphasis that the Centre Party's initial advances into urban areas were partly the result of electoral alliances with the Liberals. The co-operation between the two parties was not without its stresses and strains.

However, after the 1968 election, Liberal leader, Sven Wedén, proposed a fully blown fusion. The Centre leader Gunnar Hedlund saw merits in the idea but, after consulting senior party colleagues, he declined, realising that the project would meet resistance in his party. Further contacts took place in 1969, whilst in the election campaign of 1970 the parties published a joint brochure where it was stated that if the election went well on both sides, the possibility of a merger would be investigated again.[17]

In the event, both parties did improve on their respective results from 1968, although Hedlund still feared that the Centre Party was not ready for such a step. Fälldin, who took over as party leader in 1971, was also strongly in favour of a merger although he, too, was aware of the resistance among party members. In the 1973 election, the Centre Party was very successful, but the Liberals lost 40 per cent of their votes compared with three years earlier. It came as a surprise to them, therefore, when Fälldin proposed a merger of the two parties a month and a half after the election. The Liberal leader since 1969, Gunnar Helén, was none the less ready to negotiate. Indeed, Helén, it seems, showed considerable willingness to compromise, despite the fact that his party was only one-third of the size of the Centre Party. The new party name would have included the words the Centre Party, and Fälldin would have been its leader. The merger negotiations broke down when the Party Council of the Centre Party rejected the plans at a stormy meeting in November 1973.[18] Fälldin later admitted that he had seriously misjudged the mood of his party. He even considered resigning the leadership and claimed that his miscalculation on the issue caused irreparable damage to his position, even though he remained party leader for another twelve years. Interviewed in 1998 Fälldin still believed that a merger would have been in the long term interests of both parties and insisted that, in hindsight, he should have resigned when it was rejected by his own party.[19] Fälldin contended that the failure of the proposed merger with the Liberals was crucial in understanding the decline of the Centre Party, claiming that the merged party could still [in 1998] have been the second biggest in Sweden.[20] Such an assertion appears at best questionable.

Another event, which many commentators argue represented a watershed in the Centre Party's fortunes took place shortly after the 1976 election. In the campaign, Fälldin made an unconditional commitment not to commission any more nuclear power reactors and to phase out nuclear power by 1985. At the time, the Centre Party was faltering in the polls, and the Social Democratic government looked likely to hang on to power. Fälldin's pledge, however, made at a broadcast press conference, changed the whole mood of the campaign. Poll data strongly suggest that Fälldin's decision to 'bind himself' (in Lewin's phrase) was decisive for the outcome of the election and this in turn meant that Sweden got a non-socialist government for the first time in 40 years. But, while the anti-nuclear pledge may have been productive in the short term, it led to grave consequences after the election. The government negotiations with the Moderate and Liberal parties proved extremely tough, and the Centre Party had to make significant concessions on nuclear power. Crucially, it agreed that one reactor in the Barsebäck plant in the deep south, would be commissioned. This led to a 'betrayal debate', which severely damaged the credibility of Fälldin and his party.[21]

Fälldin later argued that the three-party agreement included a commitment to new and stricter demands on the handling of nuclear waste. But his statement at the time, that he 'had not made it all the way' in the negotiations, became something of a symbol of his failure to live up to his unconditional campaign pledge.[22] It is not an exaggeration to assert that Fälldin's leadership credentials were seriously compromised by this concession. The damage was not repaired when the Centre Party resigned from the government in 1978, over the commissioning of two further reactors. Clearly, many different factors contributed to the subsequent decline of the Centre Party, but many see the failure to live up to the campaign pledge on nuclear power as the starting point of the party's downturn.

The history of the Agrarian-Centre Party can be divided into three historical phases, each preceded by a critical event or sequence. The first phase between 1921 and 1957 can be described as the 'Limited Strategy' phase. The critical event that preceded it was the merger of BF and JR into one party, something that facilitated a coherent effort to mobilise the agrarian population. This phase was characterised by limited electoral and political ambitions. The party was intent on protecting the interests of the agricultural sector and concentrated on mobilising the rural vote. It was, however, a successful strategy, which paid dividends in terms of political influence and participation in government. Nevertheless, the urbanisation process meant that the limited strategy gradually became outdated. A continuation of the existing strategy would have led to inevitable marginalisation. This prompted the second critical event, or series of events, namely, the change of name in 1957-58, the independent proposal in the referendum on pensions and the abandoning of the coalition with the Social Democrats in 1957. The phase that followed could be termed 'Successful Adaptation'. It was characterised by a strategic response to the decline in its traditional support base. More clearly than before, the Centre Party pledged its allegiance to the non-socialist bloc and distanced itself from its former coalition partners, the Social Democrats. The party successfully broadened its electoral appeal and, as a consequence, enjoyed a near continuous increase in support.

The third phase, which is still continuing, could be called the 'Decline' phase. Precisely what precipitated it is open to question. It could be argued that the failed merger with the Liberal Party in 1973 was a crucial turning point. Certainly, the party's share of the vote declined almost continuously after 1973. Equally, it might have been even more damaging if the plans for a merger had gone ahead. There was widespread resistance in both parties, and talk of an organised defection of disaffected Liberals had the merger taken place.[23] After all, although the Centre Party's poll fell back by one percentage point between 1973 and 1976, it actually gained votes in absolute terms, because the voting age was lowered from 20 to 18. At least as plausible as the catalyst for electoral decline was Fälldin's broken campaign pledge on nuclear power in 1976. Both Fälldin and the party suffered seriously after this event. Of course, other factors have subsequently contributed to the decline, but the fact that Fälldin and the party bound themselves to a radical anti-nuclear policy, only to have to make significant concessions once in government, led to a credibility crisis, which in hindsight proved irreparable.

## The Organisational Structure of the Agrarian-Centre

The Centre Party has a strong organisational tradition and frequently refers to itself and its affiliated organisations as the 'Centre movement'. Moreover, despite significant variations in electoral support, the party has been the second biggest membership party in Sweden for most of the post-war period. During the first two historical phases, from the 1920s until the 1970s, its organisational presence was significant in many rural areas of the country. During the second phase, it also established an organisational base in urban areas, although the vast majority of the party's members came from rural areas. The 'Centre movement' provided a wide range of political and non-political activities for its members. The organisational presence was reinforced by links to the farmers' interest organisations and the agricultural co-operative movement. The latter were never formalised in the way they were between the Social Democratic Party and the trade unions.[24] Rather, they took the shape of informal personal links. Unlike Norway, the most influential agrarian pressure group, *Riksförbundet Landsbygdens Folk* (RLF) was formed in 1929, over a decade after the first farmers' parties had been formed. Furthermore, there has been a clear decline in these informal interest group connections. The amount of joint representation between the parliamentary Centre Party and the national executive of the RLF (with successor) declined in the 1970s, and disappeared completely in the late 1980s.[25]

As can be seen in Table 1.3, the party's claim to movemental status has been justified by reference to its membership strength, although this has witnessed a continuous decline for two decades. At the end of 1998 the party had 66,561 members, not including affiliated organisations. This was less than half the number of members in 1980. The decline also affected the affiliated organisations. The Women's Organisation had 33,919 members in 1998, compared to nearly 75,000 in the late 1970s. Nevertheless, it has held on to its position as the largest party political Women's Organisation in Sweden since 1970. The Youth Organisation was very strong for many years, claiming a membership of over 100,000 in the 1940s and 1950s. By the late 1990s it had declined to below one tenth of its peak strength, and the official figure in 1998 was 6,349. Despite the decline, the Centre Party remains organisationally strong compared to the other Swedish parties. If the main party and Women's Organisation memberships are combined - the best way of comparing the memberships of Swedish parties - the Centre Party was still the second biggest in Sweden in 1998 with 100,723 members. This was approximately 70,000 behind the Social Democrats, but 13,000 more than the Moderate Party and well ahead of all other parties. However, the Centre Party has on average the oldest members of the major Swedish parties, which would suggest that the decline will continue.[26] The level of activity among the party members also compares well with other parties, and between 1979 and 1994 the Centre Party had the second highest level of activity. Just as with membership, however, the party has suffered a decline in activity. According to one estimate, the number of activists was roughly halved between 1979 and 1994.[27]

The claim to a movemental tradition is reflected in the party structure. The party conference meets every year. There is also a Party Council (*Förtroenderåd*) comprising representatives from the party regions, which meets twice a year. Despite having lost its formally defined decision-making power in 1969, the Party Council is a very important organ, which the party leadership cannot overlook. It was the Party Council that effectively put an end to plans for a merger with the Liberal Party. In addition, there are regular meetings of the regional party chairs. Thus, the party structure allows plenty of potential contact between the leadership and sub-national party units. Equally, the formal membership influence in the Centre Party declined somewhat following a revision of the party rules in 1969, which downgraded the power of the Party Council.[28]

Table 1.3  Swedish Agrarian/Centre Party Membership, Selected Years, 1930-1998

| Year | Party | Women's Organisation | Youth Organisation |
| --- | --- | --- | --- |
| 1930 | 30,770 | - | 20,189 |
| 1940 | 63,250 | 8,714 | 91,187 |
| 1950 | 121,506 | 52,115 | 109,249 |
| 1960 | 119,012 | 60,092 | 91,290 |
| 1970 | 116,798 | 65,639 | 45,019 |
| 1975 | 135,576 | 72,209 | 42,924 |
| 1980 | 137,057 | 73,307 | 37,106 |
| 1985 | 125,318 | 69,599 | 30,112 |
| 1990 | 110,406 | 60,718 | 19,042 |
| 1994 | 88,588 | 47,878 | 10,201 |
| 1998 | 66,561 | 33,919 | 6,349 |

**The Agrarian-Centre's Electoral Support**

During its first historical phase, the party relied exclusively on the rural electorate. Indeed, Mohlin has shown how, in these formative years, it was particularly successful in mobilising votes in areas that suffered from poor communications, where the agricultural sector was strong and where the previous level of political organisation was low. Both BF and JR were formed around the time the suffrage was extended to include virtually all men, and the two parties merged when the suffrage was extended to include women. Thus Mohlin's findings, based on ecological analysis, indicate that in its earliest years, the party's vote did not derive solely from farmers, but also from other, previously non-mobilised voters in rural areas.[29] None the less, there is no doubt that the party relied heavily on voters connected with the agricultural sector. However, structural changes worked to the party's disadvantage. In 1960, 12 per cent of the voters were farmers; in 1998 the proportion was 2 per cent.[30] This meant that the party was obliged to look beyond its traditional core groups to gain electoral strength. It was quite successful in this in the 1960s and 1970s. As can be seen from Table 1.4, the proportion of the party's vote comprising salaried employees almost trebled between 1960 and 1968, and has remained between 30-40 per cent thereafter. Conversely, the proportion of the party's vote made up of farmers more than halved, and stayed around 20 per cent from the 1970s onwards.

Interestingly, the proportion of working class voters remained relatively stable between 1960 and 1998 although the social profile of Centre Party voters changed considerably in that period. In 1960, it was still very much a farmers' party. The proportion of farmers among the party's voters was about four times as high as among the electorate as a whole. During the 'Successful adaptation' phase, the decline of the farmers was offset by increased support from white-collar professionals. The over-representation of farmers has not disappeared, but it dropped significantly during the 'Decline' phase. In 1998, 18 per cent of the Centre Party voters were farmers, compared to 2 per cent of the electorate. In contrast, the proportion of salaried employees has increased.

Table 1.4  The Social Composition of the Swedish Centre Party Vote, 1960-1998

| Year | Farmers | Other self-employed | Salaried employees | Working class | Students | n |
|---|---|---|---|---|---|---|
| 1960 | 48 | 7 | 10 | 35 | - | 181 |
| 1964 | 47 | 10 | 14 | 29 | - | 355 |
| 1968 | 28 | 9 | 28 | 34 | 1 | 455 |
| 1976 | 19 | 7 | 32 | 39 | 3 | 565 |
| 1979 | 23 | 7 | 29 | 36 | 5 | 432 |
| 1982 | 22 | 11 | 31 | 33 | 3 | 380 |
| 1985 | 26 | 8 | 30 | 33 | 3 | 266 |
| 1988 | 19 | 10 | 33 | 34 | 4 | 274 |
| 1991 | 16 | 6 | 37 | 38 | 3 | 201 |
| 1994 | 21 | 10 | 30 | 32 | 7 | 183 |
| 1998 | 18 | 7 | 39 | 25 | 11 | 88 |

*Sources*: Petersson 1977, p. 14; Holmberg 1981, p.300; Holmberg 1984, p. 82, Gilljam and Holmberg 1987, p. 179; Gilljam and Holmberg 1993, p. 200; Gilljam and Holmberg 1995, p. 101; Swedish election studies data.

Table 1.5 shows the distribution of the farmers' vote since 1960. The Centre Party dominance is obvious until 1998 when the Christian Democrats caught up. This was the first time since election studies began that the Centre Party was not by far the best-supported party among farmers. The decline in farmers' support for the Centre Party dates back to the 1980s. Yet the 18 per cent of the Centre Party votes stemming from farmers (Table 1.4) is still by far the largest proportion in any Swedish party. Despite a relative decline in loyalty, farmers remain a core component of support for the ailing party.

**Table 1.5 Party Vote of the Swedish Farmers, 1960-1998**

| Year | Centre | Moderate | Liberal | Soc. Dem. | Christ. Dem. | Greens | Others | n |
|---|---|---|---|---|---|---|---|---|
| 1960 | 70 | 16 | 6 | 7 | -- | -- | 1[1] | 151 |
| 1964 | 64 | 13 | 12 | 8 | 2 | -- | 1[2] | 262 |
| 1968 | 64 | 21 | 8 | 4 | 2 | -- | 1[3] | 195 |
| 1976 | 70 | 15 | 5 | 8 | 1 | -- | 1[4] | 150 |
| 1979 | 65 | 23 | 5 | 7 | 0 | -- | 0 | 152 |
| 1982 | 70 | 11 | 3 | 13 | 1 | 2 | 0 | 117 |
| 1985 | 64 | 16 | 8 | 6 | 5 | 1 | 0 | 108 |
| 1988 | 63 | 17 | 5 | 11 | 1 | 3 | 0 | 76 |
| 1991 | 45 | 23 | 1 | 4 | 17 | 4 | 6[5] | |
| 1994 | 55 | 20 | 3 | 6 | 6 | 6 | 4[6] | 69 |
| 1998 | 37 | 16 | 0 | 2 | 35 | 5 | 5[7] | 43 |

[1] Left Party Communists.
[2] Includes Left Party Communists (0.5 per cent).
[3] Left Party Communists.
[4] Left Party Communists.
[5] New Democracy.
[6] Includes Left Party (3 per cent).
[7] Left Party.
Sources: Oskarson 1994, p. 50; Holmberg 1981, p.300; Holmberg 1984, p. 82, Gilljam and Holmberg 1987, p. 179; Gilljam and Holmberg 1993, p. 200; Gilljam and Holmberg 1995, p. 101; Swedish election studies data.

A related aspect of the Centre Party's changing support base is the geographical distribution of its vote. The party's successful penetration of the urban electorate in the 1960s and 1970s meant that its profile as a rural party was significantly reduced. In 1973, when the party enjoyed its best result to date, the geographical variation of the Centre Party vote was the lowest ever. It was still a rurally based party, but to a lesser extent than earlier and indeed later. The corollary of electoral decline after 1973 has been an increasing concentration of the vote back into rural areas.[31] Thus, while the Centre Party's reliance on farmers has not increased since the late 1970s, its electoral profile has become significantly more rural during the same period. In the 1994 election, when the Centre Party received 7.7 per cent of the national poll, it was the second largest party in the Swedish countryside, claiming 28 per cent of rural voters. Conversely, 45 per cent of the party's vote derived from the countryside, more than twice as many as in any other party.[32]

The development of the party's geographical profile can thus be described as curvilinear. During its 'Limited Strategy' phase, it was exclusively a rural party; during the 'Successful Adaptation' phase, it made significant gains in urban areas, without ever losing its rural support; during the 'Decline' phase, the party forfeited most of its urban support and became a predominantly rural party again.

*The Development of a Centrist Ideology*

For many years, the Centre Party did not see itself as ideological at all, and often referred to ideologies in derogatory terms.[33] This is illustrated in a famous cartoon from the early 1960s, where four Swedish party leaders are seen standing below paintings of their respective ideological forefathers. Social Democrat Tage Erlander is below Karl Marx, Conservative Jarl Hjalmarson is below Edmund Burke, and Liberal Bertil Ohlin is below John Stuart Mill. But Centre Party leader Gunnar Hedlund is standing below a painting of himself.

From the outset, *Bondeförbundet* displayed characteristics of traditional conservatism. The party programme of 1933 included commitments to Christianity, traditional family values and the preservation of the Swedish race.[34] The last reference has sometimes been interpreted as an indication of fascist influence in the party.[35] On the whole, however, the 1933 programme was more a collection of demands on behalf of the rural population than a coherent ideology. The latter began to take shape during the years after the Second World War. The process was accelerated after the name change in 1957-1958, but was not complete until the 1970s. Since then, the party's publications have contained claims to a specific Centre ideology consisting of three main elements: decentralism, environmentalism and market liberalism. There have also been attempts to trace this ideology back to the formation of the party.[36] Thomas Korsfeldt, who occupied senior positions in the party, has argued that it is misconceived to label the Agrarian-Centre a mere interest party even during its early years. This, he claims, is based on the false assumption that political ideas are best understood in relation to the left-right conflict. Instead, the party was predicated on traditional urban-rural cultural antagonisms dating back to well before the twentieth century.[37] The ideological baggage of the Centre Party is, however, an under-researched area. Whether the political values and demands of the party constitute a set of ideals and beliefs that qualifies as a coherent ideology, independent of other ideologies, must remain an open question.

Of the three ideological elements, decentralism is the easiest to trace back in time. During the 'Limited Strategy' phase, the primary concern of the Agrarian-Centre Party was to protect the interests of the rural population in an era of urbanisation. In concrete terms, this meant asserting the case for protectionism in terms of subsidies to farm products and an improved infrastructure (health care and schools) in rural areas.[38] This, of course, was the forerunner of what now is called 'regional policy', which sets out to equalise regional differences in employment and conditions for business. It could be argued that the Centre Party's gradual adoption of the concept of decentralisation was a logical extension of its historic concern to protect the interests of the rural population. Certainly Gustaf Jonnergård, the Centre Party secretary between 1951 and 1976, has insisted that the policy of decentralisation had its origins in the agricultural policies and rural demands dating back to the party's initial phase.[39] Thus, measures that can be termed 'decentralist' can be traced back to the formation of the party. When decentralisation became a leading catchword in the party's rhetoric is another matter, however. It first appeared in the party programme in 1959, just after the change of the party name was completed, but it took another decade before it started to appear regularly in the party's policy pronouncements.

Environmentalist elements in the Centre Party's ideology are generally regarded as having begun to appear in the 1960s. In the party's own literature, it is claimed that environmental demands can be traced back to the 1950s. This is supported by Christensen's research based on manifesto data, and it can be argued that some of the party's policies from even earlier can be interpreted as environmentalist.[40] It is, however, somewhat tenuous to attribute these demands to more profound environmental concerns. It was mostly a question of highlighting the negative consequences of urbanisation, such as the deterioration of abandoned farmland. Thus, the 1959 programme averred to the deleterious consequences of urbanisation, industrialisation and the exploitation of natural resources, but made no explicit references to the environment. However, such references appear in the programme of 1970.[41] A few years later, opposition to nuclear power became a profile issue for the Centre Party. The pioneer of the Swedish anti-nuclear campaign was Centre Party MP Birgitta Hambraeus, who in 1972 tabled a parliamentary interpellation on the dangers of nuclear energy.[42] This reinforced the green profile that had been apparent in the 1970 party programme. A subsequent factor, which worked in the same direction, was the contacts with non-partisan environmental and anti-nuclear groups, particularly in connection with the referendum on nuclear power in 1980. The environmentalist profile was subsequently developed into the concept of 'eco-humanism', which now appears frequently in Centre Party publications.[43]

The third element in the Centre ideology, market liberalism, has not always been there. While it has never been justified to label the party 'socialist', many of its policies were quite far removed from what is normally meant by market liberalism. Indeed, some of its rhetoric during the formative phase manifested elements of anti-capitalism, and the party was perfectly happy to accept significant amounts of market regulation. The 'cow trade' with the Social Democrats in 1933 is a notable example of this.[44] While the party had traditionally been sympathetic to small-scale capitalism – both farmers and entrepreneurs – a more elaborate commitment to the market economy came only after the name change in the late 1950s. This was an integral part of the attempt to become a mainstream non-socialist party directed principally against the Social Democrats. However, until the 1970s, the party was at pains to keep the Moderate Party (Conservatives) at arm's length. In the 1960s, the emphasis was on co-operation with the Liberals. This 'middle bloc' co-operation was reflected in the production of joint electoral material. Its purpose was to ensure that the attack on the Social Democrats came from the centre of the party system, with the Conservatives as junior partners. As noted earlier, the Liberal/Centre pact involved advanced plans for a merger although, when this came to naught in 1973, the co-operation between the two parties slowly declined and has been insignificant since the mid 1980s. Interestingly, the Centre Party has always been very reluctant to refer to itself as a 'bourgeois' (*borgerligt*) party, a term frequently used by the Liberals and Conservatives. Instead, it prefers to call itself 'non-socialist' in precisely the manner of its Finnish sister party.

During the period when Thorbjörn Fälldin was at the helm (1971-1985), the Centre Party adopted a more accentuated anti-socialist profile than before. For most of the 1970s, Fälldin was regarded as spearheading the non-socialist challenge to the Social Democratic hegemony. Put another way, the party was further from any major cross-bloc deals with the Social Democrats during Fälldin's stewardship than under any previous or subsequent leader. Fälldin has later explained how he was treated arrogantly by representatives of the regional agricultural board when he was a young smallholding farmer in the 1950s and his experiences from this period evidently led to a deeply rooted scepticism towards the Social Democratic 'strong society' and its attendant bureaucracy.[45] As party leader he attached considerable importance to denouncing socialism and was one of the fiercest critics of the Social Democrats' wage earner funds scheme, which was introduced in 1983. It was also apparent that the personal chemistry between Fälldin and the Social Democratic leader, Olof Palme, left much to be desired.[46]

After Fälldin's departure from the leadership, the pro-market profile was toned down, and the Centre Party sometimes stood out against the dominant Conservative Party in the four-party coalition government between 1991 and 1994. The Centre leader Olof Johansson in fact left the government in June 1994 over the issue of a bridge project across the Öresund straits between Sweden and Denmark. During their economic cooperation between 1995 and 1997, moreover, the Centre Party helped a Social Democratic minority government carry unpopular austerity measures through parliament. None the less, the party has maintained its programmatic commitment to market liberal principles, albeit with some qualifications. The 1990 party programme holds that the best conditions for sustainable development are a 'market economy with social and environmental aims' based on individual ownership.[47] In recent years, the party has pressed for a loosening of labour market regulations by giving employers more freedom in selecting which employees will be subject to redundancies, for example.[48]

The Centre's ideological development can be summarised as follows. During the 'Limited Strategy' phase the party lacked an ideology. Its *raison d'être* was the pursuit of interest politics on behalf of the agricultural sector and the rural population. During the 'Successful Adaptation' phase, it developed an ideology with decentralism, market economics and environmentalism as the main components. It may be possible to trace these elements further back in the party's history, but it was in the 1960s that they began to shape a coherent set of ideas. During the 'Decline' phase, the party has maintained this ideology, possibly with a slightly reduced emphasis on market economics.

## The Centre Party and Europe

The Nordic Centre Party family has been far from united on the question of European integration. Venstre in Denmark has been enthusiastically in favour of the EU as well as EMU. The Norwegian Centre Party has been fiercely opposed to EU membership. The Finnish and Swedish Centre Parties have been split. EU- related issues have been a constant thorn in the Swedish Centre Party's side since the early 1990s. The party was split in the 1994 referendum on accession, and at the time of writing there is an internal debate about whether Sweden should join the EMU. For many years, however, the 'European issue' was uncontroversial. From the early 1960s to the late 1990s, the party supported the policy of the Social Democratic government that the Swedish policy of non-alignment and neutrality was incompatible with full EC membership. There was a readiness to contemplate less binding forms of association, and the party supported the trade deal with the EC that the government negotiated in 1972. As Lundgren Rydén has shown, however, the Centre Party's arguments for staying outside the EC differed from those of the Social Democrats. Both parties agreed that Swedish security policy ruled out membership, but the Centre Party, and especially its Youth Organisation, also held that EC membership would lead to the further centralisation of political and economic power.[49]

In late October 1990, the Social Democratic government made the unexpected announcement that it intended to apply for EC membership. On exactly the same day, the Centre held an extraordinary party conference at which the drafting of a new programme was a principal issue. Naturally, the conference delegates did not have time to digest and assess the implications of the Social Democratic initiative, but the programme that was adopted did leave the door open for a more flexible EC policy than in the party programmes of 1970 and 1981.[50] Officially, the party gave cautious support to the formal application in July 1991, but internally a split was emerging. In August 1992, the 'Centre No to the EU' grouping was formed. Moreover, whilst an extraordinary conference in May 1994 decided to support a Yes vote in the referendum to be held in November that year, it was only after a fifteen-hour debate and a sizeable minority had voted against.[51] The party chairman, Olof Johansson, kept a very low profile during the campaign and did not publicly advocate a Yes vote until a week before polling day. Instead, the most conspicuous Centre Party member during the campaign was Hans Lindqvist, who was a leading figure for the No side.[52] Indeed, survey research shows that 54 per cent of Centre Party supporters voted against EU accession in the referendum.[53]

A new cloud soon appeared on the horizon in the form of the EMU issue. Several consecutive party conferences backed resolutions opposed to Sweden joining the EMU. This was initially in line with the policy of the Social Democratic government, which in 1997 decided not to join at the time of the initial launch on 1 January 1999. However, the Centre Party's arguments go further than the Social Democratic 'wait and see' policy to insist that Swedish membership of EMU is not compatible with the Centre Party's view on democracy and decentralisation.[54] Indeed, the Social Democratic decision in March 2000, to say yes in principle to EMU membership has meant that the Centre Party is now one of a minority of parties [also the Greens and Leftist Party] that are explicitly opposed. There is an active pro-membership minority in the party, but an attempt to reverse the anti-EMU policy was rejected at the party conference in June 2000.

*Mass Party, Catchall Party or What?*

It could be argued that the Centre Party displays some of the characteristics of a mass party. Its emergence from a loose base outside parliament and its claim to be a 'Centre Movement' are compatible with such a classification. It started life as a class party, drawing on support from the farmers and, until the early 1930s, there were severe restrictions on the acceptance of non-farmers as members.[55] It did not, however, meet the criteria of a devotee party, since membership was never restricted to the most committed, or 'conscious', farmers.[56] Thus, the 'Limited Strategy' phase manifested itself not only in policies, but also in organisational structure, even though the most severe restrictions on membership were gradually eased. The party adopted an approach similar to that of the Social Democrats, in which the farmers, and subsequently the rural population more generally, were to be organised into a popular movement that would exert pressure on government.

The main question, however, is whether the nature of the party has changed since its early years. It would seem plausible to suppose that the 'Successful Adaptation' phase involved a shift from a mass integration party to a catchall party. This did not need to be the case, however. Indeed, Kirchheimer explicitly stated that the 'Swedish Agrarians' could not 'aspire to a catchall performance'.[57] He identified five catchall criteria, of which three are organisational – strengthening the leadership, downgrading ordinary members and broadening and diversifying its links to interest groups. In addition, a catchall party reduces its ideological baggage and tries to distance itself from its original class character.[58]

In respect of the organisational criteria, it is difficult to find evidence that the party's members have been downgraded. True, there has been a serious decline in membership since the late 1970s, accompanied by a decline in active membership. There is, however, no evidence that these have been the consequence of a conscious leadership strategy. On the contrary, all the available evidence suggests that the loss of members has been of great concern to the party leadership. The party literature deplores the loss of members, although taking comfort in the fact that the party still compares favourably with most other Swedish parties, and repeatedly points to the necessity of increasing recruitment efforts.[59] Nor can it be sustained that the party has strengthened the role of the leadership at the expense of ordinary members. The rule change in 1969, which formally demoted the Party Council to the status of advisory organ, could be interpreted this way, but there are many factors that point in the opposite direction. The Party Council was powerful enough to block the plans for a merger with the Liberals in 1973, and the national party conference has on several occasions played a vital role in party policy, as for example the consecutive conference decisions against EMU membership. While there are groups in the party that seek to reverse this policy, it is not possible to do so without the approval of the conference. This is not to say that the Centre Party is a model of internal party democracy. There are other parties in Sweden that display more democratic characteristics. But there is not much evidence of a relative strengthening of the leadership at the expense of the ordinary members.

As far as contacts with interest groups are concerned, the Centre Party has longstanding, but informal links with farmers' organisations. There is, however, much to suggest that these ties have weakened. There has been no personnel overlap between the party's parliamentary group and the executive of the central agricultural producers' organisation, *Lantbrukarnas Riksförbund,* since the late 1980s. Nor has there been anything comparable to the Social Democratic rhetoric to the effect that the trade unions and party are fighting the same battle, albeit on different fields. Rather, the party has been increasingly concerned to keep the agricultural organisations at arm's length. The links were closest during the 'Limited Strategy' phase, started to decline during the 'Successful Adaptation' phase and have been very weak indeed during the 'Decline' phase. Crucially, the party has not tried to compensate for this decline by building bridges to other organisations. Instead, it has conformed to the

## The Swedish Centre Party: The Poor Relation of the Family? 23

general pattern in Swedish politics of parties avoiding developing unduly close contacts with sectoral interests. The party's environmentalist concerns have led to some contacts with environmental organisations, but these links have not been systematic. A possible reason is the existence of the Green Party, which has found it somewhat easier to earn the trust of environmental organisations.

Kirchheimer's fourth criterion is that the catchall party de-emphasises its traditional social base, its *classe gardée*. The Centre has certainly done its best to convince the electorate that it is not only a party for farmers. Thus, Christensen has shown how the amount of space devoted to agricultural policy in the party's manifestos has been drastically reduced since the 1960s, having taken up the lion's share in the 1940s and 1950s.[60] Yet the process of de-emphasising the connection to farmers started long before the 'Successful Adaptation' phase. As early as the 1930s, it dropped the conditions that made it difficult for non-farmers to join the party. Moreover, the name change in 1943, from *Bondeförbundet* to *Landsbygdspartiet Bondeförbundet*, reflected its ambition to embrace the entire rural population. Accordingly, while the shift to the 'Successful Adaptation' phase signified an attempt to broaden the party's base to include urban voters, the shift away from a primary concern with the agricultural sector had begun much earlier.

Finally, a catchall party is said drastically to have reduced its ideological baggage. The question of its ideological development is one of several under-researched aspects of the Centre Party. It could be contended that what the Centre Party did when it entered the phase of 'Successful Adaptation' was not to throw out its ideological baggage, but to acquire an ideology. If the conventional wisdom that the party pursued little more than interest politics during the 'Limited Strategy' phase is accepted, then this seems a plausible conclusion. Even if it is conceded, along with the Centre Party, that significant parts of today's ideological ingredients of de-centralism, environmentalism and market economics can be dated back to the embryonic days of *Bondeförbundet*, it does not alter this conclusion. There is very little evidence to suggest that the party has become de-ideologised. It could certainly be argued that there have been ideological changes and adjustments, not least during the 'Decline' phase, However, these have been to refine rather than to weaken the ideology. An example is the term eco-humanism, which can be regarded as a way of integrating environmental concerns into an ideological framework.

Taken together, the evidence does not sustain the case for the Centre Party having transformed itself into a catchall party, at least if

Kirchheimer's criteria are strictly applied. It has of course developed in a catchall direction in the sense that it seeks to recruit votes from all parts of the country and from all segments of society. There is no doubt that during its most successful period, the party was effective in competing for the general non-socialist vote. The fact that it is now back to square one in terms of its appeal, with the important difference that the square is smaller than before, can hardly be seen as the result of a conscious strategy. It could of course be that the problem lies with Kirchheimer's own operationalisation. Forsberg argues that the party was a mass party in 1922 (during the 'Limited Strategy' phase) as well as in 1958 (when it entered the phase of 'Successful Adaptation'). In 1973 (when it was about to enter the 'Decline' phase), it still retained some mass party characteristics, but had moved in the direction of the catchall model. However, Forsberg uses slightly different criteria from Kirchheimer, and the main way in which the party had moved in a catchall direction was in its use of the media, which was more focused on reaching out to new potential voters. The relationship between leadership and members displayed mass party characteristics even in 1973.[61]

## Conclusion: The Centre Party's Dilemma

The factors that contributed to the success of the Centre Party in the 1960s and 1970s were diverse. On the one hand, the party was seen as the backbone of the challenge to the governmental dominance of the Social Democrats. On the other, the party attracted votes for its stance on environmentalism and regionalism, and as a 'middle party' that kept a strategic distance from the Conservatives on the political right. This was a successful combination, and the anti-nuclear power position in particular was a vital factor in the party's accession to government in 1976. The problem was that, while successful in opposition, this combination proved difficult to manage when in power.[62] The party faced a betrayal debate no matter what it did. The commissioning of new nuclear reactors in 1976 was a crucial event that caused long-term damage to the party and not least its leader, Thorbjörn Fälldin. But if Fälldin had opted fully to honour his pledges on nuclear energy, he would have faced another betrayal debate and the charge that he had destroyed the chances of forming the first non-socialist government for 40 years. Paradoxically, the mix of policies and centrist location, which was so important during the phase of 'Successful Adaptation', also contributed to the party's decline. Certainly, it is a long time since the Centre Party was seen as the main challenge to the Social Democrats. This role has belonged to the Conservative Party since the start of the 1990s and there are no signs that this will change in the foreseeable future. In fact, the Centre Party has gradually lost some of its former non-socialist bloc identity during its 'Decline' phase. Olof Johansson's resignation from the Conservative-led government was symptomatic of this, as was the parliamentary co-operation with the Social Democrats between 1995 and 1997. These examples indicate that, of the successful mix of environmentalism and non-socialist economic policies, the party has opted for the former during the 'Decline' phase. Whether the decline could have been halted with a different strategy must remain an open question.

The European integration issue highlights the continuing dilemma for the Centre Party. An EU-critical position is in tune with the party's core support in rural Sweden. A more EU-positive policy, for example reversing its opposition to EMU, would risk losing this core. At the same time, the party must look beyond its most loyal support groups to have any chance of regaining any of its former strength. At its prime, the Centre Party represented a viable alternative for floating non-socialist voters. In order to recapture some of these volatile voters, the Centre Party must avoid projecting too radical an environmental stance, or appearing narrowly an interest party for farmers and the rural population. Whilst a shift to a pro-EMU line could revive the party's electoral fortunes, it could also lead to the virtual extinction of a party that is already teetering on the brink of parliamentary oblivion.

Related to the Centre Party's electoral dilemma is its organisation. Despite an ageing and declining membership, the party still has a strong organisation in comparison to the other non-socialist parties. The Centre Party prides itself on its internal democracy and its strength in local politics. Yet the relatively high degree of internal membership influence has enabled EU opponents to build a platform in the party and, after the referendum, to provide a base for EMU resistance. It would be risky for the leadership to alienate such a significant proportion of the party organisation. Through all this runs the Centre Party ideology, with its mix of decentralism, environmentalism and market liberalism. In the Swedish debate, decentralist and environmentalist concerns have tended to be used as arguments against the EU and EMU, while pro-market arguments have tended to support EU and EMU. These dividing lines are not hard and fast, but there is little doubt that the mixture that constitutes the ideology of the Centre Party contains strains and contradictions in respect of particular policies.

It is no exaggeration to state that the Swedish Centre Party is in crisis. It has been in electoral decline more or less continuously since 1976 and, if this decline continues, the party will lose its parliamentary status at the next general election in 2002. Recent opinion polls suggest that this might well happen. Once the pride of the Nordic Centre party family, the Swedish party is now something of its poor relation. The EMU issue illustrates the wider dilemma. Groups within the party organisation, as well as among the core voters, would feel betrayed if the party de-emphasised its environmentalism and adopted a more wholeheartedly pro-market position. But failure to make such a change could mean that the party will be trapped as an isolated and declining political force.

## Notes

1. Party ideology: e.g. Jonnergård 1985a; Larsson 1983; history: e.g. Sjunnesson 1936; Johansson and Thullberg 1979; affiliated organisations: e.g Davidsson (ed.) 1959; Dahlgren, Elgström and Larsson (eds) 1985; biographies: e.g. Jonnergård 1985b; Kjellman 1990; Bjärsdal 1992. Articles covering a wide variety of aspects appear in publications in connection with the party's anniversaries, e.g. Larsson (ed.) 1985.
2. Jonasson 1981; Larsson 1980; Mohlin 1989; Forsberg 1999; Lundgren Rydén 2000. The latter work also deals with the Social Democrats.
3. Micheletti 1992; Christensen 1997. The latter is based on Christensen's graduate thesis in Norwegian.
4. Larsson 1980, p. 1; Bengtson 1985, p. 67f, Fiskesjö 1985, pp. 75-85.
5. Lewin 1988, p. 109f; Fiskesjö 1985, p. 85.
6. Fiskesjö 1985, pp. 90f.
7. Mohlin 1986, p. 20f.
8. Centre Party 1997a, p. 13.
9. Fiskesjö 1985, pp. 90ff.
10. Lewin 1988, chapter 5.
11. Larsson 1980, p. 27ff; Norborg 1982, p. 23ff.
12. Larsson 1980, p. 68f; Forsberg 1999, p. 74ff.
13. Jonnergård 1985, p.p. 15f; 18f; Larsson 1980, pp. 69-72; p. 75.
14. Larsson 1980, pp. 118-122.
15. Larsson 1980, especially pp. 118-122. See also Forsberg 1999, especially pp. 96f.
16. A *Temo* poll in late February 2000 estimated support for the Centre Party at 3.8 per cent; a few weeks later a *Demoskop* poll indicated that the party was backed by 3.7 per cent of the electorate.
17. Möller 1986, pp. 80-84.
18. Möller 1986, pp. 84-89.
19. Fälldin and Lagercrantz 1998, pp. 107-111.
20. Fälldin and Lagercrantz 1998, p. 111.
21. Lewin 1988, pp. 253-261.

22 Fälldin and Lagercrantz 1998, p. 149-152; Lewin 1988, p. 258.
23 Möller 1986, p. 88.
24 Larsson 1980, p. 44; Forsberg 1999, p. 146.
25 Hansson 1999.
26 Widfeldt 1999, p. 200.
27 Widfeldt 1999, p. 140ff. Activity is operationalised as having attended party meetings a few times per year.
28 Widfeldt 1999, chapter 3.
29 Mohlin 1989.
30 Oskarson 1994, p. 56; data from the Swedish Election Study 1998.
31 Gilljam and Holmberg 1993, p. 221.
32 Gilljam and Holmberg 1995, p. 107.
33 Lewin 1967, p. 366.
34 Johansson 1985, p. 101f.
35 See, for example, Lindström 1985, pp. 136-144.
36 See Jonnergård 1985a; 1985b.
37 Korsfeldt 1985, pp. 125f.
38 Jonnergård 1985a, p. 22.
39 Jonnergård 1985a, p. 24.
40 Christensen 1997, p. 393ff.
41 Wieslander 1964, pp. 65-78; Wieslander 1974, pp. 142f.
42 Lewin 1988, p. 239.
43 For example in the Centre Party programme of 1990 and the election platform for the 1998 election. See also Larsson 1983.
44 Lewin 1988, p. 140ff.
45 Fälldin and Lagercrantz 1998, pp. 44-49; Elmbrant 1996, p. 121.
46 Fälldin and Lagercrantz 1998, pp. 127ff; Elmbrant 1996, p. 174.
47 Centre Party 1990, p. 40.
48 Centre Party 1998, p. 7.
49 Lundgren Rydén 2000, p. 145; p. 154.
50 Wieslander 1974, p. 153; Centre Party 1981, p. 90; Centre Party 1990, p. 87.
51 Lundgren Rydén 2000, pp.243-248.
52 Esaiasson 1996, p. 36f.
53 Holmberg 1996, p. 226f. This percentage applies both to those who voted for the Centre Party in the parliamentary election of September 1994, as well as those who claimed to support the party at the time of the referendum in November that same year.
54 Centre Party 1997b, p. 13f.
55 Thermeanius 1933:45.
56 Cf. Duverger 1964, pp. 70ff.
57 Kirchheimer 1966, pp. 187f.
58 Kirchheimer 1966, pp. 190f.
59 See, e.g., Centre Party 1989; Centre Party 1997; Centre Party 1998, Centre Party annual reports, e.g. 1975, 1978, 1984, 1988, 1994.
60 Christiansen 1997, p. 397.

61 Forsberg 1999, pp. 53f; 71f; 147.
62 Christensen 1997, p. 397.

## References

Bengtson, T. (1985), 'Organisationen', in Larsson, P. A. (ed.), *Från bonderörelse till centrörelse. Jubileumsboken 1985*, pp. 66-74. Stockholm: The Centre Party.
Bjärsdal, J. (1992), *Bramstorp. Bondeledare - kohandlare - brobyggare*. Stockholm: LTs förlag.
Centre Party (1981), 'Partiprogram'. Party programme, decided by extraordinary national party congress, 13-14 February 1981.
Centre Party (1990), 'Partiprogram'. Party programme, decided by extraordinary national party congress, 26-27 October 1990.
Centre Party (1997a), 'Medlem i Centerpartiet' (brochure issued to new members of the party). Stockholm: Centerpartiets riksorganisation.
Centre Party (1997b), 'Aktuell Centerpolitik. Ställningstaganden vid Riksstämman i Haparanda 1997' (brochure summarising decisions taken at the 1997 national party congress). Stockholm: Centerpartiets riksorganisation.
Centre Party (1998), 'Nya mitten - tillsammans lyfter vi Sverige. Valprogram för Centerpartiet i 1998 års val'. Manifesto for the 1998 parliamentary election.
Centre Party (1999), 'Förnya samarbetet i Europa. Program inför valet till Europaparlamentet den 13 juni 1999'. Manifesto for the 1999 European election.
Christensen, D. A. (1997), 'Adaptation of Agrarian Parties in Norway and Sweden'. *Party Politics* vol. 3, no. 3., pp. 391-406.
Dahlgren, A., Elgström, O. and Larsson, H.A. (eds) (1985), *Kvinnor Påverkar*. LTs förlag.
Davidsson, H. (ed.) (1959), *Ungdom väljer väg*. Stockholm: SLUs förlag.
Duverger, M. (1964), *Political Parties*. London: Methuen.
Elmbrant, B. (1996), *Palme*. Stockholm: Fischer & Co.
Esaiasson, P. (1996), 'Kampanj på sparlåga', in Gilljam, M and Holmberg, S. (eds), *Ett knappt ja till EU. Väljarna och folkomröstningen 1994*. Stockholm: Norstedts Juridik.
Fälldin, T. and Lagercrantz, A. (1998), *En bonde blir statsminister. Thorbjörn Fälldin samtalar med Arvid Lagercrantz*. Stockholm: Bonniers.
Fiskesjö, B. (1985), 'Bondepartiets framväxt och konsolidering', in Larsson, P. A. (ed.), *Från bonderörelse till centerrörelse. Jubileumsboken 1985*, pp. 73-96. Stockholm: The Centre Party.
Forsberg, S. (1999), Jönköping: JIBS Research Reports no. 1999-2.
Gilljam, M. and Holmberg, S. (1987), *Väljare och val i Sverige*. Stockholm: Bonniers.
Gilljam, M. and Holmberg, S. (1993), *Väljarna inför 90-talet*. Stockholm: Norstedts Juridik.
Gilljam, M. and Holmberg, S. (1995), *Väljarnas val*. Stockholm: Norstedts Juridik.
Hansson, D. (1999), 'Partier och intresseorganisationer i Sverige'. Paper delivered at the 12th Nordic Political Science Association meeting, Uppsala, August, 19-21.
Holmberg, S. (1981), *Svenska väljare*. Stockholm: Publica.
Holmberg, S. (1984), *Väljare i förändring*. Stockholm: Publica.
Holmberg, S. (1996), 'Partierna gjorde så gott de kunde', in Gilljam, M and Holmberg, S. (eds), *Ett knappt ja till EU. Väljarna och folkomröstningen 1994*. Stockholm: Norstedts Juridik.

Johansson, T. and Thullberg, P (1979), *Samverkan gav styrkan*. Stockholm: LTs förlag.
Johansson, T. (1985), 'Den tredje vägen. Krispolitiken, folkhemmet och världskriget', in Larsson, P. A. (ed.), *Från bonderörelse till centerrörelse. Jubileumsboken 1985*, pp. 97-112. Stockholm: The Centre Party.
Jonasson, G. (1981), *I väntan på uppbrott. Bondeförbundet/centerpartiet i regeringskoalitionens slutskede 1956-1957*. Uppsala.
Jonnergård, G. (1985a), 'Idéutvecklingen', in Larsson, P. A. (ed.), *Från bonderörelse till centerrörelse. Jubileumsboken 1985*, pp. 20-33. Stockholm: The Centre Party.
Jonnergård, G. (1985b), *Med Gunnar Hedlund i politiken*. Stockholm: LTs förlag.
Jonnergård, G. (1985c), *Så blev det centerpartiet. Bondeförbunds- och centeridéerna från fyrtiotalet fram till 1960*. Stockholm: LTs förlag.
Kirchheimer, O. (1966), 'The Transformation of the Western European Party System', in LaPalombara, J. and Weiner, M.. (eds), *Political Parties and Political Development*, pp. 177-200. Princeton: Princeton UP.
Kjellman, Ö (1990), *Från arbetarpionjär till centerpionjär. En bok om John Kjellman*. Stockholm: The Centre Party.
Korsfeldt, T. (1985), 'Brytningstid (1945-1960)'. in Larsson, P. A. (ed.), *Från bonderörelse till centerrörelse. Jubileumsboken 1985*, pp. 113-126. Stockholm: The Centre Party.
Larsson, H.A. (1980), *Partireformationen. Från bondeförbund till centerparti*. Lund: CWK Gleerup.
Larsson, H.A. (1983), *Grön idé, ekohumanism*. Stockholm: The Centre Party.
Larsson, H.A. (ed.) (1985), Från bonderörelse till centerrörelse. Jubileumsboken 1985. Stockholm: The Centre Party.
Lewin, L. (1967), *Planhushållningsdebatten*. Stockholm: Almqvist & Wiksell.
Lewin, L. (1988), *Ideology and Strategy. A Century in Swedish Politics*. Cambridge, New York and Melbourne: Cambridge UP.
Lindström, U. (1985), *Fascism in Scandinavia, 1920-1940*, Stockholm: Almqvist & Wiksell international.
Lundgren Rydén, L. (2000), *Ett svenskt dilemma. Socialdemokraterna, centern och EG-frågan 1957-1994*. Göteborg: Department of History.
Michelletti, M. (1990), *The Swedish Farmers' Movement and Government Agricultural Policy*. New York: Praeger.
Mohlin, Y. (1986), 'Bondeförbundets politiska geografi', in Berglund, S. and Dellenbrant, J. Å. (eds), *Svensk partiregionalism*, pp. 20-33. Stockholm: Liber.
Mohlin, Y. (1989), *Bondepartierna och det moderna samhället. En studie av svensk agrarianism*. Umeå: Department of Political Science.
Möller, T. (1986.), *Borgerlig samverkan*. Uppsala: Diskurs.
Norborg, L. A. (1982), *170 år i Sverige. Svensk samhällsutveckling 1809-1979*. Stockholm: Esselte Studium.
Oskarson, M. (1994), *Klassröstning i Sverige. Rationalitet, lojalitet eller bara slentrian*. Stockholm: Nerenius och Santérus förlag.
Petersson, O. (1977), *Valundersökningar. Rapport 2. Väljarna och valet 1976*, Stockholm: Statistiska Centralbyrån.
Sjunnesson, O. (1936), *Bonderörelsens uppkomst och utveckling*. Malmö.Thermeanius, E. (1933), *Sveriges politiska partier*, Stockholm: Gebers.
Widfeldt, A. (1999), *Linking Parties with People? Party Membership in Sweden, 1960-1999*. Aldershot: Ashgate.

Wieslander, H. (1964), *De politiska partiernas program.* Stockholm: Prisma.
Wieslander, H. (1974), *De politiska partiernas program (4th ed.).* Stockholm: Prisma.

# 2 The Norwegian Agrarian-Centre Party: Class, Rural or Catchall Party?

DAG ARNE CHRISTENSEN

The Scandinavian agrarian parties once comprised a distinctive family of political parties (Beyme 1985, Berglund and Lindström 1978). In recent years, the family has split up (Berglund and Lindström 2000). The Finnish Centre Party and Danish Liberals (*Venstre*) are large parties boasting significant electoral strength. The Norwegian and Swedish parties, in contrast, are generally small parties. Indeed, the Swedish party may find it difficult to cross the four per cent barrier and maintain its parliamentary standing at the next general election in 2002. There are other differences. The Danish Liberals are a strongly pro-EU party, while the Norwegian Centre Party is united in its opposition to EU membership. The Finnish and Swedish Centre parties have been internally divided on European integration. Yet despite their differences, the Scandinavian agrarian parties testify to an axiomatic truth in politics, namely that political parties seldom go out of business. The renamed Norwegian Agrarian Party has, like its sister parties, survived in an industrial setting. Formed in 1921 as a distinct class party, it represented a rural response to the conflict in the commodity market between producers and consumers of food (Rokkan 1970). The Norwegian Agrarian Party in short emerged as a single-issue party, articulating the interests of the farmers and predicated on an urban-rural cleavage in the party system. Since its origins, however, the environment surrounding the party has changed dramatically.

Although, historically, class differences have been the primary determinant of electoral behaviour in Scandinavia, the Norwegian Agrarian Party had to face the fact of a shrinking electorate in the period after the second world war. As indicated in Figure 2.1, the extensive structural rationalisation of farm holdings and increased migration to the cities undermined the party's natural support base. The social class base for a pure agrarian party no longer existed. Today public and private services are the largest employer, their dominance being comparable to agriculture in the nineteenth century (Sundberg 1999). Women and men, moreover, comprise equal shares of the work force. There has been a flight from agriculture and fishing, as well as a significant decline in the size of the manual workforce.

**Figure 2.1 Employment in Agriculture and the Population in Urban Areas in Norway, 1950-1990**

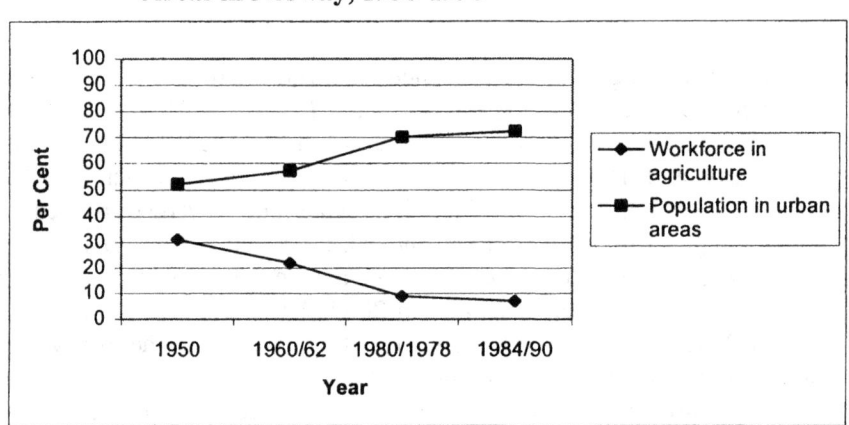

In reality, these socio-economic developments left the Agrarian party with little option but to expand its electoral appeal or face inevitable decline. Class agrarianism had to be replaced by something else. The first overt response to the challenge of urbanisation was taken in 1959 when the party changed its name from Agrarian Party (*Bondepartiet*) to Centre Party *Senterpartiet* (Elder and Gooderham 1978). Obviously the idea behind the change of name was to render the party attractive to a larger share of the electorate. However, symbolic changes are rarely enough, and the success of the re-designated party has been modest in electoral terms.

The principal focus in this chapter is on how the Agrarian-Centre Party has met the challenges of modernisation. In essaying a response, recourse is had to Kirchheimer's (1968) celebrated 'catchall party thesis'. Two questions in particular stand out. First, did the party pursue a catchall party strategy? Second, if this was not the case, what course of action did it follow? Other related questions are addressed. How did the party redesign its policy in order to mobilise new voters? Is the party manifesto still oriented towards the protection of rural interests? Has the party managed to appeal to a cross-section of the electorate?

The analysis of the transformation of the Norwegian Agrarian Party is divided into five parts. The first outlines the theoretical framework, whilst the second contextual section briefly sketches the party political setting in Norway. The third section traces the origins of the Agrarian Party. The fourth identifies the different options discussed before the party renamed itself in 1959. Finally, the fifth part applies Kirchheimer's catchall model to the transformation of the Norwegian Agrarian Party.

## Party Change: Some Theoretical Considerations

At times of electoral decline parties inevitably ask themselves fundamental questions about the way forward. In Kirchheimer's submission, the answer is that a party always goes where the voters are. In a review of the literature on party change two findings stand out. First, Kirchheimer's catchall party thesis is difficult, if not impossible, to test. Among the political parties in Western democracies there is little empirical evidence of a trend towards the adoption of catchall strategies (Wolinetz 1990). Second, as Green and Shapiro have observed, political parties normally face four options at times of electoral decline. In their words, 'The strategic imperative to go where the voters are is pitted against other imperatives – go where your heart is, go where the campaign funds are, go where you hope to lead the voters, or stay where you're stuck' (Green and Schapiro 1994: 159).

Political parties pursue a wide range of strategic options, although, ultimately, these can be reduced to four main types – the search for electoral support, policy influence, governmental status and internal party unity (Strøm 1990: 566, Sjøblom 1968, Harmel and Janda 1993). An office-seeking party tries to gain control of political power, the policy-seeking party tries to have an impact on public policy and the unity-seeking party is preoccupied with keeping the party organisation together. Kirchheimer's (1968) model views political parties as vote-maximisers driven by the desire to attract as many voters as possible. In this context, parties and party leaders are cast in the role of entrepreneurs motivated by political power and attracting the necessary votes to achieve it. However, on the basis of the empirical evidence, it is hard to specify one single goal in the study of party change. Rather, party objectives are contingent on their differing environments. Within the framework of a multiparty coalition system, like the Norwegian, it is not even necessary to articulate widespread popular concerns to gain access to political power. Hence, political parties may give varying weight to the four options over time.

Bearing the above-mentioned caveats in mind, what does a catchall party look like? According to Kirchheimer, it is characterised by a distinct political and organisational style. In respect of policies, the catchall party will a) drastically reduce its ideological baggage in order to profit from short term (tactical) electoral considerations, and b) de-emphasise its class character in order to catch a wide spectrum of voters. Organisationally, the catchall party will c) downgrade the role of individual party members, d) strengthen the role of the national party leadership, and e) seek to gain access to a wide variety of interest groups.

## The Party Political Setting

The historic Norwegian parties were born out of the struggle to achieve parliamentary democracy between 1870 and 1920. The original cleavages in the Norwegian system were territorial and cultural. The provinces opposed the capital; the peasantry challenged the officials of the king's administration; and the defenders of the rural cultural traditions resisted the steady spread of urban secularism and rationalism (Rokkan 1970: 235). During the first two decades after the establishment of universal suffrage (including women) in 1913, the functional-economic conflict cut across the earlier territorial-cultural cleavage and produced a complex system of alliances and political configurations.

The traditional Nordic five-party model that emerged around 1920 consisted of the Communist Party, the Social Democrats, the Liberals, the Agrarians and the Conservatives (Berglund and Lindström 1978). From 1945 to the beginning of the 1960s, the left-right cleavage dominated Norwegian politics. This was a period of economic growth and prosperity and the rapid process of urbanisation also strained the relationship between periphery and centre. In 1961-1962, moreover, the European Community (EC) became a salient issue for the first time, cutting across the left-right cleavage and producing a changed political climate and the incipient fragmentation of the party system (Sparre Nilson 1981). The EC issue is a good example of how a 'foreign policy issue' can impinge on most areas of national politics. It appears, as Sparre Nilson has argued (1981), that there is a close and necessary connection between the issue of EC membership and the territorial centre-periphery dimension. From 1963 to the early 1970s the left-right cleavage again dominated the scene. In the 1970s the earlier cycle was repeated. First there was a resurgence of the EC dimension that led to heightened political conflict and party fragmentation.

Then the left-right cleavage reasserted itself. The debate over Norway's relationship with Europe was put on the back burner for two decades and was eventually revived by the Conservative Party in 1989. In 1992 the Labour Party's conference gave the Labour government the approval it needed to apply for membership.[1] From 1990 to 1994 the conflict over European Union (EU) membership dominated Norwegian politics. Opposition to Norway joining has been strong and stable and there was an impressive correlation of .88 between the negative votes in the 1972 and 1994 referenda when local authorities (*kommuner*) are used as the units of analysis (Lindström and Svåsand 1996).

Moral-religious conflict has played a subordinate, but not insignificant, role in Norwegian politics. Thus, a Christian People's Party (*Kristelig Folkeparti*) was established in 1933.[2] Parties of this type may seem incongruous in the Nordic countries, with their established Lutheran churches and the absence of substantial religious minorities, but the Christian People's Party has benefited from a tradition of revivalist groups and moral rearmament organisations. The latter have constituted a factor of no little importance in Norwegian politics. Between the two world wars, prohibition was a dominant issue and the temperance question still remains important to a number of voters. In addition, both the question of abortion and the teaching of Christianity in schools have been salient.

The Norwegian party system of the 1970s strongly resembled that of the 1920s. However, the Left Socialist Party had replaced the old Communist Left which vanished as a sizeable party. From the beginning of the 1960s to the second half of the 1970s Norwegian politics was influenced by two main sets of issues. The left-right conflict and an EC conflict between the periphery and the centre.

The principal features of the party system are an historically strong but declining Labour Party, together with a bloc of non-socialist parties, which, in addition to the main socio-economic cleavage, reflect an urban-rural divide and differences in cultural values. The Labour Party dominated government until 1965 when it was replaced by a non-socialist coalition.[3] In the Storting election in 1973 the tendency toward fragmentation that had been discernible in the party structure since the early 1960s increased markedly (Valen and Martinussen 1972a). Labour, which had polled 46.5 per cent of the vote in 1969, was reduced to 35.2 per cent in 1973. This 'earthquake election' occurred in the wake of the 1972 EC referendum, when membership was rejected by 53 per cent of the electorate. The issue shattered the historic alignments in Norwegian politics. The Liberals (*Venstre*), the Christian People's Party and the Labour Party were all internally split on the EC question (Valen and Martinussen 1972b). A pro-membership faction broke with the Liberals and formed the New People's Party. The anti-Europeans in the Labour Party constituted a group within the party, the Workers' Information Committee, which entered a loose merger with the Communists and the Socialist People's Party known as the Socialist Electoral Alliance, later the Left Socialist Party. On the far right of the political spectrum the anti-tax Anders Lange Party (later renamed the Progress Party) gained five per cent of the votes and four seats in the new Storting in 1973. Electoral changes of this magnitude had not occurred in Norway since around 1930. However, the next general election in 1977 largely restored the old parliamentary order, at least for the time being.

A long-term trend in Norway has witnessed a gradual weakening of the Labour Party and a corresponding increase in support for the non-socialist parties (Svåsand and Lindström 1992). Since 1981 there has been a non-socialist majority in the Storting, with the Conservative Party generally the largest non-socialist party. The relationship between the non-socialists has, however, been strained over Norway's relationship with the EC/EU and by the presence of the radical rightist Progress Party. The 1993 general election, fought principally on the EU issue, transformed the Agrarian-Centre Party, which gained nearly 17 per cent of the votes, into the largest opposition party in the Storting. Ironically, an increasingly EU-friendly Labour Party not only remained in government, but in fact gained votes.

## The Origins of the Agrarian Party

The origins of the Agrarian Party can be traced to the economic mobilisation of the farmers and the establishment of a Farmers' Union (*Norsk Landmandsforbund*) in 1896 (later renamed *Norges Bondelag*). The Union was spawned of dissatisfaction on the part of the farmers with the two existing parties, the Liberals (*Venstre*) and the Conservatives (*Høgre*). Instead of working to influence the representatives of these two parties in parliament, many farmers felt they needed their own party in order effectively to promote their economic interests. In 1919 the Farmers' Union set up a committee with the task of resolving the 'party question' and, by extension, how the political activity of the Union should develop. However, the committee was divided on whether or not it should go ahead with plans for launching a political party. Although a majority of its members ultimately opposed the plan, a majority at the Union's national conference in 1920 decided to go ahead with it. The Agrarian Party was founded on 19 June 1920 as the political arm of the Norwegian Farmers' Union.

The Agrarian Party was designed to be a single-issue party for a specific stratum of agriculturists. Importantly, the social base of the party did not embrace the farming population as a whole so much as the large landowners organised in the Farmers' Union. Re-stated, the Union and the party were an expression of the mobilisation of the commercial farmers in the most economically developed eastern parts of Norway (Nordby 1991:140-41). The Agrarians participated in their first election in 1921.[4] This gave the nascent party its greatest share of the non-socialist vote in areas were the Farmers' Union boasted its highest level of membership. In the western parts of Norway, where economic development was less advanced, both the Farmers' Union and the Agrarian Party struggled to gain a foothold (Aasland 1974: 254-256). The support of the farmers in these areas was captured first by the Liberals and later, in the economic crisis of the 1920s, by the Labour Party (Furre 1971a: 164).

Compared to its Scandinavian sister parties, the Norwegian party was a classic case of an externally created party à la Duverger. It rested on a pre-existing (interest group) base outside the legislature. Indeed, the Norwegian Farmers' Union did not draw a formal distinction between its political and economic functions in the 1920s. The party blended into the economic organisation of the farmers locally and the same people were at the heart of the local party, local union and local sales organisation. Throughout Norway the organisational development of the party took place as a process of penetration, not by the party itself, but by the Farmers' Union. The party lacked real autonomy and was in effect a puppet of the Union. Aasland (1974: 250) concludes that 'what the Union actually did was to make its existing organisation stronger for its primary purpose, whilst establishing a new party organisation which it kept control over without giving it any influence in return'. As late as the 1940s, the Agrarian Party's finances rested on the membership dues paid to the Union. Significantly, the party was characterised by very weak leadership throughout the 1930s. The formation of the first government led by the Agrarian Party in 1931 illustrates the point, since Jens Hundseid, who was both party leader and parliamentary leader, failed to get elected as Prime Minister! (Hauge 1980: 56). Hundseid took over as Prime Minister when Peder Kolstad died in 1932, but could not even get support for a ministerial reshuffle when he wanted to remove the minister of law, Lindboe, and the minister of defence, Quisling (Gabrielsen 1970: 99).

The ideological foundation of the party was built on a specific agricultural identity closely related to the interests of the larger landowners. When it came to agricultural policy, the party canvassed protectionism from the start. The economic crisis in the 1920s was defined as a 'price crisis' and, as it grew worse, the party saw it as imperative to organise the sale of products in order permanently to stabilise prices. Furre (1971a) has described how the Agrarian Party regarded itself as a corporation for farm interests and claimed to represent economic interests not adequately voiced by the existing party system. Kristinsson (1991:125-126) has shown that a number of young agricultural technocrats played an important role in the party's parliamentary group from the very outset. Gabrielsen (1970: 205) in turn has observed that the attitude of these technocrats towards party policy was to press 'an aggressive agricultural course and a harder class attitude than the older generation of MPs'.[5] The combination of farmers and agricultural technocrats in the party leadership may be one factor explaining the strict class strategy pursued by the party in the pre-1945 period. Ultimately the hardships of the 1920s paved the way for the so-called [red-green] 'crisis agreement' between the Labour Party and the Agrarian Party in 1935.[6] In return for Agrarian support for a package of innovative social security reforms, the Labour Party provided measures of agricultural protection. In addition, this 'historic class compromise' between workers and farmers facilitated a programme of welfare legislation through which all citizens were included in the redistribution of public goods (old age pension, unemployment insurance etc.). Consequently, the Agrarians made a significant contribution to the first wave of social policy reforms. However, the 'crisis agreement' did not lead to a more permanent 'red-green' alliance as in Sweden.

The aftermath of the Second World War confronted the Agrarian Party with new challenges. During the war its organisation had been dormant, whilst a negative attitude had developed towards the party as a result of the fact that several of its leading personalities had sympathised with the Nazis. Agrarian Party politicians, like Jens Hundseid, were arrested (Gabrielsen 1970). The editor of the party newspaper, *Nationen*, Thorvald Aadahl, had sympathised with the neo-Nazi *Nasjonal Samling* ('National Unity') and was forced to step down. In 1934 the Agrarian Party had even negotiated [albeit unsuccessfully] with several fringe radical rightist groups about the possibility of a common political platform. Most importantly, however, the name of the arch Nazi collaborator, Vidkun Quisling, was linked to the party since he participated in the Agrarian minority government between 1931-1933. This was despite the fact that

Quisling broke with the party in 1933 to head his own party, the aforementioned *Nasjonal Samling*. The adverse public climate prompted the Agrarian Party leadership to consider not taking part in the 1945 parliamentary election. Certainly the other parties displayed a reticent attitude towards the Agrarian Party and some believed it would not survive the 1945 election (Holmen 1971: 75). In the event, with 8.1 per cent of the vote, the party lost eight of its previous eighteen MPs at the polls that year.

Importantly, the first question raised by the Agrarian Party leadership in 1945 was not how to reform the party, but how to restore it. A Youth Organisation was established in 1949 and a Women's Organisation in 1953. The Farmers' Union adopted an officially neutral position towards the party in 1946 (Feiring 1972). The newspaper, *Nationen*, which had been under Union control, was taken over by the party. In addition the party mobilised new members in the post-war period. In 1947-1948 the party had 29,000 members; in 1957 this figure had risen to 64,000. Most of the voters had returned to the party when the name debate was placed on the agenda in 1952.

In its first two decades, policy seeking had been the primary goal of the Agrarian Party. Put simply, the interests of the farmers were given primacy. Moreover, content with its electoral performance on the threshold of the 1950s, the Agrarians saw no reason to engage in catchall politics. Subtly though, the policy style of the post-war period differed from the class-dominated politics of the 1930s. Legislative agreements and interparty compromises now became the staple characteristics of Norwegian political life.

**The Name Debate 1952-1959**

The Agrarian Party was not in a hurry to modernise itself. The question of changing the party's name, for example, first came up in 1952, but it took seven years before it gained acceptance at an extraordinary party conference in 1959. The discussion launched by the party leadership concerned ways in which the party might appeal to new segments of the electorate. Would voters still be willing to rally around a party named the Agrarian Party?

At the party conference in 1953, a committee was appointed to assess the alternatives (Gabrielsen 1970, Holmen 1971). Its chairman, Jon Leirfall, saw no need to rush the issue, however, and the committee's first meeting was held no less than one year later in October 1954! Thereafter, several options were discussed, although the committee members ultimately failed to agree on a common proposal. Three alternatives were prominent in their deliberations:

1. The *Class Party option*. The 'traditionalists', mostly party veterans, wanted the party to stay 'where it was stuck'. They saw no need for change. As a leading spokesman of the class party option, E. Vatnaland stated that: 'the farmers need their own party – they have common interests that are incompatible with the interests of the population at large' (Holmen 1971: 31).[7]

2. The *Rural Party option*. The 'rural wing' wanted to refurbish the party's name so as to include the word 'rural' or 'countryside' in it, and thus to go where 'the party's heart was'. A leap into the unknown was too risky: the party's natural constituency comprised people living in the countryside. The name-change committee chairman, John Leirfall, backed this alternative. He saw Norwegian politics as a battle between the irreconcilable interests of the centre and the periphery.

3. The *Catchall Party option*. The 'reformers' wanted the party to go 'where the voters were', i.e. they aimed at a nationally based party. Their main argument was that little would be gained by renaming the party the 'Rural Party'. The party's chairman, Per Borten, voiced the views of the reformers and opposed a name that would identify the party with different segments of society.

Eventually, however, a majority of the name-change committee plumped for the middle way, i.e., a name with 'rural' (*bygd*) in it. One of its members, Einar Hovdhaugen, favoured a name with a wider appeal and came up with the proposal 'the Norwegian People's Party' (*Det Norske Folkeparti*). Another went for the Class Party option.

The debate at the 1955 party conference was short and the conclusion unequivocal. A change of name was too risky. A test vote among delegates indicated that 57 wanted to change the party's name whereas 63 were opposed to it. A ballot of members the same year also showed that the balance inclined towards the Class Party option. Out of the 5055 members that took a stance on the issue, 2708 (53.6 per cent) wanted to keep the old name (Dale 1980: 117). Fearing open division, conference decided to postpone the issue. As Gabrielsen (1970: 197) has observed "the issue split the delegates in two and further debate was useless". The 1957 party conference did likewise and decided to keep the issue off the agenda.

When the Party Council discussed the issue in 1958 and overwhelmingly (46 votes to 9) supported a change of name, the debate within the party was rekindled. The 'reformers' now had the upper hand, and the 1959 party conference would be obliged to take a stand. However, in their eagerness to rename the party, the leadership failed to agree on which alternative should be presented to conference. As late as the day before the start of proceedings, the Party Council could still not reach a consensus on a new name. Conference delegates were hesitant but opted by 118-19 to call the party the 'Norwegian Popular Sovereignty Party' (*Norsk Folkestyreparti*). The new name was met with a mixture of amusement and ridicule in the press. A curious situation arose when, as a consequence, the party leadership decided that the conference decision had to be reversed, and that an extraordinary gathering later the same year should take a 'permanent decision'. This time conference did not hesitate and, after a short debate, the Centre Party (*Senterpartiet*) was born. The Swedish sister-party's success under the new Centre Party label made it easier for conference delegates. Yet another test vote showed 76 delegates in favour of 'Centre Party', 46 for 'Rural Party' (*Bygdepartiet*), and 10 for 'Farmers Party' (*Bondepartiet*). The party organ *Nationen* commented that 'if the press had not hammered home how ridiculous the first party conference decision was, the name "Centre Party" would not have gathered such strong support' (Nationen 13 June 1959). The newspaper added that, in an effort to appease the traditionalists, 'Agrarian Party' would still appear in small letters on the Centre Party's election lists. Hence, it was not a party eager to modernise itself that left the 1959 party conference. One party veteran wrote that (Dale 1980:114), 'at the leadership level the party agreed to build a new ideological platform, but the gap between intention and realisation was huge'.

## Centre Party Electoral and Legislative Performance

The new designation gave the party no immediate electoral dividend. However, the Agrarian-Centre experienced a slow but steady upturn in its electoral fortunes in the period 1949-1973. Voter support grew from 7.9 per cent in 1949 to a peak of 11.1 per cent in 1973 (see Figure 2.2). However, in the three elections in the 1980s, the party's support fell back to around 6.5 per cent. Once the EU issue was back on the agenda again in the early 1990s, the Centre Party anticipated big gains. Yet the 1991 local election and the 1993 parliamentary election turned out to be aberrations. In 1993 its vigorous anti-EU stance transformed the former Agrarians into the biggest opposition party with 16.8 per cent of the votes. Four years later, following a second Norwegian 'no' to Europe in the 1994 referendum, the intensity of anti-EU feeling had died down somewhat and the Centre Party's parliamentary group was halved. There do not appear to be any short-term factors to explain the Centre Party's sharp rise in support apart from the question of European integration. Figure 2.2 indicates clearly that this single issue has explained the lion's share of the increase in the Centre Party's vote. Whilst in most Norwegian parties there has been a significant discrepancy between the party elite and rank-and-file supporters on Europe, the Agrarian-Centre was united both in 1972 and again in 1994 (Lindström and Svåsand 1996). Equally, the European issue has not enabled the party to gain a lasting foothold among new sections of the electorate.

**Figure 2.2 The Norweigan Centre Party's Electoral Support, 1936-1997 (%)**

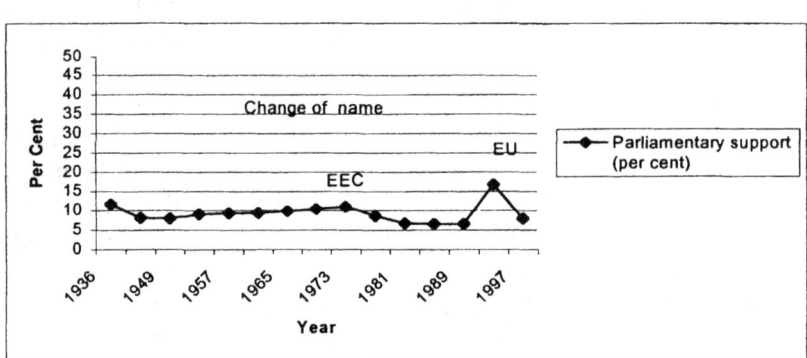

Traditionally Norweigan multiparty politics has produced two main governmental alternatives that can be located along a left-right continuum. In the pre-1961 period Norway could even be characterised as a 'dominant' party system in that Labour governments usually controlled effective parliamentary majorities. In other words, they were able to rely on shifting alliances in parliament – joined by the left wing opposition on some issues and one or more of the bourgeois parties on others (Strøm 1990: 225-226). On occasions, Labour even polled a greater proportion of the votes than the British Labour and Conservative parties under a plurality electoral system. Since the 1961 election, however, no single party has gained an electoral or parliamentary majority in Norway (Svåsand and Strøm 1997). Over the last four decades, Norwegian voters have normally been confronted by two competing government alternatives – either a non-socialist coalition or a minority Labour government dependent upon active support from the Left Socialist Party (*Sosialistisk Venstreparti*) or the small parties 'in the middle' (including the Centre Party). The non-socialist parties have often formed explicit electoral alliances before elections.

In a multiparty system, possessing relevant policies is not enough when a party communicates with voters. It must also be able to demonstrate its relevance for government and policy-making. In coalition systems, like the Norwegian, this may be problematical. On the one hand, co-operation is necessary if a party wishes to influence policy; on the other, co-operation requires compromises that can reduce a party's credibility. In addition to prioritising specific issues in elections, parties also have to choose which party(ies) will be their opponent(s) or coalition partner(s). This choice has to correspond in some measure to the party's election programme. Within the Centre Party, discussions have concentrated on three coalition alternatives. 1) A centrist government comprising the Liberals, Centre and Christian People's Party. This option was favoured in the 1960s and 1990s. 2) A non-socialist coalition involving the three aforementioned parties, plus the Conservatives. This option has been the principal alternative to a Labour Party government since 1965. 3) A 'red-green' alliance between the Centre Party and the Labour Party. This alternative was preferred by the Centre Party's Youth organisation in the 1960s, but gained little or no support within the parliamentary party.

Traditionally, the Centre Party has given precedence to a sector-orientated 'office-seeking' strategy (Rovde 1989, Kristinsson 1991, Christensen 1992). The concerns of the agricultural sector have been by far the most important factor explaining this course of action. The party participated in a non-socialist government from 1965 to 1971 when regional policy became an important issue in Norwegian politics. Co-operation, especially with the Conservative Party, made compromises on regional policy necessary for the survival of the government, but these led to internal conflict within the Centre Party. The left wing wanted to break with its coalition partners so as to articulate a more radical regional policy, while the right wing gave priority to non-socialist co-operation.

The 1990s, however, has witnessed a change in parliamentary strategy. This coincided with the advent in 1991 of Anne Enger Lahnstein as the party's first female leader. Lahnstein declared, as the Swedish sister-party had done in the 1960s, that the categories 'left' and 'right' were obsolete. 'The middle is a third centre of gravity and an alternative to both left and right' (Centre Party election handbook 1991: 237). The Centre Party challenged its old coalition partner, the Conservatives, insisting that the latter espoused policies that were anathema to the Centre. This new 'centrist' parliamentary strategy also seems to be the one pursued by Odd Roger Enoksen, who succeeded Lahnstein in March 1999.

Between autumn 1997 and spring 2000, the Centre Party joined the Christian People's Party and Liberals in a fragile centre-based coalition. Together the three parties controlled only 42 seats in the Storting or 25 per cent of all parliamentarians. The coalition claimed to be the only alternative capable of altering the configuration of alliances in the assembly. Numerically very weak, the Bondevik coalition proved remarkably durable. It survived three budgets. To secure the passage of the first two, deals were done with the right wing parties, while the Labour Party reluctantly worked with the government on the budget proposal for 2000. It was not an electoral victory that helped the three parties into office but the Labour Party leader, Torbjørn Jagland's bad tactical miscalculation. Before the 1997 election he announced that his minority government would resign if Labour failed to win 36.9 per cent of the votes (the amount it polled in 1993). It failed to do so, and this opened the way for a centrist government that nobody could possibly have envisaged six months before the election. The three parties issued their joint governmental programme in May 1997 and, astonishingly, four months later they were in office.

It was not easy to say who governed Norway between 1997 and the resignation of the Bondevik cabinet over the issue of gas-fired power stations in 2000. The coalition faced a legislative majority on several issues that were of vital importance to the Centre Party. These included questions related to European integration. In addition, the three governing parties differed on the European Economic Area (EEA) agreement,[8] the Centre Party opposing it while the Christians and Liberals supported it. The Centre Party also found it hard to get their coalition partners to veto EU regulations.[9] The Centre Party's participation in government put it under strong pressure from a critical membership. Several high-ranking party members at the county (*fylkeskommun*) level demanded that the Centre should leave the government if it could not get its partners to veto controversial directives issued by the EU. These included regulations on food colouring and preservatives and genetically modified food.

## Class, Rural or Catchall Party?

This section focuses on the Centre Party's efforts to modernise itself. It considers the catchall option alongside the two other alternatives discussed in connection with the change of name in the 1950s, the class party option and the rural party option. The analysis takes the catchall party thesis as its starting point and asks if the Centre Party has 1) manipulated its ideology for electoral reasons? 2) attracted support from a cross-section of the electorate? 3) downplayed the role of individual party members? 4) renounced its formal links to the Farmers' Union and sought contact with a wide variety of different interest groups?

The modernisation of the Centre Party in the 1950s involved adopting a new name but not a new party programme. It saw no need to engage in catchall politics; indeed, it was rather pleased with its performance. Moreover, as Dale (1980: 123) has observed, it was 'the farm and rural interests that were in the forefront in the name debate'. Significantly, the Centre Party's first new statement of basic principles was not adopted until 1965, seven years after the party renamed itself. Its title was 'The will to assume responsibility' and it contained liberal use of the slogan 'decentralising people, power and capital'. Above all, it was directed towards mobilising rural communities.

**Figure 2.3 The Amount of Space in the Agrarian-Centre's Manifestos Devoted to Regional Policy, Environment and Agriculture, 1945-1989 (%)**

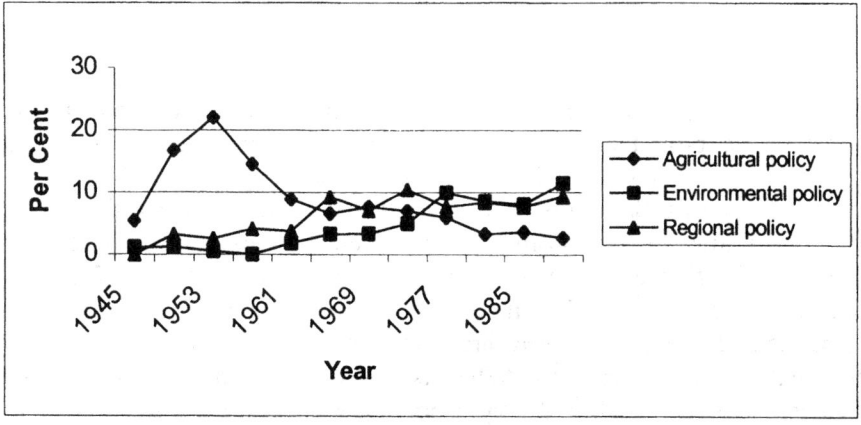

The Centre Party has moderated its class character and developed a broader political platform since the 1950s. Issues other than those directly related to agriculture have been incorporated into its manifestos. Based on data from the European Manifestos Project, Figure 2.3 shows how much space the party has devoted to three vital policy areas. Agriculture reflects traditional party concerns whilst regional policy and environmental issues have been crucial elements in the party's redefinition of its identity. It can be seen that the amount of space the Norwegian Centre Party has allocated to agricultural questions has decreased over time, while regional policy and environmental issues have assumed greater prominence. The party's change of name in 1959, however, had only a minor impact on the party's policy profile. Perhaps more revealing than the figures is what the manifestos indicate about the nature of agricultural policy. The Centre Party's manifestos have been marked by an increasingly positive attitude towards state intervention in the agricultural sector. The traditional call for income equality between agriculture and industry has, of course, been present in the manifestos of the Centre Party throughout the period.

**Table 2.1    Space Devoted to Agriculture Relative to Industry in the Manifestos of the Norwegian Agrarian/Centre, 1957-1985**

| Year    |     |
|---------|-----|
| 1957/58 | 4:1 |
| 1969/70 | 2:1 |
| 1977/81 | 2:1 |
| 1985    | 3:1 |

*Source*: Steen 1988: 326.

In terms of regional policy, the conflicting interests between rural and urban areas provided the basis on which the Centre Party sought to mobilise core voters. Indeed, the party scarcely acknowledged the phenomenon of urbanisation until the late 1970s and remained thoroughly orientated towards the promotion and protection of rural and regional interests. Its first action programme for the cities came in 1977. What stands out from Table 2.1, moreover, is that even in 1985 agriculture, fisheries and forestry received three times the space devoted to industry in the Centre Party's manifestos. Whereas the Swedish Centre Party addressed the concerns of small industry from 1959, direct proposals aimed at stimulating the growth of small firms were not incorporated into the Norwegian party's manifestos before 1965. In fact, the Norwegian Centre Party's new programme in 1965 was taken more or less wholesale from the Swedish Party's 1959 programme. Its key words were 'decentralising people, power and capital' together with 'equal living conditions for the rural population'. The party engaged itself, among other things, in the fight to prevent the closure of rural schools and opposed the merging of local authorities. With the Rural Party option as the main thrust, the party directed itself towards new support groups in the countryside.

Table 2.2 indicates that Norwegian farmers have developed an attitude of dependency on the state in respect of their incomes. For example, between 1983-85 they received over half their income in the form of state subsidies. Clearly, therefore, the farmers have much to gain from the state and are favourably disposed towards a government that does not prioritise economic efficiency. Preserving a strong element of state intervention in Norwegian agricultural policy has been a primary concern of the traditionalists within the Centre Party. Thus, the Centre has been active in the deliberation of agricultural issues in the Storting. Between 1987 and 88, approximately 25 per cent of agriculture-related questions raised in parliament emanated from the party, although it comprised only 7 per cent of MPs at the time (Dagens Næringsliv 6 March 1991). That is why the likelihood of finding a single supporter of the European Union in the Centre Party's ranks is effectively nil.[10]

Table 2.2  Income from Sales and State Subsidies as part of Net Farm Income, 1959-1985 (%)*

|  | 1959 | 1969 | 1976-78 | 1983-85 |
| --- | --- | --- | --- | --- |
| Income sale | 93 | 87 | 75 | 44.6 |
| State subsidy | 7 | 13 | 25 | 55.6 |
| Total net income | 100 | 100 | 100 | 100 |

* Net income includes sale of agricultural products, state subsidies and other incomes deducted.

Key political issues also form part of the 'structures of opportunity'. In Norway the EEC/EU question has reinforced the impression of the Centre Party as being primarily concerned with regional and farm interests. Between 1969-73 Norwegian politics was dominated by the matter of

Norway's relations with the European Community. The Centre-led coalition under Per Borten was in office when the third application for membership was lodged, but stood down a year before the first EC/EU referendum in 1972 (Trøite and Vold 1972). The interests of the farmers took centre stage in the debate, making it impossible for the Centre Party to profile itself as anything other than a farmers' party. In the EEC referendum in 1972, 84 per cent of the farmers and fishermen voted against membership (Kristinsson 1991: 207). The 1973 election gave the Centre Party 11.1 per cent of the votes, its best result since changing its name. However, the party did not manage to integrate the anti-EEC interests into a broad, still less lasting coalition. The parallel with the 1993 election is remarkable. Then, the party opposed the EEA agreement as well as Norwegian EU-membership and achieved its best performance ever with 16.8 per cent of the poll. Of the Centre Party's voters 94 per cent opposed membership in the European Union in 1994.[11] This time the potential for the Centre Party to retain some of its new followers appeared greater as a result of changes in Labour Party policy. The latter's strategy in the aftermath of the 1972 referendum was to recapture lost voters by emphasising regional policy and agricultural policy. After 1994 Labour Party policy has been characterised by a more pragmatic stance on these issues, creating (in principle at least) some electoral space for the Centre Party.

The centre party has not displayed evidence of de-ideologisation. In fact, many political commentators have argued just the reverse. The EU issue fuelled a massive Centre Party critique of modern capitalism and even the Conservatives began to view the Centre Party's economic policies as too extreme. Indeed, Narud (1999) has shown how voters have tended to shift their placement of the Centre Party on the political spectrum. In previous studies voters placed the Centre Party to the right of the Labour Party, but in 1997 the two parties had changed position. In addition, the distance between the Conservatives and the Centre Party has increased. Significantly, at its conference in 1993, the Left Socialists sought to include the Centre Party in its governmental sights, in addition of course to the Labour Party. The current Centre Party leader, Odd Roger Enoksen's efforts to press the issue of the public ownership of vital industries illustrates the same tendency.

The social profile of the Centre Party's vote is not compatible with the catchall party option (see Table 2.3 and Figure 2.4). Its core voter remains employed in agriculture and lives in rural areas. None the less, whereas the party received nearly three-quarters of its 1957 vote from farmers and fishermen, this had fallen to one-third in 1989. What stands out, moreover, is the party's appeal to the 'new middle class'. Since 1957 the party's share of the vote from salaried employees has increased by 31 per cent and by 1997 the predominant share of the Centre vote came from the new middle class. Typically these middle class voters are employed in the public sector and have their background in rural areas (Valen 1981). The party is also over-represented among men and the older generation (Bjørklund 1999).

Table 2.3 The Norwegian Centre Party's Voter by Occupation, 1957-1997 (%)

|  | 1957 | 1965 | 1969 | 1973 | 1977 | 1981 | 1985 | 1989 | 1993 | 1997 |
|---|---|---|---|---|---|---|---|---|---|---|
| Farmers* | 74 | 71 | 59 | 55 | 43 | 31 | 33 | 41 | 19 | 26 |
| Workers | 17 | 13 | 20 | 24 | 28 | 32 | 12 | 22 | 26 | 24 |
| Employees** | 8 | 11 | 16 | 16 | 24 | 24 | 28 | 23 | 39 | 39 |
| Self-employed | 1 | 4 | 5 | 6 | 5 | 13 | 12 | 4 | 7 | 5 |
| Others | - | - | - | - | - | - | 15 | 10 | 9 | 6 |
| Total | 100 | 100 | 100 | 100 | 100 | 100 | 100 | 100 | 100 | 100 |
| N | 104 | 188 | 186 | 165 | 87 | 87 | 129 | 111 | 316 | 134 |

*Farmers includes fishermen
** Private and public employees in one category

Geographically the Centre Party stands out as an ideal-type rural party. Between 70-80 per cent of its supporters live in rural areas. It has been especially strong in Trøndelag and the western parts of Norway. This regional profile has been stable over the whole period although the party has increased its support in the coastal areas of western and northern Norway as a result of its stronger engagement in fishery policy. The 1993 election, however, marked a complete break with the past. The EU-dispute even helped the Centre to gain ground in urban areas. However, by 1997 the party had forfeited its newly won electorate, whilst in the 1999 local elections the party's suffered a severe setback in the cities. It presently lacks representation in cities like Oslo, Kristiansand, Hamar and Porsgrunn. In Horten, Trondheim, Bergen, Arendal and Skien, the Centre has only a solitary member on the local councils. The party leader, Enoksen, has stated that reversing the disappointing electoral results in the cities is the primary challenge facing the party organisation in the run-up to the 2001

## 50  From Farmyard to City Square?

parliamentary elections.[12] The Centre's representatives on the city councils are also demanding a coherent Centre Party policy on city development.[13]

**Figure 2.4  The Norwegian Centre Party's Support in Rural and Urban Communes**

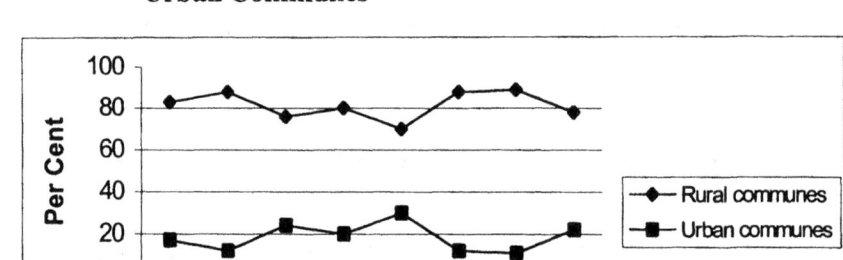

The data in Table 2.4 indicate the existence of strong inter-party competition for the farm vote and suggest that the Centre Party has underperformed among its core electorate. The tendency was for the party to gain a stronger hold on the primary sector vote in the 1970s and 1990s and this constituted a barrier to a comprehensive change of policy. Although most farmers in Norway vote for the Centre Party, the Norwegian Agrarian-Centre Party has never been alone in defending the interests of the farmers and rural economy. When the transformation of the party began in the late 1950s, the farmers were divided among several parties. The Labour Party and the other parties in the centre (the Liberals and Christian Democrats) were particular competitors of the Centre Party for the smallholders' vote (Berglund and Lindström 2000). The larger landowners, on the other hand, have split their vote between the Agrarian-Centre Party and the Conservative Party. This made the catchall option risky. Moving too far away from traditional party policy, it was feared, might lead the party's core supporters into the arms of its competitors. The risk was heightened because the other parties could offer almost identical policies with regard to the farm interests. An alternative strategy was to compete for votes among the smallholders that had traditionally supported the Labour Party. This Rural Party option seemed the safer bet and, accordingly, the party pursued a 'regional' strategy of prioritising the interests of the primary sector as a whole and not just the interests of the medium-sized and larger farm holdings.

**Table 2.4 The Primary Sector Vote by Party, 1965-1997**

| Party | 1965 | 1969 | 1973 | 1977 | 1981 | 1985 | 1989 | 1993 | 1997 |
|---|---|---|---|---|---|---|---|---|---|
| Left Socialist Party* | 0.7 | 0.5 | 0.7 | 1.1 | 0.0 | 2.1 | 6.4 | 2.2 | 5.2 |
| Labour Party | 23.2 | 17.9 | 12.7 | 11.8 | 20.6 | 18.8 | 24.0 | 21.5 | 10.4 |
| Liberals | 8.8 | 4.3 | 3.3 | 3.9 | 4.4 | 1.0 | 2.4 | 1.1 | 5.2 |
| Christian People's Party | 7.0 | 8.2 | 16.0 | 11.8 | 7.4 | 14.6 | 12.0 | 6.5 | 16.9 |
| Centre Party | 48.5 | 59.8 | 60.0 | 56.9 | 39.7 | 44.8 | 36.0 | 63.4 | 45.5 |
| Conservative Party | 11.4 | 9.2 | 5.3 | 12.7 | 22.1 | 17.7 | 10.4 | 4.3 | 5.2 |
| Progress Party** | - | - | 2.0 | 0.0 | 2.9 | 0.0 | 7.2 | 1.1 | 10.4 |
| Others | 0.4 | 0.0 | 0.0 | 2.0 | 3.0 | 1.0 | 1.6 | 0.0 | 1.3 |
| N | 272 | 184 | 150 | 102 | 68 | 96 | 125 | 93 | 77 |

\* Socialist People's Party to 1975
\*\* Anders Langes Party to 1975

Kirchheimer has made the point that every election is a new and unpredictable event, although that was not really the case in Norway until the late 1980s. Thereafter, the Norwegian electorate became more heterogeneous and unstable and class voting declined markedly (Lane et.al 1993). Today, more people vote differently from one election to the next – 43 per cent changed allegiance in 1997 – and the volume of voter traffic across traditional boundaries – such between socialist and non-socialist parties – has increased. The declining incidence of class voting, the increase in last-minute choices ('eleventh-hour voting'), growing volatility and weakened partisan identification have all meant that the electorate presents more challenges for the party tacticians today than earlier. Carefully planned catchall strategies, for example, can be of little worth in an electoral environment where the electronic media have a decisive and independent impact on the political agenda. One of the reasons for the stability that Lipset and Rokkan (1967) observed, when formulating their 'freezing' of party systems hypothesis was the adaptability of political parties. As indicated earlier, new electoral concerns, especially environmental issues, have been integrated into the Centre Party's political profile.

52 *From Farmyard to City Square?*

It is important to consider the extent to which the Centre Party conforms to the 'top-down' organisational style predicted by Kirchheimer. In general the party possesses an organisational structure broadly similar to the other Norwegian parties. The party conference, held every second year, determines party policy and elects the leadership. The Party Executive (*Sentralstyret*) is composed of the party chairman, a deputy chairman, five other members and the chairman of the Youth Organisation. If not already elected, the leader of the parliamentary group is co-opted as a member. In addition to the Party Executive, the party discusses current issues and issues of principle in the Party Council (*Landsstyret*) which comprises the parliamentary group, the Party Executive, two representatives from the Youth and Women's Organisations and one each from the press and party secretary associations.

The Centre Party has not downgraded the importance of its membership. The number of members increased between 1961 and 1966, a time when the party tried to refurbish its image. In 1948 the party had 29,000 members whereas by 1961 the figure had risen to 32,000. It was not until the 1960s in fact that the party developed a mass political organisation comparable to that of the Labour and Conservatives parties. What stands out from Table 2.5 is that the Centre Party increased its membership in the 1960s but has experienced a modest, but steady decline in membership ever since (see also Svåsand 1994).

Table 2.5 **Norwegian Centre Party Membership, 1961-1997**

| Year | Number of members |
|---|---|
| 1961 | 61,000 |
| 1966 | 67,154 |
| 1971 | 61,728 |
| 1976 | 56,542 |
| 1980 | 54,939 |
| 1985 | 46,923 |
| 1989 | 48,503 |
| 1995 | 46,627 |
| 1997 | 39,766 |

It is hard to say whether the Centre Party leadership has strengthened its position over time. True, there has been a low level of leadership turnover. Typically, party leaders have tended to be re-elected for several terms.[14]

However, the party leadership, as in most Norwegian parties, is dependent on the support, or at very least the broad acquiescence of party activists. Party programmes are developed by a centrally appointed committee that submits its proposal to the Party Executive. Early in an election year, a draft proposal is circulated to the party branches and they are invited to propose additions and/or amendments. Eventually a revised proposal is presented to the party conference in the spring where it is adopted.

Finally, it is difficult to square the catchall option with the social characteristics of either party members or the party elite. Heidar (1997) has shown that farmers and fishermen account for between 40 and 60 per cent of the party's members. The steady downward trend in membership obviously reflects the decline in the size of the agricultural community. Organisationally, the social profile of Centre members is a long way from being a mirror image of a catchall party. The most important change that has occurred in the lifetime of the Centre Party has been the removal of the normal links between the political and economic arms of the farmers' movement. However, it is important to stress how extremely strong the bonds once were. In the 1920s the Agrarian Party programme even had to gain acceptance at the leadership level in the Union. The party veteran, Jon Leirfall (1989: 21), has recorded how the Union paid the party to look after its interests. Although the formal ties have been broken, informal contacts remained strong until the 1980s and there was extensive personnel overlap between the two organisations. There was a tradition of Centre Party MPs being represented at leadership level in the Farmers' Union[15] and the party in turn voiced the interests of the Union in parliament. However, this situation of close mutuality appeared to end in the 1990s. The Bondevik centrist coalition of 1997-2000 even launched plans to reduce state subsidies to the agricultural sector and there is no longer a parliamentary majority in the Storting when it comes to agricultural subsidies. High agricultural subsidies seem to be a lost cause for the Centre Party which in turn has largely accepted the situation. Yet whilst the Centre Party has played down its relationship with the Farmers' Union, there is no evidence to suggest that it has tried to build bridges to other interest organisations. There has in fact been a general tendency in Norwegian politics to play down the linkages between parties and interest groups.

## Conclusion: New Bottle, Same Old Content?

Alan Ware (1996: 329) has noted that a firm that consistently fails to make a profit will eventually go out of business. Yet it seems that a party can remain very much in existence even if it does not expand its electoral base and/or languishes for long periods in opposition. Ware's observation applies extremely well to the Centre Party. The party has not witnessed the changes in strategy and style that Kirchheimer predicted. It does not possess a heterogeneous support base and it lives for, and off the periphery. It is heavily under-represented in urban areas and the social profile of the party's voters reveals that it has not attracted lasting support from a broad cross-section of the electorate. The party holds on to an extremely loyal, though dwindling clientele. The only real exception to the rule was the 1993 general election. When it comes to policy, the party has moderated its class character and adjusted its appeal. However, policy is still primarily directed towards the regional and rural interests – interests that may still be seen as incompatible with those of the urban areas. The party defends the periphery against the centre, and the nation against supranational centres such as Brussels. The party's focus from 1965 has been on the decentralisation of people, power and capital. The only short-term issue that has affected the Centre Party's electoral support has been the EC/EU issue, which has reactivated two deep-seated historic cleavages, the centre-periphery axis and the urban-rural axis.

The Agrarian-Centre Party has survived for eight decades and presently operates in a political environment that is radically different from its early years. Thus far, it has been able to play a not insignificant role in Norwegian politics with the support of mostly between six to ten per cent of the electorate. According to Kirchheimer, vote seeking is the primary goal of political parties. However, this chapter has stressed office seeking as the foremost aim of the Centre Party. For example, the vote-seeking benefits could hardly explain the Centre Party's participation in the Bondevik coalition (1997-2000), since the party witnessed a steady decline in the opinion polls thereafter. The policy-seeking benefits do not provide an adequate explanation either since the Bondevik government was extremely weak and faced an adverse parliamentary majority on crucial issues. The Centre Party leadership has also faced a difficult task balancing the interests within the party so that intra-party democracy does not fit the bill. What remains, by a process of elimination, are the office-seeking benefits. The [unlikely] formation of a centrist coalition in 1997 was, in no small measure, designed to demonstrate to voters that it was possible to build a coalition that excluded the Conservative Party whilst at the same time offering a viable alternative to a minority Labour Party government. In sum, vote seeking does not always represent an accurate characterisation of the games played in coalition systems like the Norwegian.

## Notes

1. The Labour party was internally split on the issue and all local branches in northern Norway vigorously opposed membership. This time, however, Labour had learned from its mistakes in 1972. Then the Labour Prime Minister, Trygve Bratteli, made the issue a question of confidence in the government, pitting pro-EC Labour voters against anti-EC Labour voters. The party initiated a long and intensive consultation process within the party and the leadership did not take up a public stance until the 1992 party conference, when it eventually approved sending the application to Brussels. Labour even tolerated an anti-EU faction within the party, 'Social Democrats against the EU'. This prevented the Eurosceptics from leaving the party, and the party even improved its Storting representation at the 1993 general election.
2. The Scandinavian Christian parties differ from the Christian parties on the continent. They have not opposed national education as such and have not built up the extensive networks of functional organisations around their followers (Rokkan 1970: 106).
3. The Socialist People's Party helped topple the Labour Party minority government in 1963, bringing the non-socialists to power for the first time since 1945. Although the government fell after only a few weeks it was symbolically important because it demonstrated that there was a governmental alternative to Labour.
4. The party polled 118,000 votes and won as many as 17 seats in parliament in 1921.
5. The two Prime Ministers in the first Agrarian Party government in 1933, Peder Kolstad and Jens Hundseid, both had an agricultural education. Later, such prominent Centre Party politicians as Per Borten, Hans Borgen, and Johan J. Jakobsen graduated from the Agricultural University.
6. Identical parliamentary agreements were reached in Sweden in 1933 and in Finland in 1937.
7. Vatnaland was Member of Parliament from 1945 to 1961, and leader of the party's parliamentary group from 1948 to 1957.
8. In 1984, the EFTA and EC ministers agreed to create the so-called European Economic Area (EEA) comprising eighteen West European countries. The EEA negotiations started in June 1989 and by 1994 Norway gained full access to the single internal market, with the exception of sizeable portions of the fishery and agricultural sectors.
9. Prominent politicians, such as the former Prime Minister, Gro Harlem Brundtland, have suggested that next time Norway engages in a debate over EU membership it should arrange a referendum before the application for membership is sent.
10. On crossing the border into Sweden, however, pro-Europeans dominate the Centre Party leadership (Svåsand and Lindström 1996).
11. The referendum was held 28 November 1994.
12. Sentrum nr. 11, 23. September 1999 (Party membership paper).
13. See for instance Jill Eirin Undem, member of the city council in Tønsberg in Sentrum nr. 13 1999.
14. Since 1967 only 6 persons have filled the office of party chairman, Johns Austrheim (1967-1973), Dagfinn Vårvik (1973-1977), Gunnar Stålsett (1977-1979), Johan J.

Jacobsen (1979-1991), Anne Enger Lahnstein (1991-1999) and finally from 1999 Odd Roger Enoksen. Lahnstein turned out to be a very popular party leader and was seen as the leading figure in the movement against Norwegian membership of the European Union up to the referendum in 1994.

15  In the 1960s top Centre Party politicians like Per Borten, Hans Borgen, Jon Leirfall and Lars Leiro held positions at the leadership level in the Union of Farmers. During the Borten-led government between 1965 and 1971, the secretary general of the Union of Farmers, Dahlberg, even contributed to writing the chapter on agriculture in the government's White Paper on the EEC (Trøite and Vold 1977: 36). As late as 1989, Anne Vik, minister of agriculture, was also member of the Union's National Council.

## References

Aardal, Bernt (1994), 'The 1993 Storting Election: Volatile Voters Opposing the European Union', *Scandinavian Political Studies* 17(2): 171-180.
Aardal, Bernt and Henry Valen (1989), *Velgere, partier og politisk avstand*. Oslo-Kongsvinger: Statistisk Sentralbyrå.
Aardal, Bernt and Henry Valen (1997), 'The Storting Elections of 1989 and 1993: Norwegian Politics in Perspective', in Strøm, Kaare and Lars Svåsand (eds), *Challenges to Political Parties. The Case of Norway*. Ann Arbor, The University of Michigan Press, pp. 61-76.
Aardal, Bernt, Henry Valen, Hanne Marthe Narud and Frode Berglund (1999), *Velgere i 90-årene*. Oslo: NKS- Forlaget.
Aasland, Tertit (1974), *Fra landmannsorganisasjon til bondeparti: Politisk debatt og taktikk Norsk Landmandsforbund 1896-1920*. Oslo: Universitetsforlaget.
Berglund, Sten and Ulf Lindström (1978), *The Scandinavian Party System(s)*. Lund Studentlitteratur.
Berglund, Sten and Ulf Lindström 2000, *The Scandinavian Party System(s)*, Forthcoming.
Beyme, Klaus von (1985), *Political Parties in Western Democracies*, London: Gower.
Bjørklund, Tor (1999), *Et lokalvalg i perspektiv*. Oslo: Tano Aschehoug.
Christensen, Dag Arne (1992), Bondeparti, distriktsparti eller folkeparti: Ei komparativ analyse av fornyinga av bondepartia i Noreg og Sverige. Graduate thesis, Department of Comparative Politics, University of Bergen.
Christensen, Dag Arne (1996), 'The Left-Wing Opposition in Denmark, Norway and Sweden: Cases of Euro-phobia?', *West European Politics* 19(3): 525-546.
Christensen, Dag Arne (1997), 'Adaptation of Agrarian Parties in Norway and Sweden', *Party Politics* 3(3): 391-406.
Christensen, Dag Arne (1998), 'Foreign Policy Objectives: Left-Socialist Opposition in Denmark, Norway and Sweden', *Scandinavian Political Studies* 1(1): 51-70.
Dale, Jon (1980), '1960-åra: Spranget framover', in Jofred Storøen m.fl (ed.), *Rotfeste og framtid: Senterpartiet i medgang og motgang 1920-1980*. Oslo: Cultura Forlag.
Einhorn, Eric S and John Logue (1982), 'Continuity and Change in the Scandinavian Party Systems', in Steven B. Wolinetz (ed.), *Parties and Party Systems in Liberal Democracies*. London: Routledge.
Elder, Neil and Rolf Gooderham (1978), 'The Centre Parties of Norway and Sweden', *Government and Opposition* 13(2): 219-35.

Esping-Andersen, Gøran (1985), *Politics Against Markets: The Social Democratic Road to Power*. Princeton: NJ: Princeton University Press.
Feiring, Trond (1972), 'Jordbruksorganisasjonane etter krigen', in *Etterkrigshistorie III*. Oslo: Universitetsforlaget.
Fryklund, Björn and Tomas Peterson (1981), *Populism och missnöjepartier i norden. Studier av småborgerlig klassaktivitet*. Lund: Arkiv.
Furre, Berge (1971a), *Mjølk, bønder og tingmenn: Studiar i organisasjon og politikk kring omsetninga av visse landbruksvarer 1929-30*. Oslo: Det Norske Samlaget.
Furre, Berge (1971b), *Norsk historie 1905-1940*. Oslo: Det Norske Samlaget.
Gabrielsen, Bjørn Vidar (1970), *Menn og politikk: Senterpartiet 1920-1970*. Oslo: Aschehoug.
Green, Donald and Ian Shapiro (1994), *The Pathologies of Rational Choice Theory. A Critique of Applications in Political Science*, New Haven, Yale University Press.
Grønn-Hagen, Karen (1980), '50-åra med jevn framgang', in Jofred Storøen m.fl (ed.), *Rotfeste og framtid: Senterpartiet i medgang og motgang 1920-1980*. Oslo: Cultura Forlag.
Harmel, Robert and Kenneth Janda (1993), *Performance, Leadership, Factions, and Party Change: An Empirical Analysis'*, Manuscript presented at the 1993 annual conference of the American Political Science Association.
Holmen, Jenny (1971), Nytt navn – Ny politikk. Omkring Bondepartiets navneskifte 1959, Graduate thesis, Department of History, University of Oslo.
Kite, Cynthia (1996), *Scandinavia Faces EU: debates and decisions on membership 1961-1994*, Umeå University, Department of Political Science.
Kristinsson, Gunnar Helgi (1991), *Farmers' Parties: A Study in Electoral Adaption*. Félagsvísindastofnun Háskóla Íslands.
Lane, Jan-Erik, Tuomo Martikainen, Palle Svensson, Gunnar Vogt and Henry Valen (1993), 'Scandinavian Exceptionalism Reconsidered', *Journal of Theoretical Politics* 5(2): 195-230.
Narud, Hanne Marthe (1999), 'Politiske avstander og regjeringsalternativ ved valget i 1997', in Aardal, Bernt, Henry Valen, Hanne Marthe Narud and Frode Berglund (1999), *Velgere i 90-årene*. Oslo: NKS-Forlaget, pp. 120-143.
Nordby, Trond (1991), *Det moderne gjennobruddet i bondesamfunnet: Norege 1870-1920*. Oslo: Universitetsforlaget.
Panebianco, Angelo (1988), *Political Parties: Organizations and Power*. Cambridge: Cambridge University Press.
Petersson, Olof and Henry Valen (1979), 'Political Cleavages in Sweden and Norway', *Scandinavian Political Studies* 2(4): 313-332.
Rokkan, Stein (1970), *Citizens, Elections, Parties*. Bergen, Universitetsforlaget.
Rovde, Olav (1989), 'Borgarleg samling', in Trond Bergh and Helge Ø.Pharo (eds), *Vekst og velstand: Norsk politisk historie 1945-1965*. Oslo: Universitetsforlaget, pp. 397-450.
Sjøblom, Gunnar (1968), *Party Strategies in a Multiparty System*, Lund, Studentlitteratur.
Steen, Anton (1988), *Landbruket, staten og Sosialdemokratene. En komparativ studie av interessekonflikter i landbrukspolitikken i Norge, Sverige og England 1945-1985*. Oslo: Universitetsforlaget.
Strøm, Kaare (1990), 'A Behavioral Theory of Competitive Political Parties', *American Journal of Political Science* 34(2): 565-98.

Strøm, Kaare and Lars Svåsand (eds) (1997), *Challenges to Political Parties. The Case of Norway*. Ann Arbor, The University of Michigan Press.

Svåsand, Lars and Ulf Lindstrøm (1996), 'Scandinavian political parties and the European Union', in John Gaffney (ed.), *Political Parties and the European Union*, London: Routledge, pp. 205-219.

Trøite, Jostein and Jan Erik Vold (1977), *Bønder i EF strid. Senterpartiet og landbruksorganisasjonane 1961-72*. Oslo: Det Norske Samlaget.

Urwin, Derek (1997), 'The Norwegian Party System from the 1880s', in Strøm, Kaare and Lars Svåsand (eds), *Challenges to Political Parties. The Case of Norway*. Ann Arbor, The University of Michigan Press, pp. 33-60.

Valen, Henry (1972), 'Tre valg i utviklingens tegn', in Henry Valen and Willy Martinussen (eds), pp. 13-31.

Valen, Henry (1981), *Valg og politikk*. Oslo: NKS-Forlaget.

Valen, Henry (1992), *Valg og politikk: Et samfunn i endring*. Oslo: NKS-Forlaget.Valen, Henry og Willy Martinussen (1972a), *Velgere og politiske frontlinjer: Stemmegivning og stridsspørsmål 1957-1969* (together with P.E. Converse and D. Katz). Oslo: Gyldendal Norsk Forlag.

Valen, Henry and Willy Martinussen (1972b), 'Electoral Trends and Foreign Politics in Norway: The 1971 Storting Election and the EEC Issue', in Karl Cerny (ed.), *Scandinavia at the polls*. Washington, DC: American Enterprise Institute for Public Policy Research, pp. 39-72.

Valen, Henry, Bernt Olav Aardal and Gunnar Vogt (1990), *Endring og kontinuitet: Stortingsvalget 1989*. Oslo-Kongsvinger: Statistisk Sentralbyrå.

Ware, Alan (1996), *Political Parties and Party Systems*, Oxford: Oxford University Press.

# 3 The Finnish Centre Party: A Case of Successful Transformation?

DAVID ARTER

In his path-breaking work on the catchall 'people's party' in the mid-1960s, Otto Kirchheimer made it clear that, because of their defence of a specific clientele, Agrarian Parties could not become catchall parties.

> 'Neither a small, strictly regional party such as the South Tyrolean People's party nor a party built around the espousal of harsh and limited ideological claims, like the Dutch Calvinists; or transitory group claims, such as the German refugees; or a specific professional category's claims, such as the Swedish Agrarians; or a limited action programme, such as the Danish single-tax Justice Party, can aspire to a catchall performance' (Kirchheimer 1990: 55).

But could Agrarian Parties re-designated as Centre Parties specifically to broaden their electoral appeal be expected to do any better? As a rule, Kirchheimer notes, only major parties can become successful catchall parties (Kirchheimer 1990:55) and the Finnish Agrarians were the largest single parliamentary party with 23.0 per cent of the vote when they changed their name to Centre Party in 1965.

Although the literature on *party system change* and indeed *party change* abounds with references to it, the notion of the catchall party is extremely difficult to operationalise and therefore test. What, exactly, does a catchall party look like? Clearly, it is not enough to define it as simply a party with a heterogeneous support base (Wolinetz 1979: 5). Rather, it is necessary to examine the extent of changes in a party's electoral support, the constraints on extending beyond its 'core constituency' or *classe gardée* and the strategies designed to achieve this end. Even then, it is difficult to establish that, incontrovertibly, the pursuit of particular strategies has led to particular outcomes. As Peter Mair has observed: 'Strict criteria concerning what constitutes a "catchall party" or a "mass party" are not easily conceived' (Mair 1989:258) and testing the model is fraught with problems. In any event, Kirchheimer argues that parties with very specific group or regional claims are too narrowly based to achieve a 'life-saving transformation' (Kirchheimer 1990:55).

Recent work on the electoral adaptation of Scandinavian farmers' parties has focused on Iceland, Norway and Sweden (Kristinsson 1991) and, curiously, there has been little or no mention of the Finnish case (Christensen 1997: 391-407). As the example of the West German Social Democrats' Bad Godesberg programme in 1959 appears to illustrate, however, it might reasonably be hypothesised that catchall strategies are particularly attractive to parties at times of electoral decline and/or periods of extended political opposition. Thus, the Swedish Agrarians changed their name having plummeted to an electoral nadir of 9.4 per cent in 1956. Yet the Finnish Agrarian Party (*maalaisliitto*) was the largest single party in 1962 and there appeared no *prima facie* reason to engage in catchall strategies. Against this backdrop, the present chapter concentrates on three interlinked questions: a) Why did the Finnish Agrarians adopt catchall tactics in the early 1960s? b) What were the catchall strategies it pursued? c) Has an archetypal mass-class or single-interest party, contrary to Kirchheimer's thrust, been able both to diversify its support base and refashion its organisation in line with the 'catchall model'?

The Finnish case study is in seven sections. In order to appreciate the scale of the task confronting the party in extending its electoral constituency beyond its core farm support, the first part examines the historical strength and class base of the Finnish Agrarians in a comparative Nordic perspective. The second analyses the socio-economic changes (exponential industrialisation and urbanisation) underpinning the case for electoral adaptation and the re-designation of the party in 1965. The third part constitutes a brief note on the electoral record of the modernising party from its change of name to the present. The fourth considers whether the Centre Party has been a genuine pivot party *à la* Keman. The fifth examines the challenges facing the Centre Party as an opposition party since 1995. Sixth, there is an application to the Finnish Agrarian-Centre Party of the catchall strategies enumerated by Kirchheimer. Finally, there is a more detailed consideration of the extent to which the Agrarian-Centre Party has broadened its voter base to become a catchall party.

It is argued that the Finnish Agrarian-Centre possesses the most heterogeneous support of all the Finnish parties. It is the only party with substantial backing among the Finnish-speaking farmers and the only party with levels of support significantly above its national average in the 'other Finland' – that is, the relatively sparsely-populated regions outside the southern third of the country. In its traditional core areas in northern and eastern Finland in particular the Centre Party *is* a catchall party with roughly equal amounts of support from the farmers, blue-collar and white-collar workers. Equally, whilst a catchall party in the breadth of its support, the Agrarian-Centre has lacked the primary structural characteristics of a catchall party as defined by Kirchheimer and remains a mass political organisation.

## The Historic Strength and Class Base of the Finnish Agrarians

It was not so much the emergence of farm-specific parties in the Nordic region that was distinctive – peasant parties arose across central and eastern Europe in the period before and after the first world war – as the fact that they persisted until the late 1950s in Sweden and Norway and until 1965 in Finland. In Finland, moreover, when the Agrarian Party followed its Swedish and Norwegian sister parties and changed its name to Centre Party, it was not only the largest single party but also the leading party of government and had been the 'hinge group' in coalition-building since the first years of independence.

The Finnish Agrarian Party was formed in 1906 largely out of breakaway elements from the two nineteenth-century nationalist parties, the Old Finns and Young Finns (Hakalehto 1986: 61-194).Technically, the new grouping *maalaisliitto* should perhaps be translated as Agrarian Union since its founding-fathers preferred to avoid the term *'puolue'* (party) which carried a pejorative association with the nineteenth-century proto-parties. The suffix *liitto* symbolised a community of values – a *gemeinschaftlich* tradition – that had deep rural roots. In any event, the nascent party stressed socio-economic issues over and above matters of 'high politics' such as the constitutional question – that is, the strategy to adopt towards Russification and Czarist violations of Finland's basic rights as a Grand Duchy. On the constitutional question, incidentally, it was closer to the principled stance of the Young Finns than the more concessionary line of the Old Finns.

At 66 per cent in 1910 the proportion of the economically active population engaged in agriculture was significantly higher than in Norway and Sweden. However, far more pertinent for the emergence of the Finnish

Agrarians were the concentrations of independent family-sized farms in the north-west (Oulu and Vaasa) and south-east (Karelia) of the country. It may be, as Kari Hokkanen has argued, that the embryonic Agrarian Party was *in principle* a party of the whole countryside and not narrowly a farm producers' party (Hokkanen 1998: 4). But in practice the Finnish party's vote derived from the independent small farming population. Indeed, in recruiting support almost exclusively from the stratum of independent farmers, the Nordic Agrarian parties were more evidently class parties than their more celebrated social democratic-labour counterparts. In the Finnish case, 'class agrarianism' took deep root in the party during the 1920s and 1930s, whilst in the aftermath of two losing wars against the Soviet Union between 1939 and 44 there was a further deepening of the divide between (agricultural) producers and (urban) consumers (Hokkanen 1996: 379). In 1948, 81 per cent of the Agrarians' support derived from farmers (Sänkiaho 1991: 31).

A broad picture of the significantly greater electoral strength of the Finnish Agrarian Party compared with its Norwegian and Swedish counterparts can be gained from Table 3.1. In the ten *Storting* elections between 1921 and the party's change of name in 1959, the Norwegian Agrarians polled an average of 11.3 per cent, marginally the weakest of the three farm-specific parties. The Swedish party's profile was not significantly different. In the eleven elections to the *Riksdag*'s lower chamber between 1920 and the adoption of the title Centre Party in 1957, the Swedish Agrarians averaged 12.2 per cent of the poll. The average poll of the Finnish Agrarians in contrast was more than double that of the Norwegian party and nearly double that of the Swedish Agrarians.

**Table 3.1  The Average Agrarian Poll in Norwegian, Swedish and Finnish General Elections, 1919-1962**

| Country | Per cent | Best Poll Year | Period Average |
| --- | --- | --- | --- |
| Norway | 15.9 | 1930 | 11.3 |
| Sweden | 14.3 | 1936 | 12.2 |
| Finland | 27.3 | 1930 | 22.9 |

In the fifteen *Eduskunta* elections between 1919-62, the Finnish Agrarians averaged 22.9 per cent of the vote and they obtained 27.3 per cent in 1930.

Excluding the first post-independence general election in 1919, the Finnish Agrarians' vote did not fall below one-fifth of the total poll.

In seeking to understand the greater electoral strength and all-round 'relevance' of agrarianism in Finland – in Sartori's sense of eligibility for government – five main points need emphasis. First, there was the Finnish Agrarians' central role in the completion of state-building between 1917 and 1919 (the independent farmers fought on the victorious White side during the 1918 civil war) and in promoting a republican constitution for the new successor state (Arter 1978: 91-123). Having been the only party consistently to defend the newly-independent Finnish republic throughout the period 1917-19, the Agrarians broke new electoral ground in the south and west of the country at the polls in March 1919 and emerged as the leading non-socialist party with 42 of the two-hundred *Eduskunta* seats. In Czechoslovakia in 1918 the Agrarians changed their name to Czechoslovak Republican Party and gradually broadened their support to include urban voters. The Finnish party could have done the same for the Republican Club, founded in June 1918, provided a forum in which to discuss the merging of the rump of Young Finn republicans (the remainder had backed a constitutional monarchy) into the Agrarians. The Agrarian leader, Santeri Alkio, however, refused to contemplate a change of name.

Second, there was the party's promotion of a land reform programme in the 1920s which was designed as a measure of social engineering and, in providing independent holdings for the rural proletariat of crofters and farm labourers, strengthened the Agrarians' core class of supporters. The Agrarians were even able to gain the support of the radical left at the decisive third reading of *Lex Kallio* in October 1922, a law which, in creating independent smallholdings, was attempting to build a bulwark against extremism on the left. More than fifty thousand new holdings were created in the first five years that Lex Kallio was in force and in 1929 the number of independent farms outnumbered leaseholdings of over half a hectare by almost ten to one (Rasila 1967: 54).

Third, there was a vigorous resettlement programme in the late 1940s for refugees from that part of Karelia conceded to the Soviet Union, which served to reinforce the size of the family-sized farm population at a time of accelerated industrialisation. Importantly, agrarianism was imported into, and in turn consolidated the party's support base in southern Finland as a result of the re-settlement of the Karelian population. These were areas where the pattern of rural stratification before independence – a few large landowners and a mass rural proletariat of crofters and scrapholders – had not favoured the Agrarians. Thus, in the Uusimaa constituency in the hinterland of Helsinki, the Agrarians regularly elected two MPs from 1948 onwards when the Karelian settlers began to vote (Virolainen 1997: 157). The Mäntsälä commune illustrates admirably the impact of *imported agrarianism*. Between the wars, Mäntsälä was a leftist-dominated commune and in 1939 the second largest party was the radical rightist Patriotic People's Movement (IKL). The Agrarians gained only 7.7 per cent. After the Karelian settlement, however, the Agrarians became the largest single party with support around the 35 per cent mark (Hämäläinen 1997: 105-6). The same thing happened elsewhere in southern Finland and meant for example that a Karelian MP, Urho Kähönen, was elected for Turku south in 1951 (Kittilä 1958: 16-18). The advent of young Karelians, moreover, strengthened the party's organisation and attracted former crofters from the political left into the Agrarians' ranks.

Next, there was the role of the long-serving (and former Agrarian) president Urho Kekkonen (1956-81) in maintaining the Agrarians in office and the concomitant special relationship that developed between the Agrarians and the Kremlin (Arter 1981:219-234). With several other parties, *inter alia* the Social Democrats and Conservatives suspect in foreign policy terms, the Agrarians could argue that they, above all others, were the party that acted in the national interest. The Agrarians unquestionably benefited at the polls in 1962 from Kekkonen's successful resolution of the so-called Note Crisis with the Soviet Union the previous year. Electing an Agrarian-led government, it was implied, would constitute a strong affirmation of Kekkonen's handling of Finno-Soviet relations and, against the backdrop of the Note Crisis, an all-time record turnout of 85.1 per cent was recorded. If the recent evidence suggests the whole episode may well have been engineered in Moscow to ensure (the trusted) Kekkonen's re-election for a second presidential term (in February 1962), the Finnish head of state was none the less widely viewed as a national hero and some of his success rubbed off onto his former party (Arter 1999: 285-286).

Finally, there were the divisions in the Social Democrats in the late 1950s that kept them out of power for a decade and made the Agrarians and not the Social Democrats the natural governing party until 1966. By 1958 the Social Democrats, under the dogmatically anti-Communist leadership of Väinö Tanner, had split into two parliamentary groups. The main SDP group had 38 seats and the SDP opposition – which the following year formed the Workers' and Small Farmers' Social Democratic League

(TPSL) – had 13. The SDP's position was further marginalised when it ran a joint candidate with the Conservatives against Kekkonen at the 1962 presidential election, although at the height of the Note Crisis, Olavi Honka stood down 'in the national interest'. The normalisation of the SDP's relations with Kekkonen and the Kremlin began with the election of a new chairman, Rafael Paasio in 1963, whilst two years later co-operation with the radical left was proposed by [a future SDP Prime Minister] Mauno Koivisto in a May Day speech in Tampere. The party's rehabilitation was completed when it joined an alliance backing Kekkonen's [successful] re-election in 1968.

## The Agrarians' Change of Name

On the eve of Finnish independence in 1917, agriculture employed almost five times as many persons as industry, whilst in 1930 the proportion of the economically active population engaged in agriculture was exceeded in only five European countries – Yugoslavia, Bulgaria, Roumania, Lithuania and Poland (Arter 1979: 110). Following the Second World War, however, there was a sharp decline in the size of the population engaged in agriculture and forestry. A large indemnity, repayable to Russia mainly in heavy machinery, stimulated industrialisation, and the loss of substantial areas of Karelia led many emigrants, despite the resettlement programme, to take jobs in the towns. By 1960 the numbers employed in agriculture and forestry had fallen to little over one-third of the total labour force and it was only one-fifth in 1970 (see Table 3.2). Particularly marked was the post-war increase in the numbers working in commerce and the service industries. Crucially, the movement away from the land was not an even process and rural depopulation affected precisely those peripheral regions where the Agrarians had traditionally been strongest.

None the less, the barrier to party modernisation – programmatic renewal and/or a change of name – was the existence of a strong class (peasant) consciousness in the party. Throughout the 1940s and 1950s, there was deep-seated grassroots' resistance to Deputy-Chairman Johannes Virolainen's concern to broaden the base of the party so as to include all those living and working in the countryside. Virolainen recognised the realities of rapid industrialisation – which he contended should be decentralised and dispersed throughout rural Finland – and the need to respond to it. The likes of veteran Karelian and former minister, Juho

Niukkanen, however, gave forceful expression to the suspicion felt by the rank-and-file members towards the educated 'gentlemen' at the party's helm and in general to the so-called 'asphalt agrarians', that is, those politicians who were not farmers. (Hokkanen 1996: 386) In addition to Virolainen, these included V.J. Sukselainen, the party chairman between 1945 and 1964 and Urho Kekkonen, who was Prime Minister on five occasions between 1950 and 1955 and thereafter served as President for a quarter of a century. Consequently, at the Lappeenranta party conference in June 1950, Virolainen's proposal to include reference in the programme to the Agrarian Party as a centre party was given short shrift (Virolainen 1969: 428).

**Table 3.2  The Economically Active Finnish Population by Industry, 1950-1970**

| Industry | Year | | |
| --- | --- | --- | --- |
|  | 1950 | 1960 | 1970 |
| Agriculture, forestry, fishing | 45.9 | 35.5 | 20.1 |
| Industry | 21.5 | 22.8 | 25.7 |
| Construction | 6.3 | 8.7 | 8.3 |
| Commerce | 9.2 | 13.2 | 18.8 |
| Transport/communications | 5.4 | 6.3 | 7.1 |
| Services | 10.3 | 13.2 | 18.0 |
| Unknown | 1.4 | 0.3 | 2.0 |

Two factors in the late 1950s allowed the broad issue of modernisation back onto the party agenda. There was the Swedish Agrarians' change of name and subsequent electoral gains and the post-mortem that followed the Finnish party's election defeat in 1958. In August that year, Virolainen wrote an article in the Youth organ *Kyntäjä* in which he alluded to *Venstre* in Denmark as a model of how an agricultural and rural party could develop into a nationally based party (Kyntäjä 1958: 28-29). He also delegated to the Youth Section the responsibility for promoting a debate about the party's ideology. Over the autumn-winter 1959-60, moreover, Virolainen wrote a series of fifteen articles analysing the party's leading principles and this provided the initiative for an internal discussion which led to the adoption of a new party programme in Kemi in 1962. For the first time this was split into a section on 'Principles' and another on 'Practical Policies'. Before that, in February 1961, the Prime Minister V.J. Sukselainen's political secretary, Kalervo Siikala, in an article in the newspaper *Maakansa*, proposed that the party's designation be changed to 'Agrarian Party-Centre Party' (Keränen 1984: 86).

Virolainen's displacement of the long-serving Sukselainen as the new chairman at the party conference in Kouvola in June 1964 (almost certainly with the connivance of President Kekkonen) expedited the change of name. Virolainen used two main arguments in its favour. First, he emphasised the way Finnish society was no longer the class society it had been – in which political alignments reflected occupational divisions – and urged the need to recognise the increase in social and geographical mobility (Virolainen 1969: 430-431). Speaking at a particularly stormy meeting in Turku in March 1965, Virolainen underlined the stark reality of accelerated industrialisation, and its corollary rural depopulation and stated:

> 'In my view, one of the most effective ways of maintaining our strength [and defending the agricultural interest] is to seek to keep within our ranks at least the lion's share of those girls and boys from Agrarian Party homes leaving the countryside. If the young persons leaving the land go over to other parties and increase their numbers and the Agrarian support is correspondingly weakened, our capacity to manage agricultural matters will be decisively complicated' (Virolainen 1969: 419).

At the subsequent extraordinary party conference in Kuopio on 17 October 1965, Virolainen insisted furthermore that: 'The dividing line between the countryside and the [urban] centre should be removed since all citizens are equally worthy and deserving and everybody's work is important when viewed from a national perspective' (Virolainen 1969: 428).

Second, he urged the need to think to the middle term so as to meet the socialist threat and by extension protect the agricultural interest. As if to underline his point, Virolainen noted that the fraternal parties in Sweden and Norway had changed their names and that in Norway a Centre-led non-socialist coalition under Per Borten had recently assumed the reins of power. In backing his initiative, and voting 1036-137 in favour of adopting the name Centre Party, the Kuopio conference adopted a resolution that held that:

'The party's programme and its practical policies have always represented the politics of the centre. The new name depicts more clearly the party's role and significance in a rapidly changing society. The new name...reflects the party's placement on the political spectrum. It does not mean the subordination of the interests of agriculture and the countryside. In an industrialising society, a continuously thriving agricultural and forestry population should be able to participate fairly in the general increase in living standards' (Keskustapuolue 65: 28).

Yet in Kuopio, the Chairman of the Varsinais-Suomi organisation, Einari Karvetti, condemned the unseemly haste in jettisoning the old name and argued that a small Agrarian Party would be better equipped to make its voice heard than a large and disparate Centre Party. He concluded that: 'In twenty or thirty years time, there will be nothing left of the Agrarians' ideological foundation' (Suomenmaa 18.10.1965). Similar sentiments, incidentally, were expressed on the eve of the Swedish Agrarians' change of name by among others, the long-serving parliamentarian, Alex Rubbestad. (Jonnergård 1985: 20) In the same traditionalist class conscious vein, Pekka Nuutinen from North Savo commented derisively that: 'If somebody with a Beatles haircut seeks to represent the peasant's interests, then all is lost'! Some media interest was aroused by the fact that Sukselainen, clearly not wishing to end up on the losing side again, absented himself from the Kuopio conference (Helsingin Sanomat 19.10.1965). But, as Virolainen noted, the only real surprise was that the change of name was ultimately carried so overwhelmingly by 1036-137 votes (Suomenmaa 18.10.1965).

## The Electoral Record of the Finnish Centre Party

It is not possible in this chapter to trace in any detail the electoral and governmental performance of the Centre Party from its change of name to the present. The salient points none the less warrant emphasis. First, the adoption of catchall strategies, including a new name and new programme in the early 1960s, did not yield an instant electoral return; rather, the first decade after its change of name witnessed a sharp decline in the party's support. In 1970 the Centre Party lost its status as the largest non-socialist party and recorded its worst result since before the achievement of independence in December 1917. Throughout the period 1970-1991, moreover, the Centre played second electoral fiddle to the Conservatives (*Kokoomus*). In the six general elections between 1970 and 1987, the Centre Party polled 17.3 per cent compared with 20.2 per cent for the Conservatives.

Second, following the dramatic rise of the populist Finnish Rural Party, led by Veikko Vennamo, the Centre's vote dropped to a nadir of 16.4 per cent in 1972. The Centre Party had participated in a so-called 'Popular Front' coalition under the Social Democrat, Rafael Paasio, which also included the Communists, between 1966 and 1970. However, its association with measures to rationalise agricultural production, along with the structure of farm holdings, which heightened rural discontent and quickened the pace of emigration to southern Finland and Sweden, played into the hands of former Agrarian, Vennamo. As a reaction to Vennamo, the Centre Party shifted to the right and there were even plans to replace Virolainen with the rightist-inclined Nestori Kaasalainen (Suomi 1996: 376-380). The ranks were deeply divided, a left-wing faction called Group 70 (*Ryhmä 70*) insinuating that to meet the Vennamo challenge, Virolainen had turned his back on internal party debate, abandoned an immediate concern to broaden the party's electoral base and taken the party back to its rural roots.

Third, since 1975, the Centre Party's support has not declined, despite the rapid fall in the numbers engaged in the primary sector; rather, it stabilised its vote at 16-17 per cent in the late 1970s and 1980s. In 1990 the size of the economically active population engaged in agriculture and forestry was 9.0 per cent (see Table 3.3) whereas at the 1991 general election the Centre Party gained 24.8 per cent of the poll.

Fourth, the 1983 general election in many ways marked a turning point in the history of the re-designated party, although the Centre Party's vote at 17.6 per cent rose by only 0.3 per cent compared with four years earlier. It was the first general election since the retirement through ill health of the long-serving president Kekkonen and the modest gains were achieved in apparently adverse circumstances. There had been deep internal division about the party's nomination for the January 1982 presidential election and the Centre candidate Virolainen gained only 16.8 per cent following a lacklustre campaign. In 1983, moreover, the Social Democrats, who advanced by 2.8 per cent, were able to profit from a 'Koivisto effect', since Mauno Koivisto had been elected the first Social Democratic president by an overwhelming margin the previous year. The Conservatives (up 0.4 per cent) continued to profit electorally from being in an 'offside position', i.e. ineligible for government for so-called 'general reasons' (suspicion in Moscow). Finally, there was also a 'second-coming' for the Rural Party which polled 9.7 per cent under the leadership of Veikko Vennamo's son, Pekka. However, having persuaded the Liberal People's Party to merge with it, the Centre Party not only held its ground, but elected its first MP in Helsinki.

Table 3.3 The Economically Active Population by Occupation in 1990

| Occupation | Per cent |
|---|---|
| Technical, natural and social science, humanistic and artistic work | 24.0 |
| Administrative, managerial and clerical work | 14.5 |
| Sales work | 8.5 |
| Agriculture, forestry, fishing | 9.0 |
| Mining and quarrying | 0.2 |
| Transport communications | 6.5 |
| Industrial production work | 22.6 |
| Services | 12.3 |
| Military work | 0.5 |
| Unknown | 2.1 |

Source: *Suomen tilastollinen vuosikirja 1995* (Painatuskeskus: Helsinki, 1995), p.337

Fifth, the psychological importance for the Centre Party of the 1988 presidential election cannot be understated. Although Koivisto was comfortably re-elected, the Conservative Prime Minister, Harri Holkeri was beaten into third place by Paavo Väyrynen (who had replaced Virolainen as party chairman in 1980) and this meant that for the first time since 1970 the Centre became the largest non-socialist party.[1] Väyrynen's strong presidential election performance enabled the Centre finally to move out of Kekkonen's shadow.

Sixth, the massive growth in the size of the salaried employment sector in the 1980s – associated with so-called post-industrialisation – blurred the old class contours of politics and created real potential for the

Centre Party to make inroads into the new middle class. In the 1991 general election, fought against the backdrop of incipient recession, the Centre Party achieved its best-ever result of 24.8 per cent (see Table 3.4). It became the largest single party overall, the largest single party in no less than eight of the fourteen mainland constituencies (that is, excluding the single-member Åland islands) and in Lapland claimed an absolute majority of the vote. True, in 1995 the Centre suffered the unpopularity associated with governing through the worst economic recession in Finland's history and saw its vote fall nearly 125,000 on four years earlier. None the less, it maintained its strength in the less-populated, agriculture-dominant areas of central and northern Finland and remained the leading party in four constituencies (Kansanedustajain vaalit 1995: 15).

### Table 3.4  The Finnish Centre Party's Performance in General Elections, 1966-1999

| PARTY | SDP | CON | CENT | LA | FRP | SPP | FCL | LIB | GREEN | OTHER |
|---|---|---|---|---|---|---|---|---|---|---|
| 1966 | 27.2 | 13.8 | 21.2 | 21.2 | 1.0 | 6.0 | 0.5 | 6.5 | - | 2.6 |
| 1970 | 23.4 | 18.0 | 17.1 | 16.6 | 10.5 | 5.7 | 1.1 | 6.0 | - | 1.6 |
| 1972 | 25.8 | 17.6 | 16.4 | 17.0 | 9.2 | 5.3 | 2.5 | 5.2 | - | 1.0 |
| 1975 | 24.9 | 18.4 | 17.6 | 18.9 | 3.6 | 5.0 | 3.3 | 4.3 | - | 4.0 |
| 1979 | 23.9 | 21.7 | 17.3 | 17.9 | 4.6 | 4.3 | 4.8 | 3.7 | - | 1.8 |
| 1983 | 26.7 | 22.1 | 17.6 | 13.5 | 9.7 | 4.9 | 3.0 | * | - | 2.5 |
| 1987 | 24.1 | 23.1 | 17.6 | 9.4** | 6.3 | 5.6 | 2.6 | 1.0 | 4.0 | 6.3 |
| 1991 | 22.1 | 19.3 | 24.8 | 10.1 | 4.8 | 5.5 | 3.1 | 0.8 | 6.8 | 2.7 |
| 1995 | 28.3 | 17.9 | 19.8 | 11.2 | 1.3 | 5.1 | 3.0 | 0.6 | 6.5 | 6.3 |
| 1999 | 22.9 | 21.0 | 22.5 | 10.9 | 1.0*** | 5.1 | 4.2 | 0.2 | 7.3 | 4.9 |

*Source*: *Kansanedustajain vaalit 1995* (Tilastokeskus: Helsinki, 1991), p. 14. David Arter, 'The Finnish Election of 21 March 1999: Towards a Distinctive Model of Government?' *West European Politics* 23,1, 2000, 180-186.

* The Liberal People's Party ran as a sub-section of the Centre Party, but later reclaimed its independence.

** The 1987 vote for Leftist Alliance (LA) or its predecessor the Finnish People's Democratic League excludes the vote for the breakaway Democratic Alternative (DEVA)

*** SDP = Social Democrats; CON = Conservatives; LA = Leftist Alliance; FRP = Finnish Rural Party; SPP = Swedish People's Party; LIBS = Liberal People's Party. In 1999 the figure is for the Finnish Rural Party's successor, the 'Real Finns'

Finally, at the last general election in 1999, the Centre's only realistic chance of re-entering government, and splitting up the Social Democrats and Conservatives that formed the core of a so-called 'rainbow coalition' (this also contained the former communists in the Leftist Alliance, the Swedish People's Party, representing the national language minority, and the Greens), was to become the largest single party. This it narrowly failed to do. For the third consecutive election, the Centre emerged as the leading non-socialist party. But although gaining 2.5 per cent on its 1995 performance, the Centre was slightly weaker than the SDP. It was the largest party in six of the fourteen mainland constituencies. Yet although the party recovered lost ground in its central and northern strongholds, its performance was on average 2.5 per cent down in these constituencies compared with its striking victory eight years earlier (Arter 2000: 180-186).

## The Finnish Centre: a 'Genuine Pivot Party'?

In his study published in 1994, Hans Keman cites six West European parties as *genuine pivot parties*: the CVP/CSP in Belgium, Fianna Fail in the Irish Republic, the Christian Democrats in Italy (now of course moribund), the Christian Democratic Alliance in Holland, the FDP in Switzerland and the Finnish Centre Party (Keman 1994: 139). If Keman is correct, the latter is the only genuine pivot party in the Nordic region and, according to him, it meets the three necessary conditions for such parties:

1. They occupy the centre space in the party system

2. They possess centrality in terms of a programmatic identity distinct from left and right

3. They play a dominant role with regard to government formation and the policy-making process, i.e. they are able to bargain with parties of both left and right.

*Dominance* in Keman's terms appears the crucial variable and contains twin elements – significant electoral strength (although no numerical threshold of support is stated) and a high level of governmental participation. Clearly, the Finnish Centre Party has never been electorally dominant in the manner of the defunct DCI in Italy. Only five years after its change of name, it lost its status as the largest non-socialist party and recorded its worst result in the independence period. Indeed, it is perhaps significant that the Centre Party achieved its best post-war result, and its second-best poll ever, as an *opposition party*.

**Table 3.5 The Finnish Centre Party's Participation in Government, 1966-2000**

| Year | Prime Minister | Composition of Government |
| --- | --- | --- |
| 1966 | Rafael Paasio (SDP) | SKDL, SDP, KESK |
| 1968 | Mauno Koivisto (SDP) | SKDL, SDP, KESK, RKP |
| 1970 | Teuvo Aura (non-party) | |
| 1970 | Ahti Karjalainen (KESK) | SKDL SDP, KESK, LKP |
| 1971 | Rafael Paasio (SDP) | SDP |
| 1972 | Kalevi Sorsa (SDP) | SDP, KESK, RKP, LKP |
| 1975 | Keijo Liinamaa (non-party) | |
| 1976 | Martti Miettunen (KESK) | SKDL, SDP, KESK, RKP, LKP |
| 1977 | Kalevi Sorsa (SDP) | SKDL, SDP, KESK, LKP |
| 1979 | Mauno Koivisto (SDP) | SKDL, SDP, KESK, RKP |
| 1982 | Kalevi Sorsa (SDP) | SKDL, SDP, KESK, RKP |
| 1982 | Kalevi Sorsa (SDP) | SDP, KESK, LKP |
| 1983 | Kalevi Sorsa (SDP) | SDP, KESK, RKP, SMP |
| 1987 | Harri Holkeri (KOK) | SDP, RKP, KOK, SMP |
| 1990 | Harri Holkeri (KOK) | SDP, RKP, KOK |
| 1991 | Esko Aho (KESK) | KESK, RKP, KESK, SKL |
| 1994 | Esko Aho (KESK) | KESK, RKP, KESK, SKL |
| 1995 | Paavo Lipponen (SDP) | VAS, SDP, RKP, KOK, VL |
| 1999 | Paavo Lipponen (SDP) | VAS, SDP, RKP, KOK, VL |

KESK=Centre Party; SKDL=(Communist-dominated) Finnish People's Democratic League; SDP=Social Democrats; RKP=Swedish People's Party; LKP=Liberal People's Party; KOK=Conservatives (National Coalition Party); SMP=Finnish Rural Party; VAS=Leftist Alliance; SKL=Finnish Christian League; VL=Greens

In terms of high levels of governmental participation, Keman insists that pivot parties 'should always remain in the centre of power' (Keman 1994: 146). This is easily tested. Between the 1966 general election, the first the party fought under its new name, and 2000, there have been twenty-three governments in Finland. Three short-lived civil service 'caretakers' appointed as a last resort by president Kekkonen in the early 1970s lacked any base in parliament whatsoever and can be excluded from the

74  *From Farmyard to City Square?*

subsequent calculus. Even then, there has been much greater continuity in government than the number of cabinets might indicate, simply because compositional changes – the withdrawal of one or more parties – have not affected the Prime Ministership or the basic distribution of portfolios.[2]

However, of the twenty governing combinations with parliamentary backing (or tolerance) since 1966, the Centre Party has participated in fifteen or 75 per cent compared with seventeen or 84 per cent for the Social Democrats (see table 3.5). In terms of *governing time*, the Centre has participated in governments for twenty-six of the thirty-four years – just over 76 per cent – since its change of name whereas the figure for the SDP in the same period is twenty-eight or 82 per cent. The main difference between the two parties in governmental terms has been in the length of tenure of the Premiership. The Centre has claimed the Prime Minister's post on six occasions – Karjalainen 1970-1971, Miettunen 1975-1976 and Aho 1991-1995 – making up a total of eight years between 1966 and 2000. In contrast, the SDP has boasted the Prime Minister's post on eleven occasions, comprising a total of twenty-two years. In short, over the last thirty-four years, the Social Democrats have held the Premiership for two-and-a-half times longer than the Centre Party.

Summing up, on the most important of Keman's dimensions - dominance with regard to government formation – the Centre Party is no longer a 'genuine pivot party'. Unlike its predecessor, the Agrarians, it never really has been. True, the Finnish Centre has had significant electoral strength, at least when compared with the Norwegian and Swedish parties. Moreover, the party's percentage share of the vote in the three general elections in the 1990s was higher than at any time since its change of name. It has not though (except in 1991) surpassed that of the Social Democrats. Crucially, the Centre no longer resides at the heart of coalition governments. The turning point was 1987 whilst narrow defeat at the March 1999 general election consigned the Centre to a second consecutive period in opposition for the first time in its history.

**The Centre as an Opposition Party Since 1995**

For half a century until 1987, the Centre invariably took part in 'red-green' coalitions with the Social Democrats – the celebrated 'red earth' model – even if the relationship between the two parties was often tense and strained. Väyrynen's strategy from 1983 of ensuring that the Centre was not seen as merely the SDP's 'poodle' meant that relations between the two deteriorated to breaking point. The Centre and SDP have not co-operated since 1987. Indeed, since 1983 (with the inclusion of the Rural Party), and certainly since 1987 with the 'rehabilitation' of the Conservatives, there have been high levels of *innovation* in the process of government-formation in Finland. Increasingly open structures of party competition have led to increased coalition access and a variety of unpredictable governing combinations (Mair 1997: 209-214). Recent governments, which in addition to the Social Democrats have included the former Communists, Conservatives, Greens and Swedish People's Party, have in fact made a mockery of policy distance theories of coalition-building. Above all, the Centre has not participated in government since 1995, the longest period in opposition in its history.

After the 1999 general election, reference was made in the press to the 'Siberianisation of the Centre' and the threat of the party finding itself in the same 'offside position' as the Conservatives between 1966 and 1987 (Virkkunen 1999). An editorial in *Kainuun Sanomat* [a daily close to the party] noted that the Centre may have to contemplate a long period in opposition for 'general reasons' – not because of its relations with the East (Moscow) but with the trade union movement (Helsingin Sanomat 11.4.1999). Clearly, the trade union movement's opposition to the Centre's 'work reform programme' (discussed shortly) reduced its eligibility and, as the minister of trade and industry, Erkki Tuomioja, noted in *Keskisuomalainen*, it provided a pretext for those who did not wish to co-operate with the Centre for other reasons.

In February 2000, the Centre chairman, Esko Aho, narrowly lost the second round of presidential voting to the Social Democratic candidate, Tarja Halonen, who became the first female head of state in Finland's history. Aho gained 48.4 per cent of the poll compared with 51.6 per cent for Halonen. Barely six weeks later, Aho revealed to a startled public that he intended to spend the academic year 2000-2001 at Harvard University where he would combine lecturing and studying (Kainuun Sanomat 16.3.00). He justified his proposed 'sabbatical' by reference to his long political career (an MP since 1983) and the need to recharge his batteries. However, Aho indicated that he was willing to continue as Centre chairman and would, if re-elected, lead his party into the 2003 general election. Although Aho was elected unopposed in June 2000, his requested leave of absence was opposed by the Centre Youth Organisation and prompted expressions of concern from several leading individuals in the party. Most notably, there was the critical assessment of Olli Rehn, a deputy-chair of the party between 1986 and 94, currently working in the Finnish EU commissioner, Erkki Liikanen's office in Brussels.

Rehn likened the position of the Centre Party to the Social Democrats in 1963 when their relations with the (former Agrarian) president, Urho Kekkonen, the Agrarian Party and the Communists broke down. 'General reasons' [linked to foreign policy and the attitude of the Kremlin] prevented the Social Democrats from participating in government, bridges to the other parties were down and the SDP could not punch its weight, Rehn insisted. Similarly, he contended, the Centre was not able to do so because 'general reasons' [a heel-dragging approach to the EU] had led to its marginalisation, whilst relations with the two other large parties were strained (Rehn: 2000). Rehn insisted that the Centre's position in the political wilderness was the consequence of the fact that its ambivalent EU line had given others an excuse to leave the party out in the cold. He concluded by identifying three main challenges facing the Centre – rethinking some of its policies, adopting a more constructive and flexible stance towards the EU and reopening communication lines to the two other main parties and the trade union movement.

Taking these points briefly in turn, it needs emphasis that, in contrast to 1991, at the time of a descent into recession, when the Centre attracted a large, but unstable protest vote simply by sitting tight, so to speak, the party contested the 1999 general election on the offensive. At its June 1998 party conference, the Centre determined to promote three main campaign themes. There was the division of the nation into employed and unemployed; the case for 'blue-and-white [the national colours] ownership' and opposition to majority shares in Finland's leading companies passing into foreign hands; and, in particular, the need to implement a work reform programme. In its original manifestation, this latter was predicated on what was called a 'new tripartism' embracing the unemployed, employed and employers. Its central feature was a local contract model for small firms, permitting those with a workforce of under five persons to be exempt from the binding national agreements on working conditions. As Aho wrote in *Helsingin Sanomat*: 'Unemployment will not be significantly reduced until the taxation of work and employers' contributions are reduced, local agreements increased and service industries and work from home expanded.'

The launch of the Centre's work reform programme was manna from heaven for the SDP, which was in the electoral doldrums following a convoluted case of apparent sleaze involving one of its cabinet ministers. It was anathema in particular to the central trade union federation SAK as it interpreted the Centre's blueprint as an attack on the position of organised labour. Relations between the Centre and SAK had been strained since the days of the Aho coalition (1991-1995) – when three general strikes were threatened – and the work reform programme appeared to rub salt into old wounds. Accordingly, at its Vaasa party conference in 1999 the Centre decided to water down the package. In its diluted form, there was no mention of a local agreement on working conditions for small businesses and the right to be excluded from national agreements. But the damage appeared to be done and the Social Democrats were able to argue that Finland was only really governable with the SDP in power. By the Centre Party's conference in June 2000, the whole work reform programme had been quietly buried.

The problem for the Centre in opposition is that in the Finnish multiparty system, clearly articulated [radical] policies only rarely win elections. They are just as likely to provide hostages to fortune and present the governing parties with an easy sitting target. This is particularly so at a time of exceptionally broad-based government and consensus politics when the ruling parties can close ranks against approaches challenging the conventional wisdom. Yet even in an electronic era of leadership image, 'personality politics' and 'sound bites' (slogans with some resonance but little substance), credible alternative policies are viewed as necessary weaponry with which to shoot at the government and present the electorate with real choice. The Centre's work reform programme contained much of substance. It was, ironically, much the same as that adopted by the ruling Swedish Social Democrats. However, pilloried by the political left, it may well have cost the Centre the position of leading party after the last general election.

Much more important in all probability for bringing the Centre in 'out of the cold' than generating alternative policies will be shedding its image as something of a 'reluctant European'. Aho threatened to resign as party chairman and Prime Minister if the Centre did not formally come out in favour of EU membership. It did, although the main strongholds of opposition at the EU referendum in October 1994 were in precisely the party's strongholds in northern and eastern Finland. In opposition the Centre, whilst never opposing membership, has inclined towards a more nationalist stance and it argued (unsuccessfully) for a referendum on EMU before Finland joined as a founder member in 1999. In the guise of the former chairman, Paavo Väyrynen, presently a member of the European Parliament, the party has had the most outspoken anti-federalist in Finnish politics. Väyrynen has consistently challenged the Centre's [reputedly indeterminate] line on Europe and, amidst much publicity, he ran against Aho at the primary in September 1998 to decide on the party's presidential nomination. None the less, the Centre today tends to see EU enlargement less as a 'peace project' – contributing to building a wider 'security community' in Karl Deutsch's phrase – than a development in which it is of paramount importance to protect and promote national economic interests. It is this essentially instrumentalist orientation which sets the Centre apart from such enthusiastic Europhiles as Lipponen himself.

The Centre discovered in April 1999 that *coalition potential* à la Sartori is not necessarily increased by significant gains at the polls. Relations between the Centre and the two other large parties, the Social Democrats and Conservatives, were not good and they in turn were happy enough to continue to provide the red-blue core of ruling coalitions. The Centre was left out in the cold. This was despite Aho's [almost desperate] attempt to ensure that the party was not cold-shouldered. In the aftermath of the election, the Centre did not work for a non-socialist coalition with the Conservatives (along the lines of 1991-1995), but for a traditional 'red earth' arrangement with the SDP. On 7 April 1999, Aho arranged a personal audience with Lipponen to try and smooth over relations with the Prime Minister, and even offered to sacrifice himself and remain outside the cabinet if a 'red earth' combination could be pieced together. It seems, moreover, that Aho was ready to tell Lipponen that he was not offering to remain outside government in order to run in the presidential race. This proved unnecessary since Lipponen emphasised that governmental co-operation was not contingent on personalities. It plainly *was*, however, and the good working relationship between Lipponen and the Conservative leader, Sauli Niinistö, was of paramount importance in holding the two parties together. Significantly, unlike in 1995, Lipponen did not even telephone Aho to inform him of his decision to continue co-operation with the Conservatives (Helsingin Sanomat 11.4.1999).

**The Catchall Strategies of the Agrarian-Centre Party**

In his seminal work, Kirchheimer identifies five main catchall strategies (Kirchheimer 1990: 58-59):

1. Drastically reducing the party's ideological baggage in favour of short-term, tactical electoral considerations. In the words of Katz and Mair 'In place of the defensive electoral strategy of the mass party which laid primary stress on mobilisation and retention of a limited constituency, the party adopts an offensive strategy exchanging effectiveness in depth for a wider audience and more immediate electoral success' (Mair 1997: 102).

2. Consolidating the powers and position of a nationally-oriented leadership embodying national rather than sectional goals. Leaders are no longer primarily accountable to the members, but rather to the wider electorate.

3. Downgrading the role of individual party members so as not to detract from the projection of the desired catchall image. In Katz and Mair's terms, members are *cheerleaders* and the pattern of authority is more top-down than bottom-up (Mair 1997: 113).

4. De-emphasising the *classe gardée* in favour of catching a wide spectrum of voters in its electoral net.

5. Securing access to a wide variety of interest groups, partly for funding reasons, but primarily to secure increased electoral support via interest group intercession.

Kirchheimer's formulation focuses on the strategic reorientation of prospective catchall parties in four distinctive arenas: the ideological arena and the role of ideology in institutional adaptation; the organisational arena and the leader-member relationship; the electoral-parliamentary arena and the search for new voters; and the corporate arena with the focus on party-group linkages. How relevant were these catchall strategies to the case of the Finnish Agrarian-Centre Party?

Far from dumping excess ideological baggage, agrarianism in Finland involved in practice the narrow promotion of class interests and, ideologically, the Agrarians travelled light. As noted, however, the new party programme, adopted in Kemi in 1962, was for the first time divided into sections on 'principles' and 'practical policies' and, from the early 1960s, the Agrarians sought to project (not jettison) a distinctive centrist ideology. The party was presented as charting a middle way – a central course – between socialism and large-scale capitalism and the promotion of a catchall ideology was designed to legitimise its concern to embrace a broader base of interests. Contrary to Kirchheimer in short ideology was not sacrificed on the altar of short-term electoral considerations; rather, it was intended to inform and validate the wider policy appeal of the modernising party. The detailed set of 'Aims for the Sixties' reflected the new policy orientation in the party. Reference was made to the need for such things as a national economic plan based on the efficient use of resources in the various regions, the development of manufacturing industry in the underdeveloped north and east (i.e. small-scale rural industry) and the realisation of industrial democracy at all levels.

Kirchheimer has noted that: 'National societal goals transcending group interests offer the best sales prospect for the party intent on establishing or enlarging an appeal previously limited to specific sections of the population' (Kirchheimer 1990: 54). In the case of the Centre Party such national goals have included emphasis on the democratisation of society, including the desirability of the decentralisation of decision-making; promoting the market economy with a human face, i.e. welfare and individual security alongside wealth generation; and environmentalism ('new green' values). The protection of the farm and forestry population (old 'greenness') has not been forgotten, but sectional interests have not been allowed to prevail over a perception of the wider national interest. A good example of this was the decision of a badly-divided Centre Party ultimately to support Finnish membership of the European Union (EU) despite overwhelming opposition from the farmers. The chairman, Esko Aho's threat to resign – which he would undoubtedly have carried out – was sufficient to prevent the party appearing still primarily concerned to defend agricultural class interests in the manner of the Norwegian sister party. (Aho 1998: 132) This points to a crucial contrast.

In spite of their change of name and concern to expand from being class parties, the Swedish and Norwegian Centre parties have appeared at various times to be *single issues parties,* closely identified in the public view with an unequivocal stance on controversial questions like opposition to nuclear energy in Sweden and opposition to EU membership in Norway. This has been their greatest strength and their biggest weakness, delivering significant short-term electoral growth, but growth that proved ephemeral. In contrast, the Finnish practice of governmental co-operation 'across the blocs' – that is, involving socialist and non-socialist parties – has militated towards pragmatic policy stances and a concern to avoid marginalisation through single-issue attachment. In short, the Finnish Centre Party has not been linked to a single issue in the same way. Avoiding controversial issues may well be regarded as consonant with the pursuit of a catchall strategy, albeit one directed towards the achievement of middle-term rather than short-term gains. Indeed, the Centre ultimately dropped its controversial 'work reform programme' precisely because it proved an electoral millstone, which lost the party potential voters.

In line with Kirchheimer, the position of the Centre Party leadership has in practice been consolidated *vis-à-vis* members in an era of 'electronic democracy'. As Katz and Mair have observed: 'The rise of television as the most widely used source of political information enhances the conditions that allow, or indeed compel, parties to make universal appeals directly to voters rather than communicating principally to and through their core supporters' (Katz and Mair 1996: 13). The leader in short is (and must be) the party's principal electoral asset. It is no coincidence that in an [unsuccessful] attempt to make a decisive breakthrough in the capital city – and return two MPs for the first time ever - the party chairman, Aho, stood as a candidate in Helsinki at the general election in March 1999.

Equally, the leader is the party's principal strategist, both in and out of government. Väyrynen's determination to challenge the Social Democrats by engaging the non-socialist majority in the cabinet has been noted. At his initiative, the non-socialist ministers in January 1984 produced a nine-point policy declaration setting out goals on *inter alia* child care support in the home, electricity production, the taxation of small- and medium-sized enterprises, the reduction of unemployment (at seven per cent the highest ever) and various environmental measures (Hallituksen 25.1.1984). In consequence, relations between the Centre and Social Democrats predictably deteriorated and reached breaking point in 1987 when *before* the general election that year Väyrynen and the Conservative leader, Ilkka Suominen, did a secret deal to form a non-socialist coalition (under the Centre chairman) and exclude the Social Democrats (Almgren 1998: 136-146). Things badly misfired when the manoeuvre was blocked by President Koivisto and the result was the end of an era of red-green governmental co-operation stretching back to the Cajander 'red earth' cabinet between 1937 and 1939.

A crucial strategic consideration for the leadership today is the need to balance the coalition of interests within the Centre Party. This factor has cast the leader at times in the role of mediator, conciliator and, as noted in the case of Aho and the decision on EU accession, brinkman. Aho insists that he travelled to the Jyväskylä party conference ready to return "a former party chairman and former Prime Minister" and with his political career effectively at an end (Aho 1998: 132). The authority of his position, however, won the day and swung the party clearly behind his pro-EU stance.

**Figure 3.1 The Finnish Centre Party Organisation in 2000**

| Bottom | |
|---|---|
| Members | 220,000 |
| Local branches | 366 |
| Party districts | 21 |
| Party conference | Every 2 years |
| Top | |
| Party Council* | 134 - Comprises representatives from the party districts in relation to the size of their membership and performance in general elections. |
| Party Executive** | 31 - comprises representatives from each of the party districts, the Youth Organisation, Student's Organisation, Women's Section, Centre Journalists, parliamentary group, three advisory bodies speaking on behalf of entrepreneurs, economic interest groups and local government respectively plus the Swedish speaking Council. Meets monthly. |
| Business Committee of the Party Executive*** | Comprises party chair, deputy chairs, party secretary, three elected members from the Party Executive and the chairs of the parliamentary group and European Parliament group. Meets weekly. |

* puoluevaltuuskunta; ** puoluehallitus; *** puoluehallituksen työvaliokunta

Turning to the organisational arena, the Agrarian-Centre, like the other large Finnish parties, is hierarchically organised, with the local party branch organised territorially at the base. All local branches are members of a party district, the boundaries of which usually (though not always) coincide with a parliamentary constituency. The local branches have the right to nominate delegates to meetings of the council of the party district and are also represented at the party's conference. Moreover, all the subnational organisations are represented on the Party Council (*puoluevaltuuskunta*) (Sundberg 1992: 161-162). Figure 3.1 sets out the hierarchical structure of the Centre Party organisation. Significantly, however, it was four decades after its inception before the Agrarian Party became a class-mass party.

In other words, it was only after the Second World War that the party developed a mass political organisation and then largely in response to the challenge of re-legalised communism. As Jan Sundberg has written, competition for votes and the recruitment of members penetrated practically every village and street (Sundberg 1992: 160). Particularly during the period of Sukselainen's chairmanship (1945-1964), the Agrarians created an outstanding mass organisation and the *tupailta* or 'gathering in the farmhouse living-room' became a celebrated institution. In 1945 membership was under 30,000; by 1964 it had increased almost tenfold to 280,000 (Aho 1998: 21). At its peak the Agrarian-Centre averaged almost nine local associations per commune (*kunta*) compared with three in the case of the Communists, Social Democrats and Conservatives (Sundberg 1992: 162). In 1985 the Centre Party's membership was almost one an a half times bigger than that of all the other three large parties put together (see Table 3.6), whilst ten years later the member-voter ratio was an impressive 1:2 (Vuosikirja 1995:24). Clearly, therefore, the shift to a catchall strategy has not involved downgrading the role of individual members or de-emphasising the party's class-mass features. On the contrary, the aim was to consolidate the recruitment of the *classe gardée* at a time when a decline in its numbers coincided with increased party political competition for the farm/rural vote, initially from the Communists and after 1970 from the Rural Party too.

True, the period of rapid membership growth has definitely come to an end. By the year 2000, the membership at 220,000 (see Figure 3.1) was down almost thirty-seven thousand on five years earlier. Moreover, the professionalisation of the party leadership - an increase in the number of party officials – concomitant on the introduction of state subventions in 1967 has led to something of a decline in *membership activity* and a growing dependence on services (posters, leaflets and other propaganda) provided by central office (Sundberg 1992: 176). None the less, the

Agrarian-Centre retains the primary features of a mass party and members have not become cheerleaders. A primary election in September 1999, for example, enabled them to select the party's presidential candidate. Maintaining a mass membership, moreover, has been necessary in order to fill all the relevant positions in local government, parish councils and co-operative bodies with party members (Sundberg 1992: 179).

**Table 3.6  Membership of the Main Finnish Parties, 1945-1995**

| Year | Party | | | |
|---|---|---|---|---|
|  | SKDL/VAS | SDP | KESK | KOK |
| 1954 | 62218 | 62669 | 168651 | 90684 |
| 1962 | 61139 | 44828 | 270061 | 86737 |
| 1975 | 56561 | 99463 | 296879 | 77170 |
| 1985 | 35887 | 92032 | 298670 | 76325 |
| 1995 | 16351 | 70176 | 257473 | 47200 |

*Source*: J. Sundberg, 1996 *Partier och Partisystem i Finland* Schildt: Saarijärvi, 88-89.

In the electoral-parliamentary arena, the Agrarian-Centre strategy has in essence been to maintain its special (farm-based) clientele, whilst in Kirchheimer's words, seeking to embrace 'a variety of other clienteles' (Kirchheimer 1990:52). Electoral activity, in other words, has remained as much about the heightened mobilisation of the party's core support group as the conversion of voters to the Agrarian-Centre cause (cf Mair 1997: 95), although the latter was prioritised. There was a 'both-and' rather than 'either-or' approach and the challenge was to straddle the urban-rural, consumer-producer cleavages, that is to embrace constituencies patently lacking a community of interests.

It was with a view to having an electoral foot in both rural and urban camps that in February 1961 the Prime Minister's political secretary, Kalervo Siikala, proposed amending the party's name to 'Agrarian Party-Centre Party'. Thereafter, in December 1961, some Helsinki-based Agrarians, with the understanding of the party leadership, founded a puppet party, the Finnish Centre Party (*Suomen Keskustapuolue*). The main figures behind it were Siikala and the writer Jouko Tyyri, whilst the party chairman was the Agrarian minister of justice, Pauli Lehtosalo. The aim was to capitalise on the strong pro-Kekkonen, pro-Agrarian climate (in the wake of the successful resolution of the so-called Note Crisis) to capture support in the urban 'deep south'. However, the puppet party managed only six thousand votes in Helsinki and even less in the hinterland constituencies of Uusimaa and Häme South. Although this Finnish Centre Party (mark 1) came to nought, Siikala has argued that it expedited the Agrarians' change of name (Keränen 1984: 86-87).

Following the latter, the Centre Party set its sights on attracting the first generation of urban dwellers with roots and relatives in the countryside. By the 1980s, moreover, post-industrialisation had brought diminished subjective class identity, weakened partisan identification and increased electoral volatility. By 1991 only 44 per cent of Finns – compared with 65 per cent in 1975 – placed themselves voluntarily in a social class and, in the case of the Centre Party, the figure was only 34 per cent (Pesonen, Sänkiaho and Borg 1993: 115-116). The massive growth in service sector employment in particular offered the Centre a route to an urban support base.

Finally, on the question of the party-group link, the Agrarian-Centre Party has had a strong corporatist connection throughout the independence period and, in Sundberg's submission, remains a corporative party. He has insisted that: 'The Centre Party, with its extremely large membership base, is dependent on the much smaller agricultural producers' organisation [MTK] which provides the party with a core of active members, economic support and staffing assistance' (Sundberg 1992: 168). Yet it is important to note that in contrast to Norway, the Finnish Agrarian Party was not founded as the political arm of the agricultural producer's organisation which, as in Sweden, it antedated. Moreover, although informal links at the elite level are strong (and the MTK leader Heikki Haavisto was appointed foreign secretary by a Centre Prime Minister, Esko Aho, in 1993), the Centre Party is not dictated to by MTK which has no formal input into the party's policy-making. Following Finnish membership of the EU, the power of MTK has in any event declined and the Centre has pursued a strategy of 'keeping its distance', not least to change the common perception that the two organisations work hand in glove.

In line with Kirchheimer, the Centre has indeed sought to secure access to the leading non-primary sector interest groups, although its relations as a governing party with the central blue-collar federation SAK in the early 1990s were at times acrimonious. The Centre has had only modest success in claiming a membership base in the main industrial and public sector unions. Approximately two-thirds of MTK members support the Centre Party. In contrast, a survey in 1996 revealed that 9.1 per cent of SAK members were Centre supporters whilst the following year the figure for the white-collar federation STTK was 12.5 per cent. Significantly, in both surveys about two-fifths of respondents declined to identify their partisan allegiance. The academic-professional association, *Akava*, has not included any political questions in its survey of members.

**From Class Party to Catchall Party?**

In proceeding to assess how far the Finnish Agrarian-Centre has been able to transform itself in just over three decades from a class party based primarily on the farmers to a catchall party with broad-based social support, Sweden and Norway offer contrasting experiences. The political cohesion of the Swedish Agrarian-Centre has been relatively low. Up to the 1956 general election, the Swedish Agrarians received only half the farming vote, the remaining half being shared by the Conservatives (25 per cent) and the Liberal and Social Democrats (a combined 25 per cent) (Lindström 1979: 7). True, at the 1956 election, when the party's vote plunged to an all-time low, farmers accounted for 77 per cent of its support. But within twenty years of the Swedish Agrarian Party's change of name – that is, in 1976 – only 18 per cent of its voters were farmers, whilst no more than 37.5 per cent of the party's supporters came from rural areas. In Norway, in contrast, the Agrarian Party ran candidates only in rural districts and in 1949, for example, virtually four-fifths of its support derived from farmers – 33 per cent small farmers and 46 per cent large farmers (Barton 1998: 76-77). Excluding the protest surge in 1993, when the Centre profited from a strong vein of anti-EU sentiment, between 70-80 per cent of the party's supporters still live in rural areas (Christensen 1997: 392).

When considering the changing nature of the Finnish Agrarian-Centre's support it is clearly important to look at i) the social composition of the Centre Party's vote. How far does it rely mainly on the backing of farmers? ii) the regional distribution of party support. How far has it extended beyond its original strongholds in the north and east and penetrated an urban electorate? Table 3.7 sets out the changing nature of the Centre Party's electorate between 1948 and 1991, whilst Table 3.8 analyses party support by occupation in June 2000.

The Finnish Centre Party: A Case of Successful Transformation? 87

**Table 3.7 The Changing Nature of the Finnish Centre Party's Support Base, 1948-1991**

| Year | 1948 | 1966 | 1973 | 1982 | 1991 |
|---|---|---|---|---|---|
| Farmers | 81 | 72 | 60 | 40 | 35 |
| Workers | 16 | 18 | 23 | 28 | 27 |
| Salaried employees | 2 | 6 | 15 | 25 | 38 |
| Managers/ Directors | 1 | 4 | 2 | 7 | 0 |

Source: Risto Sänkiaho, 'Puolueiden kannattajakunnan rakenne', in *Kansanedustajain vaalit 1991*, p.38.

**Table 3.8 Party Support by Economic Activity in Finland in June 2000**

| | | | Party | | |
|---|---|---|---|---|---|
| Occupation | SDP | Party Centre | Conservatives | Leftist Alliance | Greens |
| Workers | 35 | 20 | 9 | 42 | 16 |
| Junior employees | 16 | 11 | 17 | 9 | 16 |
| Senior level employees | 8 | 8 | 25 | 7 | 28 |
| Entrepreneurs | 4 | 10 | 13 | 3 | 5 |
| Farmers | 0 | 10 | 1 | 0 | 0 |
| Students | 5 | 7 | 10 | 3 | 26 |
| Pensioners | 31 | 31 | 23 | 34 | 3 |
| Others | 1 | 3 | 2 | 2 | 6 |

Source: *Suomen Gallup 6/2000*.

It can be seen that the Centre Party's support base comprises substantial backing from the farmers. In the first general election after its change of name in 1966, nearly three-quarters of Centre Party voters were farmers. This figure had dropped to two-fifths in 1982 and 35 per cent by 1991 when a narrow majority of party supporters were salaried employees, toimihenkilöt (Sänkiaho 1991:38). By June 2000, only one-tenth of Centre support derived from farmers. This, however, was well above their proportion of the economically active population as a whole and compared with only 1 per cent of the Conservatives' support that came from farmers. Neither of the two left-wing parties nor the Greens registered any support from the farming population. Indeed, the collapse of the Rural Party, coupled with the estrangement of the larger farmers in the southwest from the strongly pro-EU Conservatives, have meant that the political cohesion of the farmers has risen in recent years.

The proportion of the Centre's vote emanating from the blue-collar population rose from under one quarter in 1973 to nearly one third in 1995. By 2000 it had fallen back to 20 per cent. This last figure was none the less twice that of the Conservatives (working class conservatism has always been weak in mainland Scandinavia). It was, however, well down on the 35 per cent of the Social Democrats' vote deriving from the blue-collar electorate and over two-fifths of the Leftist Alliance's vote coming from the same source.

The Centre's support from salaried employees rose over sixfold in the quarter of a century after the party's change of name. In 1991 38 per cent of the Centre vote came from the salariat compared with 43 per cent for the Social Democrats and 77 per cent for the Conservatives. In June 2000 virtually one-fifth of the Centre's electorate numbered junior and senior employees. Caution must be employed when interpreting and comparing the data. The Finnish Gallup 6/2000 for example employs categories not used in the earlier source material – 'entrepreneurs', for example. It also includes the proportion of non-economically active population (students and pensioners) among the electorate of the main parties. In the Centre's case 38 per cent of its support comes from the non-economically active compared with 36 per cent in the SDP, 37 per cent in the Leftist Alliance and 33 per cent in the Conservatives. Leaving aside the students and pensioners, the Centre vote comprises one-fifth workers (the third highest proportion behind the left-wing parties), one-fifth employees, one-tenth farmers and one-tenth entrepreneurs. Clearly, this is not the profile of a class party

Turning from the socio-economic structure to the geographical distribution of its support, it can be seen from Table 3.9 that there is a strong regional skew in the structure of the Centre Party's electorate. Based on the results of the 1999 general election, it is evident that the Centre attracted 23.6 per cent of its support from the two northern constituencies of Oulu and Lapland where only 12.2 per cent of eligible voters are situated. This is a figure that is nearly four times greater than the proportion of the Conservatives' vote deriving from Northern Finland and over three times greater than in the case of the SDP. Moreover, nearly 72 per cent of the Centre's vote was drawn from the Central Belt and Northern Finland – where only 51.5 per cent of the electorate is situated – compared with 47.6 per cent for the SDP and 40.0 per cent for the Conservatives. In contrast, the Centre drew only 28.1 per cent of its support in 1999 from the populous five constituencies of Southern Finland – where 47.9 per cent of the electorate is based – compared with 52.4 per cent in the case of the SDP and 60.5 per cent for the Conservatives. In short, the Centre Party has been the only party with significantly above its national average support in the 'other Finland', that is the nine constituencies in the Central Belt and North away from the populated 'deep south'.

Simplifying only to a degree, moreover, it can be stated that the further north one proceeds from the capital city, the greater the support for the Centre. At the six general elections over the two decades between 1979-1999, the Centre averaged 19.9 per cent of the national vote. Over the same period the party averaged only 12.5 per cent in the five constituencies of Southern Finland compared with 24.7 per cent in the seven constituencies of the Central Belt and no less than 39.7 per cent in the two constituencies of Northern Finland. In the southernmost constituency, the capital city Helsinki, the Centre's average general election poll between 1979-1999 was 4.4 per cent - and it recorded a low of 2.1 per cent in 1987 – whereas in the most northerly, Lapland, the party averaged 40.4 per cent over the same period, with a record 49.9 per cent in 1991.

Table 3.9  Support for the Three Main Finnish Parties by Region at the 1999 General Election

| Region | % of eligible electorate | SDP | Centre | Conservatives |
|---|---|---|---|---|
| Southern Finland | 47.9 | 52.4 | 28.1 | 60.5 |
| Central Belt | 39.3 | 40.6 | 48.3 | 33.7 |
| Northern Finland | 12.2 | 7.0 | 23.6 | 6.3 |

The extent to which the Centre party has extended its electorate into the towns can be seen from Table 3.10, which divides the country into urban communes, semi-urban communes and rural communes. It is evident that there is a marked rural-urban imbalance in the structure of the Centre electorate and that the party's support remains disproportionately concentrated in rural communes. Just over 23 per cent of the Finnish electorate lives in rural communes whereas just over 42.4 per cent of the Centre's vote in 1999 emanated from these communes. In contrast, 60.5 per cent of Finnish voters live in urban communes, but the Centre gained only 11.9 per cent of its total poll from these communes.

Summing up, the Centre Party's electoral centre of gravity remains in its historic, agriculture-dominant core support areas in northern and eastern Finland where it remains comfortably the largest party with between just under one-third and two-fifths of the vote (Vanhanen 1991: 87-97). In the rural towns in these stronghold areas, the Centre Party has succeeded in increasing its support significantly since the 1960s and it did particularly well in 1991. Support in Vaasa increased over fourfold between 1966 and 99 and it tripled in Seinäjoki and Joensuu. At the 1999 general election, the Centre gained record results in Mikkeli and Iisalmi where it had extremely strong candidates. Particularly in its historic support regions, the Centre is a catchall party embracing urban as well as rural voters.

**Table 3.10 The Finnish Centre Vote by Types of Commune in 1999**

| % of electorate | Type of commune | % Centre vote |
|---|---|---|
| 60.5 | Urban communes | 11.9 |
| 16.2 | Semi-urban communes | 31.8 |
| 23.3 | Rural communes | 42.4 |
| 100 | Whole country | 22.4 |

*Source*: compiled from *Eduskuntavaalit 1999* (Tilastokeskus: Vantaa, 1999), pp.38, 50.

*Urban Communes* are those where 90 per cent of the population live in built-up areas or where the population of the built-up area is at least 15,000. *Semi-urban communes* are those where between 60 and 90 per cent of inhabitants live in built-up areas and the largest of these is between 4,000 and 15,000 persons.

*Rural communes* are those where less than 60 per cent of the population lives in built-up areas and the largest of these is less than 15,000 persons or those communes where at least 60 per cent but under 90 per cent lives in built-up areas and the largest of these is under 4,000 inhabitants.

Several important caveats should none the less be entered. First, the Agrarian-Centre Party has gained virtually no support at all in the Swedish-speaking communes, even those situated in its historic core regions. It was the last of all the parties formally to become bilingual and, particularly during the inter-war period, had a history of championing the Finnish language and attacking the privileges of the Swedish-speaking elite. In short it has emphatically not been a catchall party in the sense of embracing both national languages.

Second, in the six large cities in Southern Finland, the growth in the Centre vote has been slow and the level of party support modest. The average Centre poll in the cities of Helsinki, Espoo, Vantaa, Turku, Tampere and Lahti rose from a mere 2.7 per cent in 1966 to a modest 7.9 per cent in 1991 before falling back slightly to 7.2 per cent in 1999. The party has struggled to find an appropriate image in the urban south where an increasing number of voters are concentrated – the three largest cities of Helsinki, Tampere and Turku, for example, grew by 11 per cent, 11.7 per cent and 4.6 per cent respectively between 1985 and 1997. As an internal party report put it: 'For many in the south, the Centre is still seen as an agrarian, second class Conservative Party and voting for it remains difficult without a rural or regional connection'. In the large towns and cities in the south, moreover, voters not wishing to support either of the two left-wing parties or the Conservatives have other options, notably the Greens who, with 17.2 per cent of the poll, were the third largest party in Helsinki in 1999. The Greens appeal principally to young, educated, salaried voters. Of Green supporters 56 per cent are 34 years or under and 70 per cent are salaried persons (including students). The comparable figures for the Centre Party are 27 per cent and 26 per cent respectively.

Third, in the capital city, Helsinki, where the party has never succeeded in electing more than one MP, the Centre has generally fared best in those districts where the population is younger than average and comprises families with children living in rented accommodation on relatively low incomes. The east and north of Helsinki are the party's 'strong areas', although these are also the areas where the turnout has been lowest (Miettinen 1997). It was precisely with a view to mobilising extra support in these areas that Esko Aho ran in the capital in March 1999. However, despite a massive organisational effort in August 1998 – the so-called 'Helsinki Open' – during which leading figures held street meetings and distributed free vegetables(!) – Aho's result was both disappointing and instructive. He polled only 6.1 per cent of the capital city vote, a mere 0.1 per cent more than Olli Rehn secured when being elected eight years earlier.

**Concluding Remarks**

Of the three Nordic Centre parties with a capital 'C', the Finnish party appears the only one successfully to have transformed itself into a catchall party. At the last general election in 1999 its support was nearly four times greater than its Swedish counterpart the previous year and three times greater than its Norwegian sister party's performance in 1997. It possesses the most heterogeneous support base of all the Finnish parties. It is the only party with substantial backing among the Finnish-speaking farmers and the only party with support significantly above its national average in the relatively sparsely populated regions outside the southern third of the country. In its traditional core areas in northern and eastern Finland in particular, the Centre Party may be said to be a catchall party with roughly equal amounts of support from farmers, blue-collar workers and the white-collar salariat.

During the difficult electoral times that followed the party's change of name, the notable strength of the Centre's organisational network was crucial both in maintaining its core support base and, through the party's strength in local politics, in attracting new elements to the party. The growth in support for the Centre in the rural towns in the 1970s was particularly important. Generational turnover also meant the emergence by the 1980s of an educated, less obviously agrarian-based leadership. The present case-study in short lends support to Mair's statement that: 'There is no denying the reality of the shift from mass parties or mass integration parties towards a more catchall model' (Mair 1990: 119).

None the less, in the case of the Finnish Agrarian-Centre Party a number of important 'how far?' questions arise. First, given the pronounced north-south differential in the strength of the Centre's support, how far can a party with such an accentuated regional profile be described as a catchall party? Second, how far has the expansion of its support base beyond the *classe gardée* been the consequence of consciously pursued catchall strategies à la Kirchheimer and how far has it been facilitated by rapid social structural change and, in particular, the emergence of an urban salariat – that is, a new, socially and geographically mobile and electorally accessible middle class generally lacking high levels of partisan identification? Third, how far can a party manifesting the salient electoral attributes – broadly-based support – be described as a catchall party when it lacks the primary organisational features of a catchall party as described by Kirchheimer? Crucially, the party is still a mass political organisation.

Party watching would be simple if it were like bird watching. However, the present analysis suggests that the catchall species is difficult to spot even with the most powerful binoculars. In the case of the Finnish Agrarian-Centre, this is simply because it has never existed in the form described by Kirchheimer. This is not to vindicate Kirchheimer in excluding small democracies and Agrarian parties from his purview. The Finnish Agrarian-Centre has indeed transformed itself, even if not in line with Kirchheimer model, and this fact must cast further doubt on the continuing utility of one of most influential theories of party change.

## Notes

1  Interestingly, Väyrynen was favoured by Kekkonen as the Centre Party's future presidential candidate as early as 1977 (when he was appointed foreign secretary) and it is clear that the ageing president had wanted to jump over a generation in his former party (that is over Virolainen and his rival Ahti Karjalainen) when he stood down (Aho 1998: 245).
2  The brief Ahti Karjalainen government from 1970 to 1971, for example, is counted as two coalitions, following the withdrawal of the radical left in 1971. The same is true for Martti Miettunen's broad-based coalition – steamrollered into office by the president in 1975 specifically to deal with unemployment – after the departure of both left-wing parties the following year. Kalevi Sorsa's government in 1977 saw the Swedish People's and Liberal People's parties pull out the following year; there were several changes in the make-up of the Sorsa coalition between 1982 and 1983; in 1990 the Rural Party left the Holkeri cabinet; and in 1994 the Christian League left the Aho coalition.

## References

'Aho lähtee Yhdysvaltoihin luennoimaan ja opiskelemaan' *Kainuun Sanomat* 16.3.2000.
Aho, E. (1998), *Pääministeri*. Keuruu: Otava.
Almgren, E. (1998), *"Villenpoika"*. Jyväskylä: Gummerus.
Arter, D. (1995), 'The March 1995 Finnish Election: The Social Democrats Storm Back', *West European Politics* 18, 4, 94-204.

Arter, D. (1978), *Bumpkin Against Bigwig* – The Emergence of a Green Movement in Finnish Politics Tampere University: Tampere.
Arter, D. (1979), "The Finnish Centre Party: Profile of a 'Hinge Group'", *West European Politics* 2, 1, 108-127.
Arter, D. (1981), 'Kekkonen's Finland: Enlightened Despotism or Consensual Democracy?' *West European Politics* 4, 3, 219-234.
Arter, D. 'The Finnish Election of 21 March 1999: Towards a Distinctive Model of Government?' *West European Politics* 23, 1, 2000, 180-186.
Arter, D. (1999), *Scandinavian Politics Today*. Manchester : Manchester University Press.
Barton, A.H. 'Occupational Class and Vote in the 1949 Norwegian Election'. *Scandinavian Political Studies* 21, 1, 71-85.
Christensen, D. A. (1997), 'Adaptation of Agrarian Parties in Norway and Sweden'. *Party Politics* 3, 3, 1997, 391-406.
Derjabin, J. (1997), *Omalla nimellä*. Reunamerkintöjä Juri Komissarovin kirjoihin ja omaan elämään. Keuruu: Otava.
Hakalehto, I (1986), *Maalaisliitto-Keskustapuolueen historia 1* Maalaisliitto autonomian aikana 1906-1917. Helsinki: Kirjayhtymä.
Hallituksen ei sosialististen ryhmien kannanotto eräisiin ajankohtaisiin hallituspolitiikan kysymyksiin 25.1.1984.
Hämäläinen, S. 'Keskustapuolueen Uudenmaan piirin 70-vuotisjuhla Mäntsälässä' in Vanhanen 1997, 103-113.
Hannula, S. 1998 *Muutosten maailma 5* Jyväskylä: Kustannuskiila.
Hokkanen, K. 'Keskusta-aatteen fundamentit – Alkiosta Ahoon'. Esitelmä puoluevaltuuskunnan kokouksessa Kuusamossa 19.4.1998.
Hokkanen, K. 1996 *Maalaisliitto-Keskusta Historia 3*. Maalaisliitto sodan ja vaaran vuosina 1939-50. Otava: Keuruu, 1996. 1939-1950. Otava: Keuruu, 1996.
Jonnergård, G. 1985 *Så blev det Centerpartiet*. Bondeförbunds- och centeridéerna från fyrtiotalet fram till 1960. Stockholm: LTs förlag.
Jussila, O., Hentilä, S. and Nevakivi, J. (1995), *Suomen poliittinen historia 1908-1995* Porvoo-Helsinki-Juva : Werner Söderström.
'Kaksi äänestystä tarvittiin ml:n muuttamisessa keskustapuolueeksi', *Helsingin Sanomat* 18.10.1965.
Keman, Hans 'The Search for the Centre: Pivot Parties in West European Party Systems', *West European Politics* 17, 4, 1994, pp. 124-148.
Keränen, S. (1984). *Ikuinen evakko*, Johannes Virolainen Kekkosen varjossa Helsinki: Kirjayhtymä.
Keskustapuolue 65 (Kirja-Mono: Helsinki, 1966).
Keskusta maineensa vanki, *Helsingin Sanomat* 11.4.1999 (citing Kainuun Sanomat).
Keskustalta välikysymys asuntopolitiikasta, *Helsingin Sanomat* 24.9.1999.
Kirchheimer, O. (1990) 'The Catch-All Party', in Peter Mair (ed.), *The West European Party System* Oxford: Oxford University Press, pp.52-60.
Kittilä, U. 'Välähdyksiä maalaisliittotyön 40-vuotistaipaleelta', in *Maalaisliiton Varsinais-Suomen piirijärjestön 40-vuotis juhlajulkaisu 1958*, 14-20.
Kristinsson, G.H. (1991), *Farmers' Parties* A Study in Electoral Adaptation. Félagsvísindastofnun Háskóla Íslands.

Kuopion ylimääräinen puoluekokous oli demokraattisen järjestöväen kypsyyskoe', *Suomenmaa* 18.10.1965.
Lindström, U. (1979) 'Helgeandsholmen and Beyond: Centre and Periphery in Sweden', *Scandinavian Political Studies* 2, 1, 1-17.
Maalaisliiton uudet vaatteet, *Helsingin Sanomat* 19.10.1965.
Mair, P. (1997), *Party System Change*. Oxford: Clarendon Press.
Mair, P. (1989), 'The Problem of Party System Change', *Journal of Theoretical Politics* 1, 3, 251-276.
Miettinen, I & Huuhtanen, H. (1997), 'Muutokset keskustan alueellisessa kannatuksessa 1945-1995'. Internal Party memorandum.
Miettinen I. 'Keskustan alueellisesta kannatuksesta'. Muistio 7.7.1997.
Niemelä, S. 1983 *Ihmisyyden edellytykset*. Kymmenen luentoa keskusta-aatteesta Kokemäki: Satakunnan painotalo.
Pesonen, P., Sänkiaho, R. and Borg, S. (1993), *Vaalikansan äänivalta*. Porvoo-Helsinki-Juva: WSOY.
Pitkä matka punamultaan, *Helsingin Sanomat* 11.4.1999.
Randall, V. 1998 'The Catch All Thesis", *Sam Pol Nytt* 77, 17, 1-7
Rasila, Viljo 'Vuokra-alueiden itsenäistyminen ja muu asutustoiminta 1919-1939'. Itsenäisen Suomen taloushistoria 1919-50. *Historian Aitta XVII* (Porvoo:1967).
Rehn, Olli, 'Keskustan parannettava suhteitaan', *Helsingin Sanomat* 12.6.2000.
Sundberg, Jan (1996), *Partier och Partisystem i Finland*. Saarijärvi: Schildt.
Sundberg, J. (1992), 'Finland: Nationalised Parties, Professionalized Organisations', in Katz, R.S. & Mair, P. (eds), *Party Organisations*. A Data Handbook on Organizations in Western Democracies, 1960-1990 London: Sage, 158-184.
Suomi, Juhani (1996), *Taistelu puolueettomuudesta*. Keuruu: Otava.
Sänkiaho, R. 1991 'Puolueiden kannattajakunnan rakenne' in *Kansanedustajain vaalit 1991*. Helsinki: Tilastokeskus.
Vanhanen, Tatu (1991), 'Suomen keskustan aluellinen kannatuspohja'. *Politiikka* 33, 87-97.
Vanhanen, Tatu (1997), 'Keskusta uudenmaan vaaleissa 1975-1996', in Matti Vanhanen 1997, 69-102.
Virkkunen, Janne 'Kun aurinko laskee'. *Helsingin Sanomat* 11.4.1999.
Virolainen, Johannes (1969), *Pääministerinä Suomessa*. Helsinki:Kirjayhtymä.
Virolainen, Johannes (1964), 'Maalaisliitto keskusta-ideogian edustajana', in Matti Isoviita and Tatu Vanhanen )eds), *Vihreä Nuoriso*. Helsinki: Kirja-Mono, 124-137.
Virolainen, Johannes 'Tämä päivä on meille kaikille kypsyyskoe' *Suomenmaa* 18. 10. 1965.
Virolainen, Johannes (1997), 'Suomen keskustan kannatuksen lisääminen uudenmaan ja muiden etelän vaalipiirien suurissa kaupungeissa', in Vanhanen, Matti 1997, (ed.), *Vihertyvä Uusimaa IV*. Tummavuoren kirjapaino, 156-166.
Virolainen, Johannes 'Vaalitappion opetuksia', *Kyntäjä* 8, 1958, pp.28-29.
Vuosikirja, *1995, (1996 Suo*men keskusta: Korian kirjapaino, 1996).
Wolinetz, S.B. "The Transformation of Western European Party Systems Revisited", *West European Politics* 2, 1, 4-28.

# 4 The Danish Venstre: Liberal, Agrarian or Centrist?
JØRGEN GOUL ANDERSEN AND JAN BENDIX JENSEN

The Danish Venstre is the deviant case among the Nordic farmers' parties. It has never changed its name, it is not called a Centre Party and, in ideological terms, it is not a centre party. Although its name 'Venstre' in Danish means 'Left', it is a party much further to the right than its Nordic sister parties. Moreover, when the party has sought to broaden its support, it has usually done so by means of rather 'tough' (neo-)liberal policies in line with its liberal tradition. The party's name has never carried any reference to farmers but to liberalism. Yet it was a genuine farmers' party from the time of its foundation in 1870 - nearly 50 years before its Nordic sister parties - and it remained essentially a farmers' party until the 1980s.

The reasons for this deviance are twofold. First, from feudal times, the rural class structure in Denmark was dominated by medium-sized farmers rather than smallholders. Second, agriculture has always been oriented towards exports and was in fact Denmark's leading export sector until the early 1960s. None the less, like the other Nordic agrarian parties, Venstre was faced with a declining farmer population, especially from the 1960s onwards. True, it could rely for one more generation on support from those workers and white collar employees who had been socialised in farmers' families. But it had to adapt to the changing social structure. However, in accordance with the party's traditions, this adaptation took a quite different ideological course from that in the other Nordic countries. Only after the 1998 election did Venstre seek to become more of a catchall centre party and then largely by dint of its position as the dominant party of the opposition. Unlike the Social Democrats, however, Venstre has never sacrificed its original class base. In the 1990s it enjoyed no small measure of success. The party stabilised its support at about one-quarter of the votes and, in terms of membership, it is by far the largest Danish party.

## The Origins and Development of the Danish Venstre Until 1910

For the first two decades under the democratic constitution of 1849 there were no parties in Denmark in the formal sense. Parties were simply not considered legitimate. Rather, members of the parliament (*Rigsdagen*) were supposed to rise above narrow class interests and work for the common good. As late as the early twentieth century, in fact, the Speaker of the lower chamber (*Folketinget*) corrected members who used the term party. It was permitted only to employ such euphemisms as 'My friends and I'! (Hvidt 1990: 61). However, the Danish peasants had begun to organise politically as early as the 1840s and the groupings that were later to form parties were visible already in the first parliamentary assemblies.

Prior to the 1849 constitution, a local government reform in 1841 had granted a relatively widespread suffrage in local elections. The franchise was more restricted for elections to the consultative Diet of Estates that were held for the first time in 1834. Only one in forty inhabitants was entitled to vote. However, a significant proportion of farmers was eligible to cast a ballot and turnout rates were high. For the urban intelligentsia, seeking a popular platform for their struggle for a democratic constitution, the Diet of Estates provided a forum in which to forge a strategic alliance with the peasantry. Indeed, prompted by growing unrest among the lower peasantry, a 'Society of Friends of the Peasants' (*Bondevennernes Selskab*) was formed in 1846. Ironically, there was not a single peasant on the Board of the Society, although the overwhelming majority of its members were farmers or smallholders (Jorgensen 1979: 22). In any event, the absence of peasants from the Board was partly a means of legitimising the association in the eyes of the authorities. A mass organisation, the Society boasted about 16,000 members by 1851, drawn mainly from Sealand, where copyholding (leasing farmland with the right to pass on the lease to a son) had remained widespread. One of its main demands was for measures that would facilitate land reform and the creation of more privately owned farms, a process which had stalled since the first decades of the century.

For the first twenty years or so under the democratic constitution, the Friends of the Peasants became a loose grouping that involved about one half of elected parliamentarians. It organised a club for MPs called Venstre, a name that distinguished it from two other loose parliamentary groupings of national liberals and the landed aristocracy respectively. Although Venstre later became the name of the agrarian party, the Society of Friends of the Peasants was by no means a disciplined party. It would act as one when electing a chairman, for example, but lacked cohesion in the deliberation of particular legislative measures (Hvidt, 1990: 65). The Society has sometimes been described as the first political party in Denmark (Gundelach, 1986:10). But this is rather misleading both at the electoral and at the parliamentary levels.

The title of the first Danish party is usually reserved for 'The United Left' (Det forenede Venstre) which was the forerunner of the present Venstre. The United Left was formed in 1870 around three groupings that had their origins in the Society of Friends of the Peasants. Its main objectives were to create a more effective force on the left, to work for parliamentarism[1] and to articulate the interests of the peasants, the country districts, and provincial towns (Elklit, 1988: 25; Lund & Pedersen, 1970: 10). At the first election it contested in 1872, The United Left won a lower chamber majority with 53 of the 102 seats (Larsen, 1979: 53). In response, over the course of 1876-1978, most MPs outside The United Left came together in 'The Right' (Højre) which was the predecessor of the Conservatives of today (Thomsen, 1979: 106).

Inspired by the Social Democrats, and to some extent in [successful] competition with them for the hand of [particularly skilled] manual workers, Højre began, in 1883, to build a national network of party associations. The United Left urged its local supporters to do likewise, although it had less success since its followers were already relatively highly mobilised through the farmers' co-operative movement, farmers' associations and folk high schools. None the less, both parties ultimately came to approximate the ideal-type modern mass party (Duverger 1955), although they remained less centralised than the Social Democrats. The United Left's successor, Venstre, for example, did not establish a party association at the national level until 1929. Moreover, the legacy of its intra-parliamentary origins is reflected in the fact that the party associations have rarely been given any formal influence on day-to-day politics.

By the 1870s, farmers had come to dominate the lower chamber. As Table 4.1 shows, their proportion of all MPs increased from 17 to 43 per cent between 1850 and 1876. Conversely, the share of civil servants gradually declined from 48 to 17 per cent over the same period. It is not possible to present these figures by party since only the Society of Friends of the Peasants bore any resemblance to a [proto-] party.[2] It has been estimated that in 1870 around one half of the representatives of The United Left were farmers and that this figure had risen to 60 per cent by 1901. However, in addition to farmers, a relatively large number of intellectuals - school teachers, teachers from folk high schools, priests, editors and occasionally lawyers – represented the farming population in parliament (Lund & Pedersen, 1970: 18).

Table 4.1  Danish MPs by Profession, 1850-1876

| Profession | Year | | | |
|---|---|---|---|---|
| | 1850 | 1858 | 1866 | 1876 |
| Civil servants | 48 | 28 | 24 | 17 |
| Proprietors of the great estates | 5 | 12 | 11 | 6 |
| 'Intellectuals'(Lawyers, teachers, editors) | 13 | 6 | 18 | 26 |
| Farmers | 17 | 29 | 29 | 43 |
| Smallholders | 1 | 4 | 3 | 2 |
| Other professions | 16 | 21 | 15 | 6 |
| Mandates (Minus the Faroe Islands) | 100 | 100 | 100 | 100 |

Source : Hvidt, 1990: 63.

The United Left, it will be recalled, gained a majority of seats in the lower chamber in 1872. However, its influence was by no means commensurate with its majoritarian status. This was because an amendment to the 1866 constitution had restricted the franchise for the upper chamber (*Landsting*), with the result that the representation of the landed aristocracy was significantly increased. This in turn secured a majority for Højre until the end of the century (Hvidt, 1990: 154). Significantly, the 1866 constitution did not provide a solution in the event of deadlock between the two chambers, and from 1877, Højre's leader and prime minister between 1875-1894, J.B.S.Estrup, operating with the blessing of the King, frequently resorted to ruling by provisional laws. This, of course, seriously diminished the role of the lower chamber. Governments after 1894 were more co-operative but the principle of parliamentarism (cabinet responsibility) was not accepted until 1901.

The period from around 1877 to 1901, when The United Left strove for parliamentarism against a recalcitrant Right, has been called the 'system struggle'. It was a bitter struggle at times, culminating in the mid-1880s when the farmers formed rifle associations. One of the leaders of The United Left, the Speaker of the lower chamber, Christian Berg, was imprisoned for six months for 'incitement to rebellion'. The 'system struggle' also demonstrated that the United Left was anything but united.

Apart from personal rivalries, it was divided over the tactics to deploy in relation to the government (Elklit, 1988: 32; Hvidt, 1990: 330-337; Dybdahl 1978). In constantly changing configurations, groupings within The United Left intermittently sought compromises with the government. Indeed, several major deals were struck, notably on such important embryonic welfare measures as the tax-financed old age reform in 1891 which became a significant alternative to Bismarck's contribution-based social insurance model (Petersen 1990; Goul Andersen 1998). The groups most willing to co-operate with the government came together in 1885 as 'The Moderate Left', which also seems to have represented the more prosperous farmers (Elklit, 1988: 32). In 1894, the rest assumed the name the 'Left Reformist Party". It was the latter that formed the first Liberal government in 1901 having gained 76 out of 114 seats at the election that year.

In 1910, The Moderate Left merged with the Left Reformist Party and the new grouping adopted its present name, Venstre. This joining of forces was facilitated by another split in 1905 when a group of MPs were expelled following deep-seated disagreement over the issue of defence spending, a key issue separating Left and Right. They formed a genuinely new party, The Radical Left (Det radikale Venstre), which is subsequently referred to as the Radical Liberals. Although led by Copenhagen intellectuals, the Radical Liberals strongly urged social reforms for the smallholders who came to constitute a major element in the party's electorate. Throughout the twentieth century, the Radical Liberals, capitalising on a unique combination of social forces, and strategically placed between left and right, skilfully exploited their ability to control the formation of legislative majorities in parliament.

Yet another 'historic' party, the Social Democrats, made its breakthrough during this period. Founded in 1871, and sustained by a strong party organisation from the 1880s, the Social Democrats (SDP) first gained parliamentary representation in 1884. Until 1894, however, they never managed more than three seats despite increasing electoral support. This support grew strongly thereafter and, in 1909 and 1913, the SDP was the largest single party in terms of votes (albeit not seats). Until 1901, the SDP co-operated with Venstre not only in parliament but also in elections. In a plurality-based electoral system (PR was not introduced until 1915), the two parties tried to avoid running candidates against one another. However, when Venstre finally formed a government in 1901, disappointment on the Social Democratic side was great and co-operation between the two came to an end before the 1903 election. Three years later, the Social Democrats and Radical Liberals began to work together at elections and this paved the way for more general collaboration that lasted almost without interruption for nearly 60 years.

The emergence of a three party system in the 1890s and a four-party system the following decade mirrored the incipient cleavage structure. There was a rural-urban cleavage between the peasants and rural population, on the one hand, and urban interests, on the other, coupled with a [mainly urban] class conflict between working class and bourgeoisie. The timing of mass mobilisation was crucial and, as Lipset and Rokkan (1967) have hypothesised, several conditions had to be met in relation to the formation and growth of strong agrarian parties. They were:

1. that at the time of the decisive extensions of the suffrage, urban and industrial centres should be weak,

2. that the bulk of the agricultural population should be active in family-size farming and

3. that there should be important cultural barriers between the countryside and cities.

These conditions were largely met in the Danish case. At the time of the introduction of the democratic constitution of 1849, Copenhagen was the only big town, medium-sized farmers were preponderant, and there was general cultural mobilisation in the countryside. To this should be added the unique organisation of the farmers. The farmers' co-operative movement, built on the principle of one man one vote, one vote one value, came to control nearly all the manufacturing of agricultural products, as well as the manufacturing of many of the raw materials and machines needed in agriculture. Credit associations, along with savings banks and co-operative banks, financed loans for farmers; nearly all farmers were organised in farmers' or smallholders' associations; consumers' co-operatives became particularly strong in the countryside; and folk high schools and other cultural associations mushroomed. At its peak, the economic, political and cultural power of Danish farmers was enormous. Not least important was the fact that they had virtually freed themselves from a dependence on urban capitalism.

The three basic classes with their corresponding parties, interest associations, and economic and cultural movements may be illustrated by means of Rokkan's (1967: 93) triangle (Figure 4.1).

## Figure 4.1 Class Cleavages in Denmark around 1900

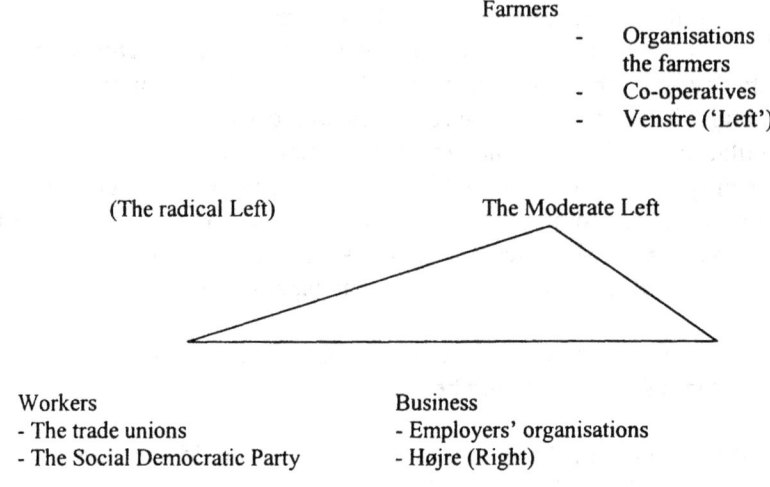

Until the mobilisation of the labour movement in the 1870s and 1880s, urban voters regardless of class, were typically associated with Højre, whereas people living in the countryside were attached to The United Left and the farmers' movement (Elklit, 1988: 164). Later, the Social Democrats added a third side to the triangle. Even though the Moderate Left [briefly] occupied the political space adjoining Højre, it never came close to establishing any formation that could bring together the urban and rural middle classes.

The initial success of the Radical Liberals reflected the increasing class conflict in the countryside. In 1885, 900 proprietors of great estates shared 40,000 tdr. hartkorn (a Danish unit of land valuation), 73.000 farmers had 290,000 tdr. hartkorn, and 188,000 smallholders had a total of only 40,000 tdr. hartkorn. Most smallholders did not possess enough land to earn a living and had to supplement their income by working for larger farmers. Smallholders typically got their land from the latter who parcelled it out and built a small house on each plot. Between 1850 and 1885, some 100.000 new plots were created, doubling the number of smallholders (Hvidt, 1990: 311). After 1885, to be sure, 'parcelling out' came to an end. However, by the end of the nineteenth century, the smallholders began to form their own associations. At the time of the first world war, these constituted the third largest class movement and they had forged strong ties with the Radical Liberals (Christiansen, 1990: 47, 49-53).

## The Danish Venstre: Liberal, Agrarian or Centrist? 103

From the outset, the Radical Liberals distinguished themselves from Venstre in their dogmatically anti-militaristic stance, their orientation towards social justice, and the way they sought to promote the interests of smallholders, *inter alia* through a government-sponsored land reform programme. Although in his opening speech to the Folketing in 1905 the prime minister emphasised that the Left Reformist Party (soon to become Venstre) would not be a party that represented only a single group in society, the fact was that after the split in 1905, the party became more exclusively a farmers' party than before and its urban support declined dramatically (Christiansen 1990: 55; see also Table 4.2 below).

Though Venstre assumed a more agrarian character, it did not become less ideological. Rather, it became more of a liberal party. Importantly, economic liberalism and the promotion of the class interests of the farmers went hand in hand, since the latter's export needs dictated a strong preference for free trade and competition, especially the removal of trade barriers. This was at the heart of Venstre's strong and unconditional support for EU membership from 1972 onwards. Until confronted with a range of environmental issues in the 1980s and 1990s, Venstre rarely found it difficult to reconcile a strong defence of the farmers' interests with its broader political goals. However, the party's version of liberalism was strongly coloured by the participatory ethic of the farmers' social movement and the folk high schools in particular. This created a legacy of tolerance and support for participation and decentralisation that facilitated co-operation with the Social Democrats and Radical Liberals much more than with the Conservatives. In fact, one of the criticisms of Venstre in the early 1990s was that it had replaced the liberalism of the folk high schools with the liberalism of the business schools.

At this stage, Venstre's contribution to laying the foundations of the embryonic welfare state in Denmark warrants emphasis. It held a lower chamber majority for the bulk of the period 1870-1910 and was thus instrumental in the passage of all major social policy legislation before the first world war. As Norgaard (2000: 3) has noted, 'the construction of early Danish welfare policy was primarily the work of Venstre, which took into account the interests of the farmers, and Højre, which was trying to strike a balance between the interests of farmers and business'. Venstre, it will be recalled, had the decisive influence on the path-breaking social reform legislation of 1891. The same was true for the laws on sickness insurance and unemployment benefits, together with the factory and industrial insurance acts, all of which were passed between 1891 and 1907. In hindsight, it is clear that, during the early chapters in Venstre's history, it was not so much its routine defence of the farming interest, as its role in facilitating the first welfare legislation, that was of lasting significance.

## Continuity and Modernisation, 1910-1960

With backing from the combined liberal groups, Venstre was able to govern on a majoritarian basis between 1901 and 1909. However, in the last-mentioned year, the majority survived for only ten weeks. Thereafter, no single party has ever held a majority in the Danish parliament. Following the 1909 election, the Radical Liberals formed a minority government backed by the Social Democrats. Indeed, whilst Venstre held the office of prime minister for about half the 1909-1924 period, and was the largest party in 1920, its heyday was over. It was not assisted by the introduction of proportional representation in 1915. From 1924-1968, Venstre took part in only three governments – 1926-1929, 1945-1947 and 1950-1953.

The reasons for Venstre's decline are fairly obvious. First, it was a victim of urbanisation. In 1873, 77 per cent of the electorate lived in rural districts, but by 1913 this figure had fallen to 60 per cent. More than two-thirds of the growth of the electorate took place in towns and cities (Thomsen, 1979: 102). Second, the Radical Liberal split in 1905 meant that the party was more cut off from urban support than it used to be. As can be seen from Table 4.2, the party was effectively eliminated in Copenhagen, a situation that obtained until the 1990s. It held its ground in the other big towns, albeit from a relatively low electoral base (14 per cent in the eighteen largest provincial towns) in 1903. Only in the rural areas of Jutland did the party maintain a predominant position well into the 1920s.

From 1924 to 1926, the Social Democrats formed their first government. Thereafter, Venstre returned to power in the form of a minority cabinet that became notorious for the severe cutbacks it made in public spending. After 1929, the Social Democrats dominated government. None the less, it warrants emphasis, particularly in view of Venstre's contribution to the pioneering social policy legislation before the first world war, that the party played a significant role in the broad inter-party compromises in the 1930s that laid the foundations for Denmark's post-war welfare state. This was not least because, lacking a majority in the upper chamber, the Social Democrats were not in a position to enact reforms without the support of either Venstre or the Conservatives.

## Table 4.2 Estimation of the Danish Parties' Share of Votes in Urban Areas, 1903-1926

|  |  | 1903 | | | 1906 | | | | 1913 | | | |
|---|---|---|---|---|---|---|---|---|---|---|---|---|
|  |  | H | V | S | H | V | RV | S | H | V | RV | S |
| Copenhagen | | 30 | 18 | 52 | 32 | 5 | 14 | 49 | 34 | 3 | 10 | 53 |
| Provincial towns | 18 biggest | 41 | 14 | 45 | 37 | 13 | 4 | 46 | 33 | 11 | 6 | 50 |
|  | The rest | 40 | 38 | 22 | 38 | 22 | 7 | 33 | 36 | 20 | 7 | 37 |
| Rural areas | Zealand and other islands |  |  |  | 19 | 45 | 36 |  | 18 | 36 | 25 | 22 |
|  | Jutland | 15 | 68 | 17 | 9 | 65 | 26 |  | 10 | 54 | 20 | 16 |
| The whole country | | 23 | 51 | 26 | 23 | 36 | 12 | 29 | 23 | 29 | 16 | 31 |

|  |  | 1918 | | | | 1926 | | | |
|---|---|---|---|---|---|---|---|---|---|
|  |  | KF | V | RV | S | KF | V | RV | S |
| Copenhagen | | 34 | 1 | 7 | 48 | 32 | 2 | 9 | 56 |
| Provincial towns | 18 biggest | 31 | 11 | 6 | 52 | 27 | 11 | 5 | 54 |
|  | The rest | 28 | 18 | 14 | 40 | 24 | 17 | 9 | 45 |
| Rural areas | Zealand and other islands | 15 | 39 | 30 | 16 | 12 | 40 | 21 | 25 |
|  | Jutland | 9 | 63 | 15 | 13 | 10 | 58 | 11 | 18 |
| The whole country | | 21 | 30 | 17 | 31 | 21 | 28 | 11 | 37 |

H = Højre. From 1915 the party changed its name to the Conservative People's Party (KF)
V = Venstre, S = The Social Democratic Party, RV = The Radical Liberals

*Source*: Thomsen 1999:122. Note that in some districts, there was co-operation between parties in 1903-1913.

In 1933 the first major revision of the social legislation of 1891-92 was passed with the backing of both Venstre and the Conservatives. The backdrop to the 1933 package of social reforms was the global economic crisis and its impact on the Danish farmers who relied heavily on foreign trade. Many farmers gave up on liberalism and joined a protest organisation called the Farmers' Union (*Landbrugernes Sammenslutning*) which demanded state intervention (in the form of lower interest rates and lower taxes) and state subsidies for agriculturalists. In the space of one year more than 100.000 farmers joined the Union and that was more than half of all farmers. Understandably, this put pressure on Venstre to play down its strong liberal views and it finally accepted a package deal with the Social

106 *From Farmyard to City Square?*

Democrats that allocated subsidies to farmers in return for social reforms of benefit to the working population (Hornemann Moller, 1994: 111-160). Somewhat less instrumentally, Venstre backed major legislation reforming the school system in 1937 even though, for the first time, the Social Democrats and Radical Liberals held a majority in both chambers and its support was not strictly necessary (Jensen, 1998: 73-83).

**Table 4.3  The Distribution of Votes at Danish Parliamentary Elections, 1920-1998**

|      | Venstre | Cons | Right W. | Centre | Socialist | Others |
|------|---------|------|----------|--------|-----------|--------|
| 1920 | 34.0    | 17.9 | -        | 12.1   | 33.1      | 2.9    |
| 1924 | 28.3    | 18.9 | -        | 14.0   | 37.1      | 1.7    |
| 1926 | 28.4    | 20.6 | -        | 12.6   | 37.6      | 0.9    |
| 1929 | 28.3    | 16.5 | -        | 12.5   | 42.0      | 0.7    |
| 1932 | 24.7    | 18.7 | 0.1      | 12.1   | 43.8      | 0.6    |
| 1935 | 17.8    | 17.8 | 1.0      | 11.7   | 47.7      | 4.0    |
| 1939 | 18.2    | 17.8 | 1.8      | 11.5   | 45.3      | 5.4    |
| 1943 | 18.7    | 21.0 | 2.1      | 10.3   | 44.5      | 3.4    |
| 1945 | 23.4    | 18.2 | -        | 10.0   | 45.3      | 3.1    |
| 1947 | 27.6    | 12.4 | -        | 11.4   | 46.8      | 1.6    |
| 1950 | 21.3    | 17.8 | -        | 16.4   | 44.2      | 0.3    |
| 1953 | 23.1    | 16.8 | 2.7      | 11.3   | 45.6      | 0.5    |
| 1957 | 25.1    | 16.6 | 2.3      | 13.1   | 42.5      | 0.4    |
| 1960 | 21.1    | 17.9 | 3.3      | 8.0    | 49.3      | 0.4    |
| 1964 | 20.8    | 20.1 | 2.9      | 6.9    | 48.9      | 0.4    |
| 1966 | 19.3    | 18.7 | 1.6      | 10.5   | 49.9      | -      |
| 1968 | 18.6    | 20.4 | 0.5      | 17.0   | 43.3      | 0.2    |

|  | Venstre | Cons | Right W. | Centre | Socialist | Others |
|---|---|---|---|---|---|---|
| 1973 | 12.3 | 9.2 | 15.9 | 25.9 | 36.7 | - |
| 1975 | 23.3 | 5.5 | 13.6 | 16.4 | 41.2 | - |
| 1977 | 12.0 | 8.5 | 14.6 | 17.6 | 47.3 | - |
| 1979 | 12.5 | 12.5 | 11.0 | 13.8 | 50.2 | - |
| 1981 | 11.3 | 14.5 | 8.9 | 17.1 | 48.2 | - |
| 1984 | 12.1 | 23.4 | 3.6 | 14.3 | 46.6 | - |
| 1987 | 10.5 | 20.8 | 4.8 | 13.9 | 49.7 | 0.1 |
| 1988 | 11.8 | 19.3 | 9.0 | 12.3 | 47.5 | 0.1 |
| 1990 | 15.8 | 16.0 | 6.4 | 11.4 | 50.0 | 0.3 |
| 1994 | 23.3 | 15.0 | 6.4 | 9.6 | 45.0 | 1 |
| 1998 | 24.0 | 8.9 | 9.8 | 11.1 | 46.2 | 0 |

The category 'Socialist Parties' includes, in addition to the Social Democrats, Communists and Socialist People's Party (a Communist splinter formed in 1959), the Left Socialists (1920), Free Social Democrats (1920), Green Party (1987-1990), Common Course (1987-1990) and the Humanist Party (1990).

The Centre Parties group includes, apart from Radical Liberals, Centre Democrats (1973-), Christian People's Party (1971-) and Justice Party (1924-1987, 1990), the Pensioners' Party (1977), Liberal Centre (1966,1968) and 'Democratic Innovation' (1998).

The Right Wing Parties include the Nazi Party (1932-1943), the Independents (1953-1966), Progress Party (1973-) and Danish People's Party (1998-).

Others include the German minority party (1920-64, 1968-71), the Economic Party (1920-1924), Farmers Party (1924), Self-Government Party' (1926), Agrarians (1935-1943), National Union (1939), Danish Union (1939-1947), and non-party candidates.

While Venstre remained an important party, the long-term tendency was one of declining support. It received almost 30 per cent of the votes until 1929 (see Table 4.3), but experienced a dramatic decline in the 1930s. In the 1950s, however, the party's fortunes revived. The full impact of the economic boom of the 1950s was not really felt in Denmark until the end of that decade. Before that, unemployment remained high, urbanisation and industrialisation proceeded relatively slowly and, in absolute terms, the number of farmers remained almost constant (Goul Andersen 1979). Venstre did not appear the victim of social change and the 1950s were in fact years of growing electoral support. Thus, profiting from the widespread political mistrust created by the Social Democratic-Radical Liberal coalition of 1953-1957 (Goul Andersen 1992: 74-75), Venstre obtained 25.1 per cent of the votes in the 1957 election, its second best election result since the 1920s (see Table 4.3). This would doubtless go some way to explaining why the party did not feel the same pressure to modernise as its half-sister, the Swedish Agrarians.

The Social Democratic Party remained the dominant force in Danish politics throughout the 1940s and 1950s. True, during the Second World War, an all-party coalition was formed under Social Democratic leadership. Moreover, when the SDP lost eighteen seats in the first post-war election (all gained by the Communists on the strength of their role in the resistance), it not surprisingly opted out of government. This opened the way for a Venstre minority cabinet that lasted until 1947 when the Social Democrats returned to power. Indeed, with the exception of a three-year period from 1950-1953, when Venstre and the Conservatives formed a minority coalition government, the Social Democrats were to stay in office for 20 years.

## The Political Significance of Venstre, 1960-2000

The 1960 election heralded a period of long-term decline for Venstre which was to last with only a few interruptions for more than 25 years (Table 4.3). It did not really affect the party's basic strategy, however, since this was primarily dictated by a concern to participate in government. There was certainly never any debate about a fundamental modernisation of the party, the adoption of a new name and/or programme.[3] True, there were a few attempts to shift the party more towards the centre. But, ultimately, the party experienced a further erosion in its urban support base. One example of a centrist orientation in the party can be noted in passing. It relates to the prominent Venstre MP, and professor of economics, Thorkil Kristensen, who was minister of finance between 1945-1947 and 1950-1953.[4] In the 1950s, Kristensen appealed to the urban middle class as a pragmatic, down-to-earth politician. In 1955 he refused to follow the party line, and voted with the Social Democrats over a crisis package. In subsequent years, moreover, he was critical of Venstre's policies. This broadside was popular among Venstre voters but not within the party where he became isolated and was finally obliged to leave by 1960. However, Kristensen had become the inspiration for a group of centrist members, mainly from Copenhagen, who advocated co-operation with the Social Democrats and Radical Liberals rather than 'bloc politics' with the Conservatives.

Yet this group did not exercise much influence and many left in 1965 to form their own party, the 'Liberal Centre' which won four seats at the 1966 general election. It drew a complete blank in 1968, however. At this time, Venstre's position in Copenhagen was tenuous. There was a steep but short-lived upturn in its fortunes in 1975, but lasting allegiances were not created. It was not until the 1990s – see Table 4.4 – that Venstre consolidated its position in the capital city.

Table 4.4 Venstre's Electoral Support in Three Regions (%)

|  | Copenhagen | The islands (which are Copenhagen suburbs) | The islands (total) | Jutland |
|---|---|---|---|---|
| 1968 | 3.4 |  | 16.1 | 26.8 |
| 1971 | 3.6 | 6.7 | 13.4 | 22.0 |
| 1973 | 3.6 | 7.1 | 11.2 | 16.1 |
| 1975 | 12.3 | 17.8 | 22.6 | 27.5 |
| 1977 | 2.9 | 4.8 | 10.3 | 16.2 |
| 1979 | 3.4 | 5.7 | 10.9 | 16.5 |
| 1981 | 2.3 | 3.7 | 9.4 | 15.5 |
| 1984 | 3.2 | 5.2 | 10.1 | 16.2 |
| 1987 | 2.5 | 3.5 | 8.1 | 14.8 |
| 1988 | 3.9 | 5.5 | 9.4 | 16.0 |
| 1990 | 7.7 | 10.0 | 14.0 | 19.3 |
| 1994 | 13.3 | 17.0 | 21.0 | 27.7 |
| 1998 | 14.5 | 19.5 | 22.3 | 27.8 |

*Source*: Statistical Yearbooks.

Important for an understanding of Venstre's strategy in the mid-1960s was the fact that it had been in opposition since 1953 (Table 4.5). Assuming a pivotal centrist position as a way back to power was clearly not an option since that role was firmly in the hands of the Radical Liberals. Venstre was in any event self-confident as the largest bourgeois party (until 1968) and considered itself the natural leader of the bourgeois bloc. The political challenge for Venstre was thus to present a credible bourgeois alternative to the Social Democrats. With this in mind, there was an extended debate in the mid-1960s about the possibility of merging Venstre and the Conservatives into a single bourgeois party. However, when Venstre's leader, Erik Eriksen, officially endorsed this idea, it generated so much internal unrest that he felt obliged to resign in 1965. Eriksen was the last farmer to lead the party. That his successor, Poul Hartling, in his celebrated 'Svanninge speech', urged the Radical Liberals to engage in closer cooperation might appear *prima facie* a basic reorientation in party strategy. Later events were to show, however, that the party had not 'sold' its liberal soul, although the short-term effect was to establish a coalition of Venstre, Conservatives and Radical Liberals. Following the 1968 election, the three non-socialist parties formed a majority government under the Radical Liberal, Hilmar Baunsgaard, which broke the fifteen-year Social Democratic stranglehold on power.

The Baunsgaard government, however, proved a big disappointment for bourgeois voters. Put somewhat crudely, the new cabinet turned out to be more social democratic than the Social Democrats in that its tenure of office between 1968 and 1971 represented a period of unprecedented growth in taxes and public spending. This paved the way for the anti-tax Progress Party and the 'earthquake' election in 1973 when the number of parties in parliament doubled and all the 'historic' parties suffered heavy losses.

With the Social Democrats much weakened after the 1973 election, and reluctant to continue in government, Venstre exploited the situation and formed a minority cabinet that rested on only 12.3 per cent of the electorate. Led by Poul Hartling, this was numerically the weakest government in Denmark since 1901. However, it managed to pursue quite different policies from those of the Baunsgaard coalition. For example, it granted tax relief, albeit failing to finance it. Moreover, when unemployment began to rise steeply in 1974, following the Yom Kippur war and concomitant oil crisis, the government took no action to prevent it. Yet with the Hartling cabinet riding high in the polls, Venstre could not resist the temptation to cash in and called an election in 1975, only thirteen months after taking office. Support for the party nearly doubled to 23.3 per cent, Venstre's best result since 1957. The government was none the less forced to resign when it failed to obtain the backing of the radical rightist Progress Party and this enabled the Social Democrats to return to office. Venstre's gains quickly evaporated and, at the following election in 1977, it plunged to a new nadir of only 12.0 per cent. The same year, Poul Hartling resigned as party leader and soon afterwards became UN High Commissioner for Refugees. He was succeeded by Henning Christophersen (1977-1984), a Copenhagen-born economist. Indeed, all the Venstre leaders since then have been economists – Uffe Ellemann-Jensen (1984-1998), and Anders Fogh Rasmussen (1998- ).

In order to abort an emerging alliance between Venstre, the Conservatives and two small centre parties – a so-called 'four-leaf clover' coalition – the Social Democratic prime minister, Anker Jørgensen, made the hasty decision to invite Venstre to participate in a left-right government in 1978. Venstre accepted, but the arrangement proved fractious and lasted for only thirteen months. Immediately after an election had been called for 1979, Venstre sought to resurrect the four-leaf clover as a governmental alternative. This did not materialise following the 1979 and 1981 elections, but when the Radical Liberals withdrew their support from the Social Democrats in 1982, a four-leaf clover cabinet, led by the Conservatives, was formed, with backing from the Radical Liberals on economic issues. Ironically, moreover, what the Social Democrats believed would point up the non-socialists' incapacity to govern, turned out to be a Conservative-Venstre coalition which, with various centre parties as allies, was able to stay in office for more than 10 years. It was forced to resign in 1993 only after a scandal about Tamil refugees.[5]

All in all, Venstre participated in government for about nineteen years in the second half of the twentieth century, nearly always in coalition with the Conservatives and, where possible, one or more of the centre parties too (Table 4.5). However, at the electoral level, the long-term trend for Venstre remained downwards. A new low point was reached in 1987 when it polled only 10.5 per cent of the votes.

The non-socialist cabinets from 1982 based their policies on a much more orthodox bourgeois approach than earlier. But gradually the Conservatives moved towards the political centre with a view to presenting themselves as a broad-based 'people's party'. In a much-quoted statement, the Conservative prime minister, Poul Schlüter, declared that 'ideology is trash'. Accordingly, Venstre began to seek a niche to the right of the Conservatives. After somewhat disappointing election results in 1987 and

1988, and an increase in support for the Progress Party, erroneously interpreted as a tax protest, compositional changes contributed to a more radical line in government. Many moderate Conservatives left politics altogether, and powerful forces within Venstre, led by the vice-chairman and tax minister, Anders Fogh Rasmussen, adopted aggressive neo-liberal rhetoric. There seemed little popular support for such a change of direction, but Venstre's ideas turned out to have a not inconsiderable appeal to young people, the better-educated and, perhaps more surprisingly, manual workers too.

Table 4.5 Venstre's Participation in Government, 1950-2000

| Year | No. of mths | Type of Government | Prime Min. |
|---|---|---|---|
| 1950-53 | 36 | Liberal-Conservative coalition (minority) | Liberal |
| 1968-71 | 44 | Liberal-Conservative-Radical Lib. coalition (majority) | Radical Liberal |
| 1973-75 | 13 | Liberal (minority) | Liberal |
| 1978-79 | 14 | Social Democratic - Liberal coalition | Social Dem. |
| 1982-84 | 16 | Conservative-Liberal-Centre Dem.-Christian (min.) | Cons |
| 1984-87 | 45 | Conservative-Liberal-Centre Dem.-Christian (min.) | Cons. |
| 1987-88 | 8 | Conservative-Liberal-Centre Dem.-Christian (min.) | Cons. |
| 1988-90 | 31 | Conservative-Liberal-Radical Liberal (min.) | Cons. |
| 1991-93 | 25 | Conservative-Liberal (min.) | Cons. |
| Total | 232 | 19 years 4 months, 39% of the time | |

*Source*: Thomsen (1994); Nielsen (1999); Andersen (1980).

A period of recession between 1987 and 1993, which pointed up a number of structural problems in the Danish economy, served as the backdrop to a period of electoral growth for Venstre that was based on an unashamedly neo-liberal approach. The party obtained 23.3 per cent of the votes in the 1994 election and 24.0 per cent four years later. This was on a par with the party's best totals in 1947, 1957 and 1975. Indeed, it is necessary to go back to the 1920s to find significantly better elections results. At the same time, Venstre was able to attract new members at a time of declining party membership. Membership increased from a low point of some 73,000 in 1992-1993 to around 83,000 in the second half of the 1990s (Figure 4.2). In spite of the fundamental decline in its core class of farmers, Venstre's membership compared favourably with that of the other large class party, the Social Democrats. In the year 2000, the Social Democrats had only 22 per cent of their 1947 membership whilst the average figure for all parties was 31 per cent. Venstre, however, maintained membership at 43 per cent of its 1947 level and, significantly, from the mid-1990s, Venstre has been the largest Danish party in terms of membership.[6]

By 1998, Venstre was the undisputed leader of the non-socialist opposition. It also appeared to have gained a firm base among urban voters. As Table 4.4 demonstrates, Venstre enjoyed short-lived success in Copenhagen in 1975, but the present breakthrough has lasted for a decade. Venstre, it seems, has gained a firm hold on groups of voters who would normally be expected to vote for the Conservatives. However, the non-socialist parties, and Venstre in particular, obtained far fewer votes than indicated in the opinion polls (Goul Andersen 1988, 1995, 1999a),[7] and this was interpreted as a reflection of popular concern about a swing to the right in welfare policies. In 1994 Venstre and the Conservatives presented themselves as a government alternative which had the backing of the radical rightist Progress Party. In 1998, however, Venstre and the Conservatives declined any contact with the parties on the radical right and they largely abstained from criticising the welfare state. None the less, the Social Democrats managed to avoid an election defeat that had seemed inevitable.

This suggested the need for an adjustment of image. Indeed, when Venstre's leader, Uffe Ellemann-Jensen, resigned shortly after the 1998 election in favour of the former vice-chair, Anders Fogh Rasmussen, many people expected a swing back to the right. Anders Fogh Rasmussen had after all been the party's chief neo-liberal ideologue, arguing in Thatcherite style in favour of a minimal state. However, he changed his tune almost overnight and launched the party on a much more centrist course. He even abstained from demanding tax reductions (this aroused some unrest among ideologically committed party members), and like his namesake, prime minister Poul Nyrup Rasmussen, he studied Tony Blair's tactics. This new strategy appears to have been relatively successful. From mid-1998 to the time of writing, Venstre has generally been the largest Danish party in the opinion polls, despite a Conservative recovery following internal division and growing support for the anti-immigrant Danish People's Party.

**Figure 4.2 Party Membership of Venstre and the Social Democrats, 1947-1999. Number of Members**

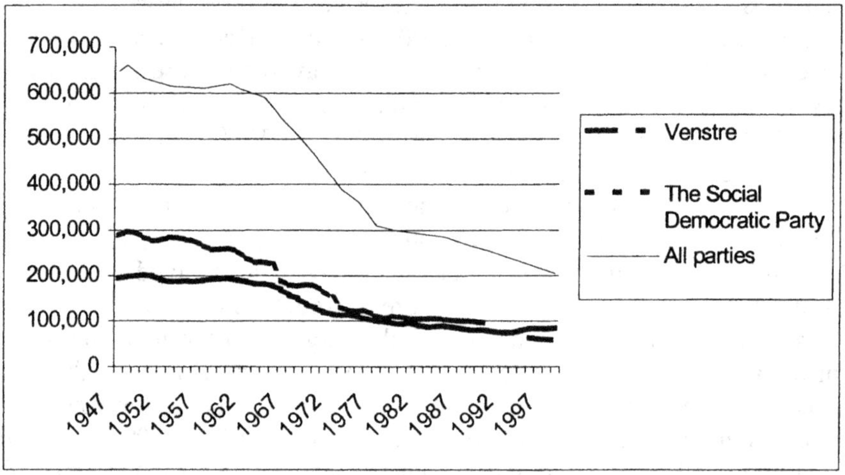

## From Class Party to Catchall Party?

The strategy of the Danish farmers' party has been quite distinct from that of its Scandinavian sister parties. In reality, they are only half-sisters. Venstre has been throughout its history an unequivocally bourgeois party. It has not sought compromises with the Social Democrats; it has not done much to win the urban middle class; and, when it has, it has been mainly by means of a neo-liberal appeal. This latter held sway from the late 1980s until the mid-1990s. Only in the second half of the 1990s, and especially after 1998, has the party tried to pursue a more centrist course. But how has the party's electoral profile evolved over time? To what extent has the party remained dependent on support from its core class of farmers, and to what extent have the farmers remained loyal to the party? To what extent, moreover, has the party been able to penetrate the urban upper-middle classes that used to vote for the Conservatives? Has Venstre simply replaced the Conservatives as the catchall bourgeois party? Finally, how has the ideological profile of supporters changed and what is the party's *policy image*? (Borre & Goul Andersen 1999). In other words, how do voters perceive the party?

It is clear that farmers have remained loyal to Venstre and their support has not varied much from one election to the next. Even the significant fluctuations in Venstre's overall electoral fortunes - such as the surge in performance in 1975 – have entailed only insignificant changes in support levels among the farmers. This is the classical picture of a class-based party and class-based party choice. There is a strong core group that is extremely loyal to the party. True, the class party succeeds from time to time in winning support from outside the *classe gardée* but in Venstre's case there has always been uncertainty about retaining this non-farmer support. This picture stands in sharp contrast to the Danish Social Democrats, where workers not only vote for the party far less than they used to do, but also have become its most unstable group of supporters (Borre and Goul Andersen 1997: Chapter 5).

**Table 4.6 Party Choice Among Danish Farmers, Selected Years 1964-1998**

|  | 1964 | 1966 | 1973 | 1975 | 1981 | 1984 | 1987 | 1990 | 1994 | 1998 |
|---|---|---|---|---|---|---|---|---|---|---|
| Venstre | 68 | 71 | 52 | 61 | 56 | 64 | 57 | 66 | 65 | 70 |
| Radical Liberals | 11 | 12 | 18 | 9 | 5 | 7 | 9 | 2 | 2 | - |
| Conservatives | 8 | 7 | 4 | 2 | 8 | 11 | 18 | 19 | 12 | 3 |
| Radical Right | 5 | 3 | 17 | 16 | 18 | 8 | 11 | 8 | 14 | 16 |
| Other parties | 8 | 7 | 9 | 12 | 13 | 10 | 5 | 5 | 7 | 11 |
| (N) | 870 | 789 | 180 | 585 | 468 | 72 | 77 | 55 | 55 | 47 |

*Source: Election Surveys: section 2 and Gallup Polls (1964,1966,1975,1981).*

*Radical Right: 1964-1966: The Independents; 1973-1998: Progress Party and (1998) Danish People's Party.*

As Table 4.6 illustrates, Venstre has never been the only party for farmers. The Radical Liberals originally brought together the smallholders and urban intelligentsia in a unique alliance. As late as 1964, nearly one-third of Radical Liberal voters comprised farmers. Moreover, the proportion of farmers voting for the Radical Liberals remained above 10 per cent until 1973 and above 5 per cent until 1987, although in the 1990s their support for the Radical Liberals almost disappeared in line with a sharp decline in the number of smallholders.

The Conservatives, too, have always been able to activate support among the larger farmers and it is a sign of weakening class cohesion among farmers that the party was much more successful in doing this in its heyday in the 1980s than in the 1960s. But for the Conservatives, farm support has been fragile support. Indeed, even though the average farm has rapidly increased to a size at which the Conservatives would not be an 'unnatural' party choice, the party has not been able to build durable allegiances among agriculturalists. In fact, the parties of the radical right have been more successful in doing so and have typically attracted at least as large a proportion of their support from farmers as their overall national vote.[8] None the less, nothing has been able to challenge Venstre's hegemony among farmers.[9]

However, as the numbers of the economically active population engaged in agriculture have declined dramatically so, too, has the electoral significance of the farmers. This has been particularly true, of course, in the case of the class party of the farmers, Venstre. Thus, in the 1960s, about one half of Venstre's vote among the economically active population comprised farmers (see Table 4.7). If farmers' wives are included, the figure would rise to 53 per cent in 1964 and 57 per cent in 1966. In contrast, in 1998, when farmers constituted a mere 1-2 per cent of the workforce, only 7 per cent of Venstre's votes derived from farmers. Given that farmers' support for Venstre is virtually a constant, the proportion of farmers in Venstre's support has of course varied with the party's electoral success.

In fact, the figures in Table 4.7 tend to underestimate the importance of Venstre's agricultural class base. In 1985, about 20 per cent of Venstre's voters were farmers. However, if farmers' spouses and people who had previously been farmers are included, the figure would rise to 35 per cent. Furthermore, if those born into a farming family are counted, the figure would reach 70 per cent in 1985 (Goul Andersen 1988: 21). The mid-1980s were lean electoral years for Venstre. But the party was still unmistakably a class party for farmers and their children and, in the long run, this was an untenable situation.

**Table 4.7  The Occupational Composition of Support for Venstre, 1964-1998**

|  | 1964 | 1966 | 1973 | 1975 | 1981 | 1984 | 1987 | 1990 | 1994 | 1998 |
|---|---|---|---|---|---|---|---|---|---|---|
| Farmer | 49 | 53 | 48 | 24 | 24 | 21 | 25 | 15 | 7 | 7 |
| self-employed | 11 | 12 | 8 | 13 | 8 | 9 | 10 | 12 | 11 | 9 |
| Non-manual | 19 | 18 | 34 | 45 | 47 | 49 | 40 | 58 | 54 | 52 |
| Worker | 21 | 17 | 10 | 18 | 21 | 21 | 25 | 15 | 28 | 32 |
| (N) | 1204 | 1061 | 194 | 1476 | 1088 | 216 | 176 | 239 | 501 | 451 |

*Source*: As Table 6. Slightly changed delineation between workers.

By the 1990s, things had changed appreciably. From a study in 1997 that included information on parents' class, it is possible to assess the scale and impact of socialisation (see Table 4.8). It is evident that the legacy of the old class structure was still strong since 17 per cent of the entire adult population (in the age range 18-74 years) was brought up in a farmer's family. Moreover, such a family background still had a large influence on Venstre's support which stood at 75 per cent among farmers, 40 per cent among those who were brought up on a farm, and 23 per cent for all others (economically active population only).[10] Thus, in addition to the 7 per cent of Venstre's voters who were actually farmers, there were 24 per cent with a family background in this class. Even so, two-thirds had no connection to farms whatsoever and hence, at present at least, Venstre is no longer narrowly a class party. It has appealed beyond the *classe gardée* before, but never to this extent and never in three consecutive elections. But from which non-farm groups does the party recruit its supporters?

## Table 4.8 Family Background and Composition of the Venstre Vote in 1994

| Family Background | Present Occupation | | | | Composition of Venstre voters |
|---|---|---|---|---|---|
| | Total | Workers | white collar | Self-employed | |
| No connection to farmers | 23 | 16 | 24 | 44 | 69 |
| Family background | 40 | 32 | 34 | 56 | 24 |
| Actually a farmer | 75 | | | | 7 |
| (N) | 1895 | 468 | 829 | 117 | 624 |
| | 369 | 87 | 128 | 18 | |
| | 60 | | | | |

*Source*: Survey for the Rockwool Foundation Study of 'Citizens and their Laws' (1997; N=3000). Data are unweighted (for details, see Hultin 1998). Entries are the proportions voting for Venstre at the 1994 general election.

It is plain from Table 4.7 that, as in most of the other parties, the urban middle class, especially non-manual employees, constitute the majority of Venstre's voters. What is notable, however, has been the unusually large proportion of workers supporting the party in the 1990s. Given that, because of the changing nature of the class structure, these figures are in some respects difficult to compare over time, the proportion voting Venstre in various occupational groups is set out in Table 4.9. The loyalty of the farmers to Venstre stands in extremely sharp contrast to the fickleness of other groups. Among the self-employed, the variation was from 8 to 35 per cent whilst among higher-level non-manuals it ranged from 6 to 29 per cent. It is also interesting to compare the situation in the 1990s with 1975 when the party peaked for the first time. In 1975 Venstre more than doubled its support among non-manual employees but remained unable to attract much support from blue-collar workers. When compared to the

The Danish Venstre: Liberal, Agrarian or Centrist? 119

workers (mainly first generation), although only in 1975 did it manage to exceed the 10 per cent threshold, and then only marginally. In 1990, the picture was broadly the same, with working class support remaining very low. This was hardly surprising perhaps in view of Venstre's strong neo-liberal appeal at the end of the 1980s. What has been more remarkable has been the unusually high support among workers in the 1994 and 1998 elections when about 20 per cent of all workers voted Venstre. Furthermore, in 1998, this was obtained in the teeth of sharp competition from the radical rightist Danish People's Party which (along with the Progress Party it replaced) has the most 'proletarian' class base of all the Danish parties (Goul Andersen & Bjørklund 1990 & 2000).

Table 4.9  Support for Venstre by Occupation, 1964-1998 and for the Conservatives in 1984

|  | 1964 | 1966 | 1973 | 1975 | 1981 | 1984 | 1987 | 1990 | 1994 | 1998 | Cons 1984 |
|---|---|---|---|---|---|---|---|---|---|---|---|
| Election result | 20.8 | 19.3 | 12.3 | 23.3 | 11.3 | 12.1 | 10.5 | 15.8 | 23.3 | 24 | 23.4 |
| Farmer | 68 | 71 | 52 | 61 | 56 | 64 | 57 | 66 | 65 | 70 | 11 |
| Self-employed | 18 | 18 | 8 | 30 | 11 | 14 | 11 | 25 | 35 | 30 | 47 |
| Higher non-manual | 14 | 13 | 10 | 28 | 11 | 9 | 6 | 22 | 29 | 28 | 34 |
| Lower non-manual | 10 | 7 | 8 | 21 | 8 | 10 | 6 | 13 | 23 | 21 | 24 |
| Worker | 9 | 7 | 3 | 11 | 6 | 7 | 7 | 7 | 19 | 20 | 15 |
| (N) |  |  |  |  |  |  |  |  |  |  |  |
|  | 870 | 789 | 180 | 585 | 468 | 72 | 77 | 55 | 55 | 47 | 72 |
|  | 754 | 725 | 194 | 656 | 849 | 140 | 157 | 111 | 153 | 133 | 140 |
|  | 1107 | 980 | 246 | 845 | 1919 | 382 | 272 | 199 | 272 | 403 | 382 |
|  | 774 | 906 | 512 | 2058 | 3643 | 749 | 827 | 766 | 857 | 599 | 749 |
|  | 2654 | 2419 | 685 | 2649 | 4032 | 647 | 660 | 515 | 714 | 719 | 647 |

Source: Election Surveys (Gallup Polls 1964,1966). Changed delineation between lower and higher non-manuals in 1966, 1975 and 1998; 1998 also slightly changed delineation between workers and non-manuals.

In the party's prime in 1984, the Conservatives also witnessed a surprising increase in working class support and were often referred to as the 'second largest workers' party'. It is interesting, therefore, to compare Venstre in 1998 with the Conservatives in 1984 as the aggregate support for the two parties was equivalent and both parties achieved their broadest-ever social support base. It can be seen from Table 4.9 that Venstre was slightly less successful among the urban self-employed and non-manual employees than the Conservatives but gained much larger support among workers. Indeed, in a large number of opinion polls in 1999 and 2000, Venstre has been the largest party among those workers who indicated a party preference (Ugebrevet Mandag Morgen no. 11, 2000).

Table 4.10 Support for Venstre and the Conservatives in Selected Occupations, 1964-1998

|   |   | 1964 | 1966 | 1973 | 1975 | 1981 | 1984 | 1987 | 1990 | 1994 | 1998 |
|---|---|---|---|---|---|---|---|---|---|---|---|
| Self-employed | Venstre | 18 | 18 | 8 | 30 | 11 | 14 | 11 | 25 | 35 | 30 |
|   | Cons | 43 | 42 | 13 | 10 | 31 | 47 | 38 | 34 | 28 | 24 |
| Higher non-manual | Venstre | 14 | 13 | 10 | 28 | 11 | 9 | 6 | 22 | 29 | 28 |
|   | Cons | 39 | 37 | 16 | 12 | 24 | 34 | 34 | 29 | 22 | 12 |
| Higher non-manual Private sector | Venstre |   |   | 8 | 31 | 12 | 9 | 8 | 27 | 39 | 40 |
|   | Cons |   |   | 13 | 14 | 33 | 44 | 42 | 34 | 27 | 14 |
| (N) |   |   |   |   |   |   |   |   |   |   |   |
| Self-employed |   | 754 | 725 | 194 | 656 | 849 | 140 | 157 | 111 | 153 | 133 |
| Higher non-manual |   | 1107 | 980 | 246 | 845 | 1919 | 382 | 272 | 199 | 272 | 403 |
| Private sector |   |   |   | 127 | 509 | 862 | 175 | 148 | 126 | 146 | 204 |

Source: Election Surveys (Gallup Polls 1964,1966). Changed delineation between lower and higher non-manuals in 1966, 1975 and 1998; 1998 also slightly changed delineation between workers and non-manuals.

In Table 4.10, Venstre's urban middle class support is explored further with a view to assessing the party's potential for affording a long-term alternative to the Conservatives among these social groups. As far as the self-employed are concerned, they seem incapable of maintaining a lasting allegiance to any particular party and often seem to plump for the non-socialist party they consider the best in the particular circumstances. Thus, support for the Conservatives from the self-employed, which used to be above 40 per cent in the 1960s, declined to 10 per cent in 1975. So far, Venstre has not been able to reach the Conservative peak in elections, although opinion polls have from time to time shown much higher readings.

The picture looks much the same with regard to the higher non-manual employees. Venstre has not succeeded in getting near to the Conservatives' best performances and, as late as 1987, only six per cent of this group voted for Venstre. Even in 1975, when the Conservatives polled a paltry 5.5 per cent of the national vote, they retained the support of 12 per cent of higher-level non-manuals. However, at that time, there was a less clear-cut divide between the behaviour of public and private employees (Goul Andersen 1999b). Remarkably, however, by the 1990s, Venstre was able to attract a level of support from senior private sector employees that compared with the best historical figures for the Conservatives. In 1994 and 1998, 40 per cent of higher-level employees in the private sector voted for Venstre. This is significantly in excess of the 1975 level and not far short of the best Conservative elections during the 'yuppie period' in the 1980s. True, these figures represent an increase from a low point of only 8 per cent in 1987. But the consistently high level of support over a decade would suggest that Venstre has managed to establish itself as a mouthpiece, and to a significant extent a point of identification for this very important core group of managers and executives. This is a new situation that augurs well for Venstre in the twenty-first century. It suggests that the party may be about to find a new core group to replace its historical core of farmers.

Taking the data in total, Venstre does not appear to be a catchall party in the sense of mobilising miscellaneous floating voters around various popular issues. It is firmly rooted in particular occupational groups, even if the social foundations have shifted from rural to urban. But, as the level of working class support indicates, Venstre *is* a catchall party in the sense that it manages to draw together unusual coalitions of voters. Moreover, since 1998, it has increasingly been catchall in the sense that it has downplayed ideology in favour of a vague (and maximally inoffensive) centrist position.

**Table 4.11 Support for Venstre within Selected Groups. Deviance from Election Result, in Percentage Points**

|  | 1966 | 1975 | 1981 | 1987 | 1990 | 1994 | 1998 |
|---|---|---|---|---|---|---|---|
| Election result | 19.3 | 23.3 | 11.3 | 10.5 | 15.8 | 23.3 | 24 |
| 18-29 years | -6 | -5 | -6 | -3 | -2 | 6 | 2 |
| 30-39 years | 0 | 1 | -2 | -5 | -4 | -2 | 0 |
| 40-49 years | -1 | 0 | 1 | 0 | -1 | -2 | -6 |
| 50-64 years | 4 | -1 | 3 | 2 | 3 | -2 | -2 |
| 65 years + | 3 | 2 | 6 | 6 | 4 | 1 | 6 |
| Basic school | 3 | -1 | 1 | 3 | -1 | -1 | 0 |
| Secondary | -9 | 3 | -1 | -4 | 0 | 1 | 1 |
| High school+ | -6 | 3 | -3 | -2 | 2 | 1 | 0 |
| Private non-manual | . | 1 | -1 | -2 | 5 | 9 | 9 |
| Public non-manual | . | -2 | -3 | -6 | -7 | -3 | -8 |
| **Composition of Venstre's supporters: deviance from all parties. Percentage points** | | | | | | | |
| Proportion of women | -3 | 1 | 1 | -1 | 1 | -3 | -6 |
| Proportion aged 40 years | -5 | -4 | -15 | -16 | -8 | 3 | 2 |

Before considering the issue of Venstre's shifting ideological stance, other aspects of the party's social profile over the period 1966-1998 may be noted briefly. In the aforementioned year, as Table 4.11 demonstrates, the party's profile was anything but promising. In particular it attracted less than proportional support among young persons and those with anything above the basic elementary level of education. Even in the successful electoral year of 1975, the age composition was slightly skewed towards the elderly and, in the 1980s, there was a strong bias towards this same group. Thus, the proportion of voters under 40 years was 15 to 16 percentage points below average. Even the gains in 1990 were too small to compensate for this. Significantly, however, in 1994 and 1998, the party contrived to have a relatively young profile. True, the legacy of the youth rebellion has kept the support at a low level among the 40-49 years cohort, and to some extent among voters in their late 30s. As far as education is concerned, the party has not had a clear profile in the 1990s and it has drawn support almost equally across all age groups, in spite of the party's strong backing among higher-level private employees and the declining importance of farmers. Two new significant 'gaps' in Venstre's social profile warrant emphasis. In 1994, and especially 1998, women were under-represented among the party's voters whilst since the mid-1980s, the same has been still more true of public employees. In 1998, Venstre was supported by 33 per cent of non-manual employees in the private sector when compared to only 16 per cent in the public sector. However, this ratio is broadly the same in the other non-socialist parties.[11] All in all, however, Venstre in the 1990s was a party with not only a sizeable but also a very broad electoral base, albeit with two main core groups - farmers and higher-level private sector employees. This is a curious combination and it is worth probing the ideological profile and policy image that lie behind it.

Table 4.12 Self-Placement on a Left-Right Scale from 1 (left) to 10 (right)

|  | 1979 | 1981 | 1984 | 1990 | 1994 | 1998* | 2000** |
|---|---|---|---|---|---|---|---|
| Social Democrats | 5.1 | 4.9 | 5 | 4.9 | 4.9 | 4.5 | 4.6 |
| Centre Parties | 6 | 6 | 6.1 | 6.1 | 5.9 | 5.6 | 5.3 |
| Venstre | 6.8 | 6.7 | 7.3 | 7.7 | 7.5 | 7.1 | 6.4 |
| Conservatives | 7.4 | 7.4 | 7.4 | 7.6 | 7.4 | 7.3 | 6.5 |
| (N) | 584 | 236 | 246 | 301 | 563 | 634 | 79 |
|  | 211 | 126 | 119 | 84 | 152 | 195 | 36 |
|  | 194 | 75 | 101 | 128 | 413 | 432 | 121 |
|  | 194 | 107 | 191 | 118 | 248 | 161 | 41 |

Where would you place yourself on this scale from 1 (0) to 10 where 1 (0) means most to the left, and 10 means most to the right? (0 to 10 scale in 1998 and 2000; otherwise 1 to 10).

*Source*: Election Surveys 1979-1998. The mid-term survey was conducted in co-operation with AIM Nielsen and Mandag Morgen, February 2000. Based on party preference at the time of interviewing.

A very simple and robust measure with which to compare Venstre's ideological profile over time is voter self-placement on a left-right scale. Data from 1979 to 2000 are presented in Table 4.12, although there are unfortunately two data breaks. In 1998, the 1-10 scale was changed to a 0-10 scale whilst in 2000 the mid-term survey was conducted by telephone, with the result that respondents could not see the scale on a showcard.[12] None the less, it is evident that Venstre has always recruited its support from well to the right of centre. True, in 1979 and 1981, the party's voters considered themselves less far to the right than Conservatives. But this changed markedly during the 1980s. Whereas all the other parties exhibited a remarkable degree of stability, Venstre's voters moved from an average position of 6.7 on the left-right scale in 1981 to 7.7 in 1990. This coincided with Venstre's period of neo-liberal mobilisation, which was conducted in an uncompromising, even aggressive tone. The Conservatives followed the move to the right to some extent, while many of that party's centrist politicians left active politics.

This was also an instance when a party (Venstre) flew in the face of public opinion. Even though Venstre voters did not share the party's hostility to the welfare state (see below), it attracted attention with its clear messages. Moreover, it did manage to a degree to make an appeal by peddling a new interpretation of society and mix of policies that were to some extent consonant with recommendations from *inter alia* the OECD. When the economic situation improved in 1993-1994, there was less room for radical policy change. Ironically, however, the ideas that came to be *implemented* in the 1990s were more radical than the relatively few changes that were carried out in the 1980s (see Goul Andersen 2000). Yet the fact remained that the non-socialist parties were not able to win the elections. Accordingly, Venstre began to adopt a much more centrist orientation. Importantly, both Venstre and Conservative voters have also moved very significantly towards the political centre since 1998. However, due to changes in the survey design, the 2000 data should be interpreted with some caution. It also seems that the image of the parties has changed. When the 1998 question was repeated in 2000, the respondents assigned both the Conservatives and Venstre a position much closer to the centre than in 1998. Unfortunately, there are the same comparability problems as above.

The traditional left-right scale does not exhaust the cleavage dimensions of Danish politics. On the contrary, voters have increasingly divided on a "new politics" axis, determined by attitudes to such issues as immigration and law and order. From voters' images of party location on issue dimensions, it is also possible to examine whether Venstre had achieved a more centrist image already by 1998.

**Table 4.13**   **Images of the Parties' Placement on a Left-Right Scale from 1 (left) to 10 (right)**

|  | 1994 | 1998 | 2000 |
|---|---|---|---|
| Venstre | 7.9 | 7.5 | 6.6 |
| Conservatives | 7.6 | 7.2 | 6.4 |

*Source:* as Table 4.12. All respondents (approximately 2000 in 1994 and 1998, about 500 in 2000).

Table 4.4 indicates that this clearly was the case. On the basis of a simple average across issue positions, it can be seen that the average placement of Venstre has changed from 1944 to 1941. The party in short has moved slightly towards the centre. Among the Conservatives the opposite is the case since, across issues, it is generally believed to have moved to the right. Venstre is still the more right-wing party but the differential *vis-a-vis* the Conservatives is down from 9 to 3 percentage points. Furthermore, Venstre is located further to the right mainly because of its pro-European sympathies which are regarded here as a 'rightist' position. Excluding Europe would make the moderation of Venstre appear even more significant.

On all issue dimensions, however, voters are in no doubt about Venstre's position to the right. As far as refugee policy and law and order are concerned, the average voter is more at odds with the Social Democrats than with Venstre. As to economic policies and public spending, the average voter is slightly more in line with the Social Democrats. On environmental issues, the average voter is out of step with Venstre whilst on European integration, the average voter is at some distance from all the large parties.

On most of these dimensions, Venstre has worked at giving signals that could change the party's policy image. On the basis of the experience from 1994-1998 it seems that it has already succeeded. This will probably bring the party more in tune with its working class supporters. On the other hand, the party runs the risk of becoming too anonymous with the concomitant risk that voters will find it difficult to discern a distinctive policy profile or they may simply consider the party too opportunistic. Whatever the case, Venstre has a clear ideological profile, and it is perceived to be far from the centre of Danish politics. This is compatible with some notions of a catchall party, but not with the most widespread definitions. The Danish party continues to be very different from its Nordic half-sisters.

**Table 4.14 Policy Image of Parties: Location on a Scale from -100 (right/new right) to +100 (left/new left), on Various Dimensions, 1998**

|  |  | Danish People's Party | Venstre | Cons. | Radical Liberals | Social Dems. | Social People's Party | Danish voters |
|---|---|---|---|---|---|---|---|---|
| Refugee policy | 1998 | -97 | -43 | -43 | 14 | 6 | 47 | -34 |
|  | 1994 | -93 | -42 | -34 | 17 | 26 | 48 | -29 |
| Law and order | 1998 | -80 | -50 | -52 | 30 | 23 | 64 | -18 |
|  | 1994 | -74 | -45 | -39 | 11 | 24 | 54 | -17 |
| Environment | 1998 | -43 | -17 | -16 | 30 | 38 | 72 | 27 |
|  | 1994 | -47 | -21 | -12 | 28 | 34 | 69 | 32 |
| Tight econ. policy | 1998 | -54 | -47 | -43 | -1 | 12 | 46 | -11 |
|  | 1994 | -64 | -57 | -46 | 4 | 40 | 58 | -9 |
| Public expenditures | 1998 | -69 | -49 | -45 | 11 | 25 | 57 | -6 |
|  | 1994 | -86 | -57 | -45 | 1 | 32 | 58 | -10 |
| European Union | 1998 | 76 | -84 | -70 | -49 | -55 | 49 | -5 |
|  | 1994 | 39 | -83 | -68 | -30 | -35 | 44 | -4 |
| Simple Average | 1998 | -38 | -41 | -38 | 5 | 10 | 48 | -7 |
|  | 1994 | -46 | -44 | -35 | 4 | 17 | 47 | -6 |

## Conclusion

From its emergence in 1870, Venstre was a class party, although from the outset it was also grounded in an ideology of economic liberalism. The two characteristics were mutually complementary as the export interests of the Danish farmers dictated a strong preference for free trade and competition. From 1905, when large sections of the urban wing, along with the smallholders, defected from the party, Venstre's electoral base narrowed even further. The party came to represent, first and foremost, the medium-sized farmers and it recruited very few votes from the towns, and the capital city of Copenhagen in particular. Despite winning a parliamentary majority in the lower chamber in 1872, Venstre was unable to form a government until 1901 when the parliamentary principle was adopted *de facto*. Backed by various groupings, the party could rule with the support of a lower chamber majority until 1909, and it held the office of Prime Minister for about half the decade 1910-1920. But Venstre's support was declining and between 1920 and 68 it participated in government on only three brief occasions.

Notwithstanding a marked decline in the number of farmers and rural dwellers in relation to the population as a whole, Venstre's electoral following remained surprisingly stable from the 1930s to the early 1960s. However, during that decade and the next, its share of the vote declined to around 12 per cent, a level that was maintained throughout the 1980s. From 1982-1993, Venstre formed coalition cabinets with the Conservatives, the latter enjoying a much larger share of the vote and holding the prime ministership. However, as the Conservatives became increasingly centrist during the 1980s, Venstre found a niche to their right. Under the influence of young party members, it adopted a rather aggressive neo-liberal rhetoric that had a surprisingly large appeal to otherwise quite moderate voters, not least among the younger cohorts. In both the 1994 and 1998 elections, Venstre secured nearly one-quarter of the vote and took on a very different appearance from being the class party of the farmers. The party has been notably successful in attracting higher-level employees in the private sector, and this group may well become a new core group for Venstre, replacing the farmers. More surprisingly, the party also has unusually large support among blue-collar workers, at least when compared with the other non-socialist parties, and it has been keen to retain this support by toning down its anti-welfare state rhetoric.

With the former vice-chairman and chief ideologist, Anders Fogh Rasmussen, at the helm following the 1998 election, it was widely expected that Venstre would intensify its neo-liberal ideology. Yet electoral successes in the 1994 and 1998 elections failed to facilitate government participation and, mindful of this fact, Anders Fogh Rasmussen chose to pursue a significantly more centrist course. This was partly motivated by considerations of vote maximisation, but also by the aspiration of increasing its appeal to the centrist parties that usually hold the key to forming a majority government. Hence, as a large party, Venstre has chosen the same centrist strategy as the Conservatives in the 1980s when they were the largest bourgeois party. As long as this pays off, and as long as economic prosperity makes a critique of welfare spending inappropriate, the party is likely to stay on its centrist course. Equally, Venstre has oscillated between centrism and 'hardline liberalism' over the years, and if the new strategy fails, the party may well return to the neo-liberal position that proved a recipe for earlier electoral success. Basically, these two orientations are variations on a theme of Paganini, that is, they are variations on the same basic policy approach. Indeed, Venstre has always espoused a broad-gauge ideology rather than seeking to gain short-term benefits by focusing on single issues.

## Notes

1. The principle of parliamentarism was not accepted (*de facto*) until 1901 and remained fragile for several years thereafter. Before that it was at the King's discretion to appoint the cabinet he wanted. The result was that The Right was the governing party for decades even though The United Left controlled a parliamentary majority.
2. As late as the 1870s a proportion of MPs was elected by a show of hands at a public meeting in the constituency. A secret ballot was not introduced until 1901.
3. In fact Venstre stressed its liberal stance by adding the suffix 'Denmark's Liberal Party' to its name when the party adopted a new programme in 1963. Equally, Venstre's leader at the time, Erik Eriksen, stressed the willingness of the party to undertake its social obligations. 'Liberal policy today has got nothing to do with laissez faire. A modern liberal policy fully acknowledges the responsibility of society to those in need'.
4. Later (1960-1969), he became the first secretary-general of the OEEC/OECD.
5. Since 1975, no Danish election has brought about a change in the composition of government. However, two changes in government did take place without an election in 1982 and 1993. The existing coalitions resigned when the Radical Liberals withdrew their support.
6. Venstre, moreover, has maintained a high membership rate among farmers. In 1990, farmers constituted 43 per cent of members. As in other European countries, the Danish Social Democrats have lost members disproportionately among workers.
7. To some extent opinion polls between elections are misleading, this is because the supporters of a large party like the Social Democrats tend to be demobilised and answer 'don't know' when asked about future party choice.

8   This holds also for the 1960s when the Independents gained more support among farmers than elsewhere. However, this party was more 'right' than 'radical', and it was originally launched in 1953 by a former Prime Minister of Venstre (1945-1947), Knud Kristensen.
9   In 1998, the Christian People's Party got some 9 per cent protest votes among farmers. It exploited the opportunity to argue strongly against a very unpopular compromise on environmental regulation between Venstre and the government which Venstre was obliged to accept in order not to appear an anti-green party to its urban voters.
10  Figures are unweighted. As a result of strong support for Venstre in opinion polls at the time of interviewing, there was some over-claiming of having voted for the party in 1994.
11  Until the mid-1970s, there were no significant political divisions between the private and the public sector, but since then, non-manual employees in the two sectors have drifted apart with public sector employees moving far to the left and private sector employees moving far to the right (Goul Andersen, 1999b; Borre and Goul Andersen 1997: 125-39).
12  There are also some indications that the latter measurement for whatever reason may be somewhat less reliable.

## References

Berglund, Sten & Ulf Lindström (1978), *'The Scandinavian Party System(s). A comparative study'*, Lund: Studentlitteratur.
Borre et al. (1979), 'Ustabilitet ved parlamentsvalg i fire nordiske lande 1950-1977' pp. 241-82 in Mogens N. Pedersen (ed.), *Dansk politik i 1970'erne*. Copenhagen: Samfundsvidenskabeligt Forlag.
Borre, Ole and Goul Andersen, Jørgen (1997), *'Voting and Political Attitudes in Denmark,'* Aarhus: Aarhus University Press.
Borre, Ole & Goul Andersen, Jørgen (1999), 'Det teoretiske grundlag for valgundersøgelsen 1998', pp. 273-82 in Johannes Andersen, Ole Borre, Jørgen Goul Andersen, Hans Jørgen Nielsen, *Vælgere med omtanke. En analyse af Folketingsvalget 1998*. Aarhus: Systime.
Christiansen, Niels Finn (1990), *'Klassesamfundet organiseres'. 1900-1925*. Gyldendal og Politikens Danmarkshistorie, Copenhagen: Nordisk Forlag.
Damgaard, Erik (1974), 'Stability and Change in the Danish Party System over half a Century', in Scandinavian Political Studies vol. 9:103-125.
Dybdahl, Vagn (1978), *'De nye klasser 1870-1913,' Politikens Danmarkshistorie bd. 12*. Copenhagen.
Elklit, Jørgen (1988), 'Det klassiske danske partisystem bliver til', in Jørgen Elklit: *Fra åben til hemmelig afstemning: Aspekter af et partisystems udvikling*, Aarhus: Politica.
Goul Andersen, Jørgen (1979), *'Mellemlagene i Danmark'*, Aarhus: Politica.
Goul Andersen, Jørgen (1995), '(Hvorfor) vinder regeringen ikke på den økonomiske fremgang? Policy vurderinger, policy effects og andre forklaringer', *Working Paper no. 2 from the Danish Election Programme*. Department of Political Science, University of Aarhus.
Goul Andersen, Jørgen (1988), *'Vælgermosaik*. Småartikler om valg og vælgere 1986-88', Working Paper, Center for Kulturforskning, University of Aarhus.

Goul Andersen, Jørgen (1992), *'Den politiske mistillid i Danmark,'* Research Report. Rockwool Foundation Research Unit/Department of Political Science, University of Aarhus.
Goul Andersen, Jørgen (1998), 'Velfærdens veje i komparativt perspektiv', *Den jyske Historiker* 82, pp. 114-38.
Goul Andersen, Jørgen (1999a), 'Appendix 2. Meningsmålinger 1994 – 1998', pp. 295-296 in Johannes Andersen, Ole Borre, Jørgen Goul Andersen, Hans Jørgen Nielsen, *Vaelgere med omtanke. En analyse af folketingsvalget 1998.* Aarhus: Systime.
Goul Andersen, Jørgen (1999b), 'Offentlig og privat', pp. 91-98 in Johannes Andersen, Ole Borre, Jørgen Goul Andersen, Hans Jørgen Nielsen, *Valg med omtanke. En analyse af Folketingsvalget 1998.* Aarhus: Systime.
Goul Andersen, Jørgen (2000), 'Welfare Crisis and Beyond: Danish Welfare Policies in the 1980s and 1990s', pp. 69-87 in Stein Kuhnle (ed.), *Survival of the European Welfare State.* London: Routledge.
Goul Andersen, Jørgen & Bjørklund, Tor (1990), 'Structural Changes and New Cleavages: The Progress Parties in Denmark and Norway', *Acta Sociologica* vol.33(3), pp. 195-217.
Goul Andersen, Jørgen and Bjørklund, Tor (2000), 'Radical Right-Wing Populism in Scandinavia: From Tax Revolt to Neo-Liberalism and Xenophobia', pp.193-223, in Paul Hainsworth (ed.), *The Politics of the Extreme Right. From the Margins to the Mainstream* London and New York: Pinter.
Gundelach, Peter (1988), *'Sociale bevægelser og samfundsændringer: Nye sociale grupperinger og deres organisationsformer ved overgangen til ændrede samfundstyper',* Aarhus: Forlaget Politica.
Hultin, Marie Louise (1998), 'Appendiks: Databeskrivelse', pp. 453-481, in Jørgen Goul Andersen, *Borgerne og lovene.* Aarhus: Aarhus University Press.
Hvidt, Kristian (1990), *'Det folkelige gennembrud og dets mænd. 1850-1900',* Gyldendal og Politikens Danmarkshistorie, Copenhagen: Nordisk Forlag.
Hornemann Moller, Iver (1994), *'Velfærdsstatens udbygning. Den anden socialreform 1933',* Frederiksberg: Samfundslitteratur.
Jensen, Michael Appel Skovbo (1998), *'Politik som strategisk handlen. Hvilke faktorer tager politikere hensyn til, når de tager beslutninger? En analyse baseret på dansk grundskolepolitik gennem cirka 100 år',* Thesis at the Department of Political Science, University of Aarhus.
Jorgensen, Erik Stig (1979), 'Politisk aktivitet og politisk organisation i den danske landbefolkning 1835-1866', pp. 13-44, in Kurt Sorensen (ed.), *Venstre. 50 år for folkestyret,* Holte: Forlaget liberal.
Larsen, Knud (1979), 'Venstreorganisationerne 1866-1929', pp. 45-77, in Kurt Sorensen (ed.), *Venstre. 50 år for folkestyret,* Holte: Forlaget liberal.
Lipset, Seymour Martin & Stein Rokkan (1967), 'Cleavage Structures, Party Systems and Voter Alignments: An Introduction', in S.M. Lipset & S. Rokkan (eds), *Party Systems and Voter Alignments,* New York: The Free Press.
Lund, Hans & Arne Fog Pedersen (1970), *'Venstre i 100 år. 1970-1901', Et folk vågner,* Copenhagen.
Morch, Soren (1982), *'Den ny Danmarkshistorie1880-1960',* Copenhagen: Nordisk forlag.
Norgaard, Asbjorn Sonne (2000), *'Party Politics and the Organization of the Danish Welfare State, 1890-1920: The Bourgeois Roots of the Modern Welfare State,'* Forthcoming article in Scandinavian Political Studies.

Pedersen, Mogens N. (1987), 'The Danish "Working Multiparty System": Breakdown or Adaption?', pp. 1-60 in Hans Daalder (ed.), *Party Systems in Denmark, Austria, Switzerland, The Netherlands, and Belgium*, London: Frances Pinter (Publishers) Limited.

Petersen, Jørn-Henrik (1990), 'The Danish 1891 Act on Old Age Relief: A Response to Agrarian Demand and Pressure', *Journal of Social Policy*, vol 19, 69-91.

Rokkan, Stein (1967), 'Norway: Numerical Democracy and Corporate Pluralism', pp. 70-115, in Robert A. Dahl (ed.), *Political Oppositions in Western Democracies*, New Haven and London: Yale University Press.

Thomsen, Niels (1979), 'Venstres vælgere. 1870-1930', pp. 45-77, in Kurt Sorensen (ed.), *Venstre. 50 år for folkestyret*, Holte: Forlaget liberal.

# 5 The Icelandic Progressive Party: Trawling for the Town Vote?

GUNNAR HELGI KRISTINSSON

The Icelandic Progressive Party was undoubtedly one of the most successful farmers' parties in any stable democracy over the course of the twentieth century. Formed in 1916, it usually enjoyed the status of second largest party and was a prime contender to head governments. Indeed, between 1927 and 1999, the Progresssive Party held the post of prime minister for a total of over thirty years and spent less than one third of the period in opposition. Its average share of votes during that time was 24.3 per cent. Apart from its obvious importance for the modern political development of Iceland, the saga of the Progressive Party is of wider interest on several counts.

First, the emergence of a sectional farmers' party in Iceland is of considerable relevance for the comparative study of party systems. Lipset and Rokkan's (1967) classic analysis of the moulding of European party systems relates their emergence until the late 1920s to the impact of the national revolution and the industrial revolution. However, it fails to provide a satisfactory account of where agrarian parties emerged and where they did not. The Icelandic case, it is argued, offers some clues in the riddle of where such parties emerged.

Second, the Icelandic farmers' party began much earlier than its counterparts elsewhere to seek electoral support from the non-farming population. As early as 1930, it ran its own list in the capital, Reykjavik, and gained no less than 12 per cent of the vote. Although its efforts to attract the non-farming population were thwarted by a split in the 1930s, persistence paid off and, by the early post-war period, it had a respectable following in the towns. Significantly, the party began to target the urban vote while still developing as an electoral force, something which appears to fly in the face of the conventional wisdom that farmers' parties seek support in the towns to offset the effects of a declining agricultural population. Factors internal to the party organisation rather than electoral sociology – the agrarian population was relatively homogenous in comprising farmers and their families – were crucial in drawing the party to the towns much earlier than the other farmers' parties.

Finally, the Progressive Party has gained a considerably stronger and more stable following outside its agrarian basis than its sister parties in Finland, Norway and Sweden. True, the Finnish party retains a share of the overall vote that is comparable to the Progressive Party. But it relies on an agrarian population which is much larger, in relative terms, than in Iceland. While the Progressive Party has its strongholds in the rural and peripheral areas, it would not remain a major party in Icelandic politics without the town votes. In sum, Kirchheimer's (1966) pessimism with regard to the chances of sectional parties transforming themselves into catchall parties seems unfounded in the case of the Icelandic Progressive Party.

**The Origins of the Progressive Party**

The Progressive Party was formed in 1916 as the party of the Icelandic farmers. It was never a peasant party demanding land reform for an underclass of tenants and agricultural labourers. Nor was it a liberal party, such as the Danish or Norwegian Venstre, with a strong agrarian basis. The term *farmer's party* is preferable to *agrarian party* when characterising the party in its early years, since it depicts its social basis more accurately. The party in fact had very little in common with peasant parties in other parts of the world. Although owner occupancy was far from the norm in Icelandic agriculture, there was relatively little structured differentiation in the countryside and farmers and their families were numerically preponderant by the time the Progressive Party was formed. Even the agricultural labourers were dwindling in numbers and were mostly the unmarried sons and daughters of farmers. Hence, land issues never featured prominently in the Progressive Party programme.

From a sociological perspective it may seem of little interest that farmers formed their own party in Iceland early in the twentieth century. In a comparative perspective, however, this is certainly not the case since relatively few democratic states boasted durable agrarian parties. This was not for want of trying, so to speak, as attempts were made in most European countries at some point to establish agrarian parties of one type or another (Urwin 1980). Barrington Moore (1966) suggests that the very existence of a peasantry represents a potential threat to democracy. Peasant parties developed in the main where democracy was not stable. But, even where agriculture had become market-oriented and democracy rested on solid foundations, only a few farmers' parties emerged.

Three major conditions, it is argued, had to be met in order for strong farmers' parties to emerge. In the first place, as Rokkan (1970 p. 129) has noted, farmers' parties did not take root where there existed a party political organ of the Catholic Church.[1] In such cases, class-specific mobilisation was unable to throw off the shackles of the dominant church-state cleavage (Berger 1972). The emergence of the Progressive Party in Iceland was thus facilitated by the fact that Catholicism had been completely eradicated during the Reformation. The task of forming the party in fact was generally made easier as a result of the religious and cultural homogeneity of the population. There were no linguistic or ethnic minorities in Iceland and almost the entire population belonged to the Lutheran state church.

A second condition for the emergence of strong agrarian parties was the existence of intense conflict between the towns and countryside that could not be contained by the established party system. This was notably the situation during the first world war as the food situation in the towns deteriorated rapidly, while the farmers, initially at least, appeared to prosper. In those nations occupying the battlefields of Europe, this conflict was held in check by the contingencies of the war effort. Elsewhere, however, conflicts over the market for food magnified what was probably a diffuse feeling of mistrust into a major political conflict. Only where agriculture was closely identified with the national interest, as in New Zealand, could such conflicts be kept within the bounds of the established party system (Graham 1963 pp. 196-197).

Finally, incipient farmers' parties struggled to surmount the high electoral barriers to parliamentary representation. In most instances where such parties were formed they benefited from modifications to the high threshold to representation created by the first-past-the-post system. In Australia this opportunity was provided by the Alternative Vote system, while in the Nordic countries, as well as Ireland and Switzerland, it was proportional representation which facilitated their task.[2] Although Iceland still used the first-past-the-post system for most seats when the Progressive Party was formed the electoral system was in fact conducive to the formation of the party.

Before the first world war the independence issue tended to dominate Icelandic party politics. Iceland gained home rule in 1904 but, until the achievement of sovereignty in 1918, the relationship with Denmark was a primary cleavage in Icelandic politics.[3] The Home Rule

Party stood for moderation in the relationship with Copenhagen and was more preoccupied with domestic progress than constitutional formalities. Its opponents, who joined forces in the Independence Party (old) in 1908, constituted a motley gathering of political currents. They took a more radical position on the independence issue than the Home Rule Party, but did not have a lot in common on other issues. They tended to be more strongly represented in the peripheral regions than the economically developed ones.

The political parties at this time were weak structures in that they were basically loose alliances of parliamentarians rather than popular mass organisations. Parliamentarians could operate freely in the national assembly without putting their seats at risk and quite a few *Athingi* members did not have fixed party allegiances. The corollary was the formation of flexible party alliances that presented government ministers with a constant threat of being ousted by parliament.

The lion's share of MPs were elected in predominantly rural constituencies and a number of these were naturally farmers. During an attempt to unify the main Althingi parties with a view to reaching a compromise solution on the relationship with Denmark, the farmers in the Althingi established the Farmers' Party in 1912. It was hardly a political party in the modern sense and its members were free to choose their positions on such crucial issues as the independence question. However, when the old parties re-emerged after the failure of the attempt at unification, the Home Rule Party symphathizers abandoned the Farmers' Party and reverted to their old party. The Farmers' Party none the less remained in existence as a forum for farmers sympathising with the Independence Party.

After war broke out in Europe, the Icelandic government was obliged to assume a more active role in economic management than earlier. Measures were necessary to secure an adequate supply of goods, and to counteract the unfavourable effects of rising food-prices in the towns. When the Althingi convened in 1915 there was growing urban dissatisfaction with the rising cost of living. The Reykjavik papers expounded on the difficulties in the towns and the nascent working-class movement maintained that the Althingi's lack of action clearly reflected the absence of working class MPs.

The political parties were unprepared for the crisis. The Independence Party was in a state of fragmentation after a faction had taken over in government with the support of the Home Rule Party. The rest of its MPs, including elements of the Farmers' Party close up, remained in opposition. In the autumn of 1915, the ruling parties supported a bill in the Althingi, proposed by the ad-hoc parliamentary Welfare Committee, which proposed radical measures to deal with the situation in the towns. These included a tax on some of the extra profits accruing to agriculture and fishing on account of the war. A temporary export duty would be levied on certain products in these sectors in such a way that each would contribute roughly equal shares to the total taxable income.

The farmers were outraged by the bill. They felt they were being unfairly taxed to support the town population because agriculture's share of total exports was much smaller than that of fisheries. Predictably, the farmers in parliament came out strongly against the bill and, joined by non-farmers in the opposition, they secured its rejection by the Althingi. They blocked a move to nominate a special committee to investigate the issue further and even denied the bill a second hearing. This was strongly criticised in the Reykjavik papers and subsequently a bill on war measures was accepted in a substantially modified form that was much less costly to agriculture. Disgruntlement continued to be widespread among the farmers and their confidence in the existing political groupings was badly shaken.

The Althingi debate on war measures in 1915 had major repercussions at the polls the following year. Two elections were held in 1916. One was plurality-based in either single or double member constituencies. The other was an 'at large' election using a proportional system of representation, in which party lists competed for the six seats which had previously been filled by representatives of the Danish crown. Two farmers' parties in fact contested the elections. There was the aforementioned Farmers' Party, which was seeking to establish itself as a fully fledged political party, and a party of Independent Farmers. The latter, a corollary of the events of 1915, was predicated on farm protest against the established political forces. Unlike the Farmers' Party, the Independent Farmers emanated from outside the parliamentary arena and they turned down a Farmers' Party proposal to unite, insisting that no incumbent MPs be placed on their lists in the 'at-large' election.

The elections of 1916 proved a notable victory for the farmers. In the 'at-large' election, the Independent Farmers gained 22 per cent of the votes and one Althingi seat while the Farmers' Party managed 7.5 per cent, although failing to return a member of parliament. The combined total of nearly 30 per cent of the votes received by farmers' lists mirrored their widespread dissatisfaction with the existing system. This was especially true of the result for the Independent Farmers which could be interpreted as a vote of no confidence in the old parties. The victory, however, was hardly more than a symbolic one in the sense that a political party could not be founded on the basis of a single seat in parliament. The crucial test for the parties came in the constituency elections in October 1916. Here, the Farmers' Party received 9 per cent of the votes and five seats, while the Independent Farmers won 4 per cent of votes and one seat. The appeal of the Independent Farmers in the 'at-large' election was clearly associated with their break with the established political forces at the national level. This was something which the Farmers' Party, with its record of support for the Independence Party, could not compete with. The same did not hold true at the constituency level where the individual candidates of the old parties could convince voters of their commitment to the cause of the farmers, as exemplified in the way they dealt with the crisis bill of 1915. Moreover, the Farmers' Party candidates were at an advantage compared to their Independent Farmer counterparts in that in many cases they were well-established and trusted representatives of their respective constituencies.

Between them, the two farmers' parties had succeeded in getting seven members elected out of a total Althingi of forty. When parliament met in December 1917, they were joined by an MP from the Independence Party and formed a parliamentary grouping called the Progressive Party. All were farmers and all but two had previously been associated with the Independence Party. Several designations were considered for the new party but 'Progressive Party' stuck almost by chance after a leading member had been pressed for a name. Moreover, as soon as the following year, the new party became part of a governing coalition. In the constituency election of 1919 it received 13.3 per cent of the votes and 26.5 per cent four years later.

Several factors contributed to the emergence of the Progressive Party. One, as already indicated, was the social and cultural homogeneity of the farm population. The party did not have to compete with religious or linguistic loyalties for the support of Icelandic farmers, since the nation was culturally homogenous and the Catholic Church absent. Furthermore, while the property and living standards of farmers varied to a certain extent, they constituted, in a comparative perspective, a fairly cohesive class of commodity producers. The very simplicity of agricultural production in Iceland in fact – mostly sheep and cattle – worked to the advantage of the Progressives because they did not have to accommodate the potentially divided interests of livestock- and grain farmers over the issue of tariffs, which the farmers' parties in Norway and Sweden had to deal with.

The event which triggered the formation of a farmers' party in Iceland was undoubtedly the war. A farmers' party might of course have emerged in any event – during the depression for example – but the timing of its creation can only be accounted for by the disturbing effects of the war in Europe. The existing political forces were unable to deal with the conflicting demands placed upon the government by the emergency. A prominent member of the Home Rule Party, Jon Thorlaksson, maintained that the organisational weakness of the existing parties was among the principal reasons for the turn of events.

> 'It was to be expected that differences would emerge between the town and country in relation to the new taxes levied on account of the war and high cost of living. Precisely because of these differences, and the need to reach a satisfactory compromise, the issue should have been considered within the parties before specific proposals were made, as happened later in the parliamentary session. But I am told that the Welfare Committee bill was not discussed in the Home Rule Party's parliamentary group, - although this was the party most likely to find a moderate solution – before being proposed to parliament. One of the major reasons we need parties in parliament is that group meetings should prepare issues before they appear before parliament' (Logrjetta 26. Jan. 1916).

Yet the support mustered by the farmers' parties in 1916 would clearly not have been sufficient to achieve a respectable Althingi presence under any electoral system. Without the relatively clear division between urban and rural constituencies and the overrepresentation of the latter, the farmers' parties would have had a harder task making a parliamentary breakthrough. Moreover, the continuing disintegration of the established parties was a factor working in the farmers' favour since, under plurality voting arrangements, it divided and weakened their opponents. Thus, although the Icelandic farmers' parties managed to establish themselves without proportional representation (except in the 'at-large' elections), the electoral system served to assist rather than hinder them.

The emergence of a farmers' party in Iceland reflected neither the enfranchisement, nor the electoral mobilisation of new groups of voters. A broad male suffrage, introduced in 1903, embraced more or less the entire male population of farmers who were twenty-five years of age and older. Comparisons of turnout in those rural constituencies in 1916 which the farmers' parties contested with the ones they did not, moreover, indicate that the farmers' parties did not activate new groups of voters. The farmers' parties emerged on the basis of an already highly mobilised electorate.

Simple sociological determinism in short is plainly inadequate to explain the emergence of the Progressive Party in Iceland.

## Going for the Town Votes

Although the Progressive Party was formed as a protest party of farmers, it was in some ways more flexible than its counterparts in Norway and Sweden. For one thing, of course, the name was not an obstacle to any ambition it might harbour of winning broader support. More significantly, its organisation was always much looser in nature than its Scandinavian sister parties. The Progressive Party was formed as a parliamentary party and lacked a national membership organisation until the 1930s. In the early years the parliamentary party was in a fairly fluid state, with lax discipline and a high turnover of members. In some cases, non-members regularly attended meetings of the parliamentary party group. Progressive Party candidates, moreover, generally emerged through fairly informal procedures and relied primarily on their personal networks for electioneering.

The informal nature of the party organisation permitted parliamentarians of quite different persuasions to co-exist within the party. Some were relatively conservative, while a few regarded themselves as liberal or leftist in the Scandinavian sense. Gradually, during the 1920s, the Progressives began to regard themselves as the main alternative to the Conservative Party which became the Independence Party (new) in 1929. The two parties became the main contenders for governmental office during the 1920s since the Social Democrats were too small to offer a serious challenge. In 1927, in fact, the Progressive Party brought down the Conservative government and formed a minority government with the support of the Social Democrats.

Given the lack of formal organisation in the Progressive Party there was clearly room for political entrepreneurs with broader ambitions than merely representing the farmers. Such ambitions were embodied above all in the person of Jonas Jonsson from Hriflu. An anti-establishment politician in the Scandinavian liberal tradition, he envisaged the Progressive Party from the outset as an Icelandic Venstre rather than a sectional farmers' party. He had various contacts with the labour movement and in the early years saw the latter as a natural ally of the farmers in the Progressive Party in their battle with the Conservatives. Although not originally a parliamentarian himself, he gradually built an elite network for the party based on the (agricultural) co-operative movement, the privately-owned party newspaper as well as the leadership of the parliamentary party. This network was the 'Tímaklíkan' (Timinn-clique), so called after the name of the party paper.

Only once during the 1920s did a Progressive Party candidate run in an urban constituency. That was in 1923, when a long-serving MP for the co-operative town of Akureyri put up as a Progressive, but lost his seat. It was a more or less private decision and there does not appear to have been any discussion of it whatsoever in the party. A more concerted effort was made in the local elections of 1930 when the Progressive Party presented a list in Reykjavik. The list was marketed as a centre party list, directed in particular against the large financial interests and speculators that were supposed to have control of the affairs of the capital city. The results were highly encouraging since the list won 12 per cent of the vote. The Progressive Party won a similar share of the vote in the constituency election the following year.

In fact, it was not the parliamentary party (the only institution which formally existed in the party at the time) that decided to enter the race for the Reykjavik vote. The radicals in the party seem simply to have jumped at the opportunity provided by the governing position of the party without feeling the need to go through formal procedures. Indeed, the radicals began their efforts in Reykjavik without assuring themselves that the parliamentary party would continue to follow a parliamentary strategy compatible with the most significant emphasis of the Reykjavik section, namely opposition to the Independence Party.

There was no little scepticism in the Progressives' parliamentary group about the radicals' endeavours to win the town vote. So long as they were not felt to undermine the party's basic commitment to the farm electorate, however, the cohesion of the party did not appear threatened.

The radicals were weakly represented in the parliamentary party and while the latter remained the only formal institution in the party they were at a disadvantage. In 1931 the first conference of the party introduced party statutes and a membership organisation. The parliamentary party elected the central committee while the party conference chose an executive committee to work with the central committee and with the responsibility of calling the party conference.

Jonson's desire to gain control of the parliamentary party led to serious internal unrest in 1932-1933 which in turn spawned a split and the formation of a breakaway Farmers' Party. An attempt by the Independence Party and the Social Democrats in 1931 to amend the electoral system in a direction less favourable to the Progressive Party was forestalled by Progressive Party prime minister, Tryggvi Thorhallsson, who called an election before this unholy alliance could have its way. It turned out to be one of the hardest fought in Icelandic history and resulted in a major victory for the Progressive Party, which received 35.9 per cent of votes and half the seats contested. Unfortunately for the Progressive Party the victory was not sufficient to gain a majority in the upper house of the Althingi (where the "at-large" members sat) and this resulted in a parliamentary impasse. Jonsson and the radicals favoured a strategy of continued confrontation with the conservatives in the Independence Party but a majority of the parliamentary party saw compromise as the only way to safeguard some of the electoral privileges of the rural areas. A coalition government of the two parties was formed in 1932 and this reached an agreement on electoral reform which to a considerable extent safeguarded the electoral privileges of the rural areas.

In 1932-1933, division within the Progressive Party over the appropriate parliamentary and electoral strategy was mirrored in conflict between the central committee and the executive committee. The radicals opposed the coalition with the Independence Party. In December 1932 the executive committee called a party conference, the main purpose of which was to pass a new party statute transferring powers to elect the central committee to the party conference. It would also vest a joint meeting of the central committee (25 members) and the parliamentary party (16 members after the election of 1933) with the authority to bring a greater measure of discipline into the parliamentary party. In November 1933 the revised party statute was used to expel two of the party's MPs who had scuppered the formation of a Progressive Party-SDP coalition by refusing to support it.

The result was a split in the party. Indeed, the main leaders of the parliamentary party, including Thorhallsson, along with the two expelled members and one other MP, left the party. Thorhallsson described the turn of events as follows.

> 'In the last two or three years, the Reykjavik wing of the Progressive Party has been considerably strengthened... In tandem with this, the Reykjavik section has become more influential within the party... As regards its policies, they are described as more "urban-radical". What happened was that through the appointment of a central committee comprising almost exclusively Reykjavik members, and by transferring power from the parliamentary party to the central committee, this Reykjavik section of the Progressive Party has become stronger than the farmers' section' (Framsokn, 15. Dec. 1933).

Hence, the decision to leave the party was considered justified. The Farmers' Party, formed by Thorhallsson and his supporters, had some initial success, gaining 6.4 per cent of the vote in 1934. It survived in the election of 1937, but by 1942 had disappeared completely. Paradoxically, the Progressive Party split had the effect of concentrating more of the party's attention on its agrarian support than before and electoral support outside its agricultural heartland declined substantially.

As the Progressive Party recuperated from the effects of the split during the 1940s, it began seeking urban support again. This was not, any more than the first time, preceded by an elaborate decision-making process in the party organisation. Although a membership organisation had been established in the early 1930s, during the struggle for control of the party, it never became its permanent centre of power. Effective power remained with the parliamentary party even after the split. The membership organisation operated in quite an informal manner, often as a clientelistic network, and characteristics of mass membership organisations such as membership fees or exact membership files were widely disregarded. The ideological platform of the party was fairly vague and neither the leadership nor rank-and-file parliamentarians were really constrained in the formulation of policy by the membership organisation. Despite the outward appearance of a democratic mass party, the Progressive Party retained strong features of the cadre organisation it originally was.

The party's second attempt to penetrate the urban electorate was nothing like as dramatic as the one in the early 1930s. This was primarily because it grew out of the endeavours of the parliamentarians themselves to accommodate the growing urbanisation of their constituencies. Given the single and double member constituency system in operation (except in Reykjavik where PR had been introduced) the Progressive Party's candidates in most constituencies faced an increasing challenge from the growth of towns and villages within previously rural constituencies Without a measure of support from the town population, Progressive candidates would increasingly face an uphill battle for a growing number of seats. The parliamentarians responded by extending their clientelistic networks to the seaside villages where, in some cases, they were supported by the co-operative movement, a major employer in the provincial towns. This development was reflected in the party platform, initially in an emphasis on the common interests of producers, and later in the stress on regional development policies as perhaps the single most important theme in the work of the party. The orientation towards regional development in the post-war period was a unifying factor in the party in as much as it cemented a happy marriage between old and new concerns - agriculture and support for the regional economy.

During the late 1930s, Jonsson became increasingly conservative and began to favour collaboration with the Independence Party rather than the Social Democrats. The latter, he believed, were less reliable after the Communist Party entered parliament in 1937. His old disciples in the party leadership, however, wished to retain the option of working with the left-wing parties and eventually engineered his removal from the party leadership in 1944. The radical traditions of the party thus lived on to some extent, despite Jonsson's *volte face* and subsequent demise. The post-war period in fact witnessed renewed attempts to establish the Progressive Party as a fairly radical urban alternative, advocating moderate left-wing and nationalist policies. Interestingly, the party's first Reykjavik MP was elected in 1949 primarily with the support of the so-called 'national preservationists', a group which opposed Icelandic membership of NATO. The party leader, Hermann Jonasson, was generally highly sceptical of any co-operation with the Independence Party – although this did not deter the party from forming coaltions with it – and was willing to consider ways of establishing close cooperation with the Social Democrats as a means of strengthening the middle ground in Icelandic politics. Indeed, in 1956, the Progressive Party and the Social Democrats entered an electoral alliance with the aim of winning a parliamentary majority and, thereafter, possibly merging the two parties. While the attempt failed, nearly two decades elapsed before the Progressives entered another coalition with the Independence Party.

Between 1956 and 1974 many Progressives regarded themselves as leftists. During this period the party did not form coalitions with the Independence Party and adopted a radical nationalist stance on issues such as the US military base in Iceland, the extension of the fisheries limits and trade cooperation in Europe. These policies were highly successful in attracting electoral support and, during the 1960s, the party became the second largest in the towns, surpassing both the radical leftist People's Alliance and the Social Democrats. At this time, moreover, a left-wing faction gained control of the Progressives' Youth Organisation and, beginning in 1969, sought to involve the mother party in negotiations on the unification of the left in Iceland. This gradually precipitated a rift between the leadership and the radicals. The natural location of the party, according to its leadership, was at the political centre where it could promote its core interests by working with either the left or the right. In 1974 the radicals in the Youth Organisation broke with the mother party and many of them joined the short-lived Union of Liberals and Leftists. Some even ended up in the People's Alliance and they included Olafur Ragnar Grimsson, who later became chairman of the People's Alliance and later President of the Republic of Iceland.

Since the split in 1974, the Progressive Party's radical credentials have appeared much weaker than before. The party is clearly conscious of the need to gain a stronger toehold in the towns, especially in the Reykjavik area where 60 per cent of the population now live. But it has not developed a coherent strategy to achieve this. The closest it has come is probably in relation to environmental issues, which have had some appeal, especially among the Reykjavik Progressives. But the party has been fairly moderate in this respect ('light green') and, in any event, some environmental concerns clearly do not sit easily with its more traditional clientele, which is neither 'post-modern' nor 'post-industrial'. Particularly under the leadership of Steingrimur Hermannsson (1978-1994), the party echoed its old nationalist and left wing policies, albeit not to the extent of posing as a left-wing party or excluding co-operation with the Independence Party. There have even been attempts to sell the party as a liberal party and, in the 1980s, it joined the Liberal International. But the Progressives' urban support is probably best explained in terms of its pragmatic centrist position and moderate line on the choice between state and market. With a somewhat weaker profile than before in the towns, however, the party has not recovered the kind of electoral strength it enjoyed there in the 1960s and early 1970s.

Furthermore, the Progressive Party's attempts to win urban support have proceeded in an ad hoc manner. There has been no prior decision on the principle of seeking to become a catchall party, primarily because the party organisation has not worked that way. Given the latter's rather informal and loose nature, attempts to gain support in the towns could be made without going through formal decision-making procedures. This explains why the party could begin much earlier than the farmers' parties of Finland, Norway and Sweden to make an urban appeal. Importantly, however, there was a significant difference between the two major strands in the modernisation strategy of the party. The first, the emphasis on rural development, fitted in well with the dominant interests in the party organisation, namely those of its parliamentarians. It was obviously in their electoral interests to broaden the appeal of the party to the seaside villages and towns. This extension of the party base was easily reconciled with a continued advocacy of agrarian interests, since farming was considered an integral element in the regional economy.

The second, radical strand in the party's modernisation strategy, on the other hand, constituted a potentially disruptive element. This was because it introduced policy considerations which might well conflict with the interests of farmers and the regions, especially with regard to coalition formation. Hence, the radicals sometimes had an uneasy relationship with the parliamentary majority on the question of government formation. In a sense, the radicals were always an 'alien element' in the Progressive Party which could co-exist with the rurally-dominated parliamentary party only because the party organisation was so flexible. But the potential for conflict was always there and played a major role in the two splits in the party in the 1930s and again in the 1970s. Had the party been more tightly organised and possessed a clearer policy platform, it might have been more prudent in its flirtation with radicalism.

An indication of the distinctive approach of the Progressive Party can be gained by comparing its election manifestos with those of the Norwegian and Swedish farmers' parties. Content analysis of these documents exists from 1910 to the 1980s.[4] The following features of the Progressive Party manifestos distinguish its approach from its Scandinavian counterparts. The Progressive Party manifestos were issued in an irregular manner. Not every election was fought on a manifesto; the documents themselves were very different in style and presentation; and there were no fixed rules regarding which element in the party apparatus issued the manifesto. This was essentially the result of the flexible nature of the Progressive Party organisation compared to the other parties. Individual policy issues were covered in an inconsistent manner in the Progressives' manifestos. Which issue areas were covered varied from one election to the next. An issue area might feature prominently in one election and then receive no mention at all in several subsequent elections. Even agriculture disappeared completely from the manifestos during the 1960s, although it returned in the 1970s. The manifestos have been non-programmatic in the sense that they usually do not try and give a systematic overview of the policy stances of the Progressive Party. Not only did issues frequently disappear altogether in the Progressives' manifestos, but the amount of space devoted to them varied significantly from one election to the next.

In contrast to the Norwegian and Swedish parties, there have been very few systematic trends in the issue coverage of the Progressive Party over time. The amount of space devoted to issues fluctuates wildly and in most cases without discernible long-term trends. A partial exception to this has been the area of foreign- and security policy which received greater attention in the second half of the century than earlier. But even that follows an erratic pattern. The Progressive Party is not as concerned with presenting its policy positions in its manifestos as the other parties. A large proportion of the manifestos in fact have not been concerned with the future at all, but with the past and the quality of the Progressive Party leadership, whether in or out of government. This is often the main point of the manifesto.

The weakness of its organisation gave the party a good deal of room for manoeuvre in its electoral strategies and often made it adept at choosing the most beneficial course. This came at a price, however, since an effective electoral strategy was not always easy to reconcile with the party's line on government formation. This could lead to strains on party unity and lost credibility in the eyes of sections of the party's voters.

**Seeking Office**

According to Anthony Down's (1957) economic theory of democracy, all parties are inherently office seekers. They exist solely for the purpose of obtaining the prestige, power and income which access to government provides for their members. Policy goals do not really enter into it, except as means of winning votes and office. Empirical research indicates that things are usually rather more complicated (Browne 1973). Strøm (1986) points out that the frequent recourse to minority government in Scandinavia constitutes a powerful challenge to the office seeking assumptions of coalition theory. He maintains that such features of Scandinavian politics as strong, future-oriented parties, decentralised and non-hierarchical legislatures and competitive elections can account for the propensity of the Scandinavian systems to produce minority governments.

The Icelandic case adds an interesting perspective on these comparisons. Since 1944, minority government has not, on the whole, been tolerated in Icelandic politics.[5] The reason lies not in the legislature, which is no less decentralised than its Scandinavian counterparts (Arter 1984), nor in the electorate, which is no less volatile than elsewhere in Scandinavia. (Hardarson 1995). The major difference is to be found in the manner in which the party organisations are run. The Scandinavian parties are/were mass membership organisations, rewarding their members with loyalty to a future-oriented programme. In contrast, the Icelandic ones have been driven more by clientelistic networks and the rewards of party membership tend to be as much material as programmatic.

Patronage on a small scale has always been a feature of Icelandic party politics. However, with the formation of party organisations around 1930, mass clientelism became a striking feature of the Icelandic parties. The Progressive Party, and Jonas Jonsson in particular, played an important role in this. Indeed, in his essay 'When Dreams Come True', in which he set out the fundamentals of his political strategy, Jonsson claimed credit for developments.

> 'I introduced two new methods into the modus operandi of politics. The first was to counter the advances of opponents by forming alliances – whenever possible – which would secure victory. The second was to win support by distributing positions of power and prestige to the faithful while taking none for myself. Much of the success enjoyed by the Progressive Party for a quarter of a century was due to this technique' (Jonsson 1952 p. XLIX).

The two were mutually reinforcing. Alliances were designed to secure access to power and access to power was central in managing the party networks. From the late 1920s the Progressive Party built a powerful clientelistic network, based on pork-barreling, jobs, loans, grants and licenses. This met with some initial resistance and at one point an attempt was made by a Reykjavik doctor to have Jonsson, against his will, committed to a mental hospital! During the 1930s and 1940s, however, clientelism also took hold in all the other parties, except perhaps the radical left, making the party organisations a major channel of access to a wide variety of clientelistic goods. Grimsson's (1978) description of the manner in which the Icelandic party organisations operated might well apply, he states, to over three-quarters of the Progressive Party's branches in 1976-1978.

> 'The party branches which have less than one-hundred members, especially those with only a few dozen members, generally do not maintain a regular formal existence. The necessary activities, such as appointing representatives to the constituency association, party confererence and other central organs, are quite often undertaken in an informal manner by the main local leaders getting together (sometimes in each other's homes) and deciding to appoint representatives from their own group for that particular occasion. Regular subscriptions or correct membership listings are generally not maintained and quite often a whole year or more passes between formal meetings of the branch. The same governing committee can be in existence without formal re-election for a number of years. The MPs for the respective constituencies generally instigate the activities which are

undertaken in the name of the local branches by contacting the local leaders or meeting them in informal gatherings. Thus, in fact, the organisational reality of the small local branches is simply a network of personal relationships which bears the party name with respect to particular activities but does not lead to an independent, formalised existence' (Grimsson 1978, p. 16).

Access to national government, of course, is an important pre-requisite for the running of clientelistic organisations. This is all the more so in Iceland where local government is relatively weak. The Progressive Party was ideally positioned to play the coalition game, as it was strategically placed between the large Independence Party and the much smaller Social Democrats and People's Alliance. Although the Progressives at times spoke as though the Independence Party was the main enemy, they were never, when it came to the crunch, willing to sacrifice the tactical advantage of a centre position on the altar of radicalism. The size of the Progressive Party, usually magnified by the election system, facilitated a pivotal position in the coalition game. Put another way, the Independence Party was highly dependent on the Progressive Party for access to government.

As Table 5.1 indicates, potential coalitions of the Independence Party and Social Democrats have usually lacked either the necessary majority or possessed only a very weak one. None the less, in half the instances when these parties have boasted the necessary majority – even a very weak one - they have formed a ruling coalition (1959, 1963, 1967 and 1991). Bi-partisan coalitions involving the Independence Party and the People's Alliance would have been slightly stronger numerically, but were virtually inconceivable in so far as they represented the polar opposites in Icelandic politics. A three-way coalition of the Independence Party and both left-wing parties was formed in 1944 and lasted until 1947. But differences between the Independence Party and the socialists, especially over foreign policy, have prevented more attempts of this nature. Hence tripartite coalitions, except those including the Progressive Party, have not increased the Independence Party's access to power. Indeed, no majority coalitions, except those mentioned above, have been formed in Iceland since 1926 without the participation of the Progressive Party.

The Progressive Party's policy profile in the post-war period has been characterised above all by support for the regions. It has advocated far-reaching state intervention to support the regional economy and generally adopted a pragmatic attitude towards the market economy. With regard to public finances, the party programme has been generally rather conservative, but the impact of the Progressive's participation in cabinet has depended a good deal on its coalition partners. When in power with the Independence Party, the Progressive Party has tended to pursue a tight fiscal policy, while in left-wing coalitions it has pursued a more expansionist line.[6] This has been part of the party's dilemma in the last few decades, in that it is sometimes considered to be something of an opportunist, with a 'yes yes, no no' approach on many issues.

**Table 5.1 Possibilities for Forming Two-Way Coalitions without the Progressive Party in 1946-1999 and Seats in Excess of Effective Majority**

| Year | Effective Majority | SDP-Indep party seats in excess of effective majority | People's Alliance-Indep Party seats in excess of effective majority |
|---|---|---|---|
| 1946 | 28 seats | 1 | 2 |
| 1949 | 28 seats | (insufficient) | 0 |
| 1953 | 28 seats | (insufficient) | 0 |
| 1956 | 28 seats | (insufficient) | (insufficient) |
| 1959 | 32 seats | 1 | 2 |
| 1963 | 32 seats | 0 | 1 |
| 1967 | 32 seats | 0 | 1 |
| 1971 | 32 seats | (insufficient) | 1 |
| 1974 | 32 seats | (insufficient) | 4 |
| 1978 | 32 seats | 2 | 2 |
| 1979 | 32 seats | (insufficient) | 0 |
| 1983 | 32 seats | (insufficient) | 1 |
| 1987 | 32 seats | (insufficient) | (insufficient) |
| 1991 | 32 seats | 4 | 3 |
| 1995 | 32 seats | 0 | 2 |
| 1999 | 32 seats | 9* | (insufficient)** |

*Here the Alliance has replaced the Social Democratic Party.
**The entry refers to the Left-Greens rather than the People's Alliance, which was extinct by this time.

Foreign policy has not been as central a concern of the Progressive Party as regional development, although at times it has featured prominently. During its most radical phase, from the mid-1950s until the 1970s, the Progressive Party opposed the US military base in Iceland and took part in two governments that initially planned to send the Americans home. Moreover, the party was less compromising than some of the other parties on the issue of Icelandic fishery limits during the so-called Cod-Wars. Icelandic nationalism was then a strong characteristic of the party.

The Progressive Party strongly opposed moves during the 1960s to involve Iceland in the European integration process and abstained when the issue of European Free Trade Association (EFTA) membership came before the Althingi in 1969. Moreover, although it later accepted EFTA membership, the party was highly sceptical of moves to bring about closer Icelandic co-operation with the European Union (then the European Community) during the late 1980s and early 1990s. Opposition to EU membership was, in fact, one of its main planks at the 1991 election. During the 1990s, however, its EU opposition seemed to moderate somewhat under the leadership of Halldor Asgrimsson. Although Asgrimsson is not an advocate of membership he has seemed to be considering ways of putting the issue on the agenda. While all manner of rational calculation may be attributed to this change of heart by the party, the most likely explanation is simply that Asgrimsson, who has been foreign minister since 1995, is simply keeping an open mind about Europe. So far the party organisation has not objected, but many Progressive Party voters remain sceptical towards European integration.

All things considered, the Progressive Party has been extremely successful in gaining access to cabinet office. In this, it has been indebted in part to its parliamentary strength, in part to its centrist location on the political spectrum and in part to its pragmatic party programme. The party has been sufficiently flexible to work in government with all the other parties and has been careful not to delimit its options in the coalition game. It retains a fairly distinctive profile with regard to agriculture and regional development but, in view of the way the electoral system has militated towards the overrepresentation of such interests in the other parties, this has not proved a major obstacle to coalition formation.

## The Progressive Party at the Polls

The continued electoral strength of the Progressive Party has been remarkable when set against the backdrop of a steadily declining rural and regional population. At the time it was founded, over 40 per cent of Icelanders were engaged in agriculture (excluding fisheries) and 60 per cent lived in rural areas. By 1990 only 5 per cent were engaged in agriculture and less than 10 per cent lived in rural areas. Yet the Progressive Party still managed to poll 18.4 per cent of the votes at the 1999 general election. This is no small achievement for an old farmers' party in a society where three out of five voters reside in the urban centre of Reykjavik and its surroundings.

Table 5.2  Icelandic Progressive Party Share of Votes and Seats, 1916-1999

| Year | Share of votes | Share of seats | Year | Share of votes | Share of seats |
|---|---|---|---|---|---|
| 1916 | 12.9 | 17.6 | 1956 | 15.6** | 32.7 |
| 1919 | 13.3 | 17.6 | 1959a | 27.2 | 36.5 |
| 1923 | 26.5 | 36.1 | 1959b | 25.7 | 28.3 |
| 1927 | 29.8 | 47.2 | 1963 | 28.2 | 31.7 |
| 1931 | 35.9 | 50.0 | 1967 | 28.1 | 30.0 |
| 1933 | 23.9 | 33.3 | 1971 | 25.3 | 28.3 |
| 1934 | 21.9 | 30.6 | 1974 | 24.9 | 28.3 |
| 1937 | 24.9 | 38.8 | 1978 | 16.9 | 20.0 |
| 1942a | 27.6 | 40.8 | 1979 | 24.9 | 28.3 |
| 1942b | 26.6 | 28.8 | 1983 | 19.0 | 23.3 |
| 1946 | 23.1 | 25.0 | 1987 | 18.9 | 20.6 |
| 1949 | 24.5 | 32.7 | 1991 | 18.9 | 20.6 |
| 1953 | 21.9 | 30.8 | 1995 | 23.3 | 23.8 |
|  |  |  | 1999 | 18.4 | 19.0 |

*'At large' elections not counted in share of votes or seats
**Support for Progressive Party underestimated on account of an electoral alliance with the Social Democrats which meant that the Progressives did not have candidates in a large number of constituencies.

Electoral research based on interview surveys did not begin in Iceland until 1983. An indication of the electoral basis of the Progressive Party between 1916 and 1959, however, can be gained by using ecological analysis (see Table 5.2). Ecological analysis was not possible after the latter date since the election system shifted to one of proportional representation in eight multimember consitutencies (data are not available below the constituency level). The analysis for 1916-1959 is based on ecological regression techniques using the agrarian share of the population on the one hand and the Progressive Party share of the vote on the other.[7] The analysis shows that among the agrarian population, the Progressive Party's share of the vote rose steadily from 1916, reaching around 80 per cent in the early 1930s. During the split it fell to around 50 per cent but recovered thereafter to approximate its former strength by the 1950s. While this is possibly an overestimation of the party's strength among farmers it suggests that the Progressives were indeed very strong among their core group and that the split in the 1930s affected their farm support substantially.

The same analysis demonstrates that the Progressives' support among the non-agrarian population was virtually nil to begin with, grew slightly during the 1920s and reached a peak of around 10 per cent in 1931. After the split, it fell below 5 per cent, but recovered in the 1940s and 1950s to around 10 per cent. In the last election covered, however, the first of two elections in 1959, the party managed to win around 25 per cent of the non-agrarian population.[8] Local elections in the towns during the 1960s and 1970s permit an insight into the non-agrarian support for the Progressives during that period. In the local elections of 1966 and 1970 the party obtained over 17 per cent in Reykjavik, close to 32 per cent in the largest provincial town of Akureyri, where the co-operatives were particularly strong, and an average of over 20 per cent in other towns. During the 1970s this support declined considerably and in 1982 the Progressive Party obtained 9.5 per cent in Reykjavik, 25 per cent in Akureyri and 20 per cent in the other towns.

Overall electoral support for the Progressive Party has declined since the 1960s. The first sign of things to come was the election of 1978, which followed a four-year coalition with the Independence Party, when the Progressives' support fell to 16.9 per cent. In the 1980s and 1990s the party really only had one good election. That was in 1995, after its only spell in opposition during that period, when it obtained 23.3 per cent of votes. Otherwise, its share of the vote has been between 18.4 and 19.0 per cent. Opinion polls in the late 1990s, moreover, put party support as low as 13-14 per cent on several occasions. Thus, while still effective at electioneering, the Progressive Party can no longer count on large numbers of loyal supporters to secure its pivotal position in Icelandic politics.

As Table 5.3 demonstrates, the Progressive Party's electoral profile reflects its origins as a farmers' party and its subsequent development as the party of the regions. It can usually count on 50-60 per cent of the farm vote but, apart from this, its occupational identity is not very clearly defined. There is a tendency for the party to fare slightly better among the manual occupations than the non-manual, although this is not a strong pattern. Some of the occupational characteristics of party voters simply reflect the Progressives' stronger position in the provincial regions, where the economy is based on non-specialised jobs to a much greater extent than in the Reykjavik area. The rather amorphous occupational profile of the party outside agriculture may be used to characterise the Progressives as a catchall party, although they are no different from the other Icelandic parties in this respect. Class voting has long been weak in Iceland and Hardarson reports an Alford index of 0 for the election of 1995 (Hardarson 1996).

Table 5.3 The Progressive Party's Vote by Socio-Eonomic Group, 1983-1999 (% of total group vote)

|  | 1983 | 1987 | 1991 | 1995 | 1999 |
| --- | --- | --- | --- | --- | --- |
| Farmers | 58 | 49 | 50 | 61 | 54 |
| Seamen | 21 | 21 | 16 | 26 | 25 |
| Unskilled manuals | 13 | 16 | 26 | 30 | 22 |
| Skilled manuals | 16 | 18 | 16 | 25 | 19 |
| Lower non-manuals | 15 | 15 | 14 | 30 | 19 |
| Professionals | 8 | 10 | 10 | 19 | 11 |
| Managers & employers | 9 | 11 | 13 | 24 | 16 |
| **All Respondents** | **17** | **18** | **18** | **27** | **20** |

*Source*: Data courtesy of Olafur Th. Hardarson and the Icelandic Election Study. Data based on a national random sample with response rate in all cases 70 per cent or more.

Despite its pre-occupation with regional development, the Progressive Party maintains a strong presence in the urban South-West, as shown in Table 5.4. The party's share of the urban vote in the South-West (the Reykjavik and Reykjanes constituencies) has varied considerably over time. It was 12.5 per cent in 1959 and, despite some fluctuations, it was back to a similar level forty years later. In the interim, the share of the Progressives' vote deriving from the South-West rose from just over a quarter to almost half its total vote. This reflects two things. First, the Reykjavik area continues to grow at the expense of the regions. The share of the electorate living in the South-West grew from 55 per cent to 68 per cent between 1959 and 1999. Second, the Progressive Party has been losing support to a certain extent in the regions. The continuing urbanisation of the regions may have something to do with this. There seems little reason to suspect that support for the party in the South-West or the regions cannot grow in tandem. In the main, gains and losses follow a similar pattern among the two groups of voters. The only instance in Table 5.4 to suggest otherwise, the election of 1987, can be explained by the fact that party leader, Hermannsson, relocated from his old constituency in the Western fjords to Reykjanes in that year. He made substantial gains for the party, which lost out elsewhere.

Table 5.4  Urban and Regional Components in the Progressive Party's Vote, 1959-1999 (%)

| Year | Progressive Party share of South-West vote | Progressive Party share of regional vote | Regional vote as per cent of total party vote |
|---|---|---|---|
| 1959 | 12.5 | 40.6 | 73.2 |
| 1963 | 17.3 | 42.1 | 65.7 |
| 1967 | 18.6 | 41.3 | 61.7 |
| 1971 | 16.6 | 37.7 | 61.1 |
| 1974 | 17.0 | 36.7 | 58.8 |
| 1978 | 9.1 | 28.9 | 67.4 |
| 1979 | 15.6 | 38.9 | 62.1 |
| 1983 | 10.3 | 31.6 | 64.1 |
| 1987 | 13.4 | 28.0 | 55.8 |
| 1991 | 11.6 | 32.0 | 60.9 |
| 1995 | 17.3 | 34.6 | 66.7 |
| 1999 | 12.6 | 29.9 | 53.9 |

Source: Based on data from Statistical Bureau of Iceland.

The fact that the electoral fortunes of the Progressive Party appear to proceed in the same direction in both the regions and the South-West does not necessarily mean that promoting issues to extend its support in the regions has been unproblematical. Indeed, the central question for the Progressive Party is whether there exists an optimal strategy, of the kind

Keman envisages for pivotal parties, 'leading to relatively high pay-offs in terms of votes, offices and policy-making'.[9] The Progressives' dilemma is that a strong emphasis on office seeking to satisfy its established clientele can prove counter-productive in so far as it delimits the scope of its electoral appeal.

Table 5.5  Support for the Progressive Party according to the Composition of the Government in the Foregoing Electoral Term, 1953-1995 (% of valid votes)

|  | After Progressive Party - Indep. Party Governments | After Left-Wing Governments (incl. Progressive Party) | After Progressive Party in Opposition |
|---|---|---|---|
|  | 1953: 21.9 | 1959: 27.2 | 1963: 28.2 |
|  | 1978: 16.9 | 1974: 24.9 | 1967: 18.1 |
|  | 1987: 18.9 | 1979: 24.9 | 1971: 25.3 |
|  | 1999: 18.4 | 1983: 19.0 | 1995: 23.3 |
|  |  | 1991: 18.9 |  |
| Average share of votes | 19.0 | 23.4 | 26.2 |
| No of instances | 4 | 4 | 6 |

Note: 1956 and second election in 1959 excluded.

Thus, co-operation with the Independence Party, which has been vital for maintaining a centrist position in Icelandic politics, may have been an effective strategy for gaining office, but it has had an electoral price. The Progressive Party tends to have its worst elections after such coalitions. Even co-operation with the left, which tends to deliver the Progressives much better election results, is not as effective a strategy from an electoral viewpoint as remaining in opposition. A balance might be struck between office seeking and vote winning by opting to participate in left-wing governments. But this would mean sacrificing its centrist position and in reality spending significantly more time in opposition. The party has never been willing to do this, even if there have sometimes been internal advocates of such a strategy. In any event, left-wing governments have been less beneficial to the Progressives during the 1980s and 1990s than earlier and there are indications that the increasingly important urban Progressives may be slightly more satisfied with right-wing governments than provincial ones.

**Table 5.6   Mean Issue Positions in 1999 by Respondents' Party (1=strongly agree, through 5= strongly disagree)**

|  | Left Greens | Alliance | Regional Progressives | Southwest Progressives | Independence Party |
|---|---|---|---|---|---|
| **State vs Market** | | | | | |
| State banks should be privatised | 3.54 | 3.31 | 3.34 | 2.78 | 2.5 |
| Reduce State intervention in the economy | 3.13 | 2.89 | 2.98 | 2.61 | 2.21 |
| **Foreign Policy** | | | | | |
| Support US military base in Iceland | 3.47 | 2.85 | 2.41 | 2.33 | 2.10 |
| Apply for EU membership | 3.56 | 2.62 | 3.24 | 2.71 | 2.82 |
| Support NATO membership | 3.16 | 2.48 | 2.36 | 1.98 | 1.85 |
| **Equality** | | | | | |
| State should equalise incomes | 1.95 | 1.92 | 2.08 | 2.25 | 2.67 |
| Introduce progressive income tax | 1.98 | 1.90 | 2.18 | 2.13 | 2.82 |
| Lower taxes even if it means less services | 4.05 | 4.12 | 3.92 | 3.81 | 3.63 |
| **Environment** | | | | | |
| Prioritise environment over economic growth | 2.09 | 2.35 | 2.87 | 2.74 | 2.87 |
| Prioritise power-intensive heavy industry | 3.98 | 3.48 | 3.00 | 3.06 | 2.97 |
| **Regions vs Southwest** | | | | | |
| Votes everywhere should have equal weight | 2.59 | 2.09 | 2.64 | 2.14 | 2.13 |
| Liberalise agricultural imports | 3.76 | 3.17 | 3.91 | 3.24 | 2.96 |
| Stop growth of Reykjavik area to improve conditions in regions | 2.15 | 2.52 | 2.05 | 2.60 | 2.87 |
| Change system of fisheries management | 1.60 | 1.38 | 1.99 | 1.59 | 2.03 |

Data courtesy of Olafur Th. Hardarson and the Icelandic election study.

By 1999 almost half the Progressive Party's votes came from the urbanised South-West. These urban voters have become crucial to the survival of the party as a major force in Icelandic politics. Since they plainly comprise neither farmers nor inhabitants of the provinces, it is pertinent to inquire what kind of policies they have favoured when compared with other Progressive Party voters (see Table 5.6). It should be noted that before the election of 1999, the parties on the left, that is the Social Democrats, Women's Alliance and People's Alliance joined forces in the Alliance, although part of the People's Alliance broke away and formed the Left Greens.

In relation to two of the issue areas considered, equality and environmentalism, there is not a great deal of difference between the urban and regional Progressives. On the question of equality, Progressives appear to take a middle-of-the-road position between the left-wing parties and the Independence Party. Interestingly, Progressive Party voters appear to be among the least environmentally concerned, suggesting that the efforts to project the party as environmentally friendly have largely failed. The emergence of the Left-Greens, trawling the same electoral waters, may have drawn voters away from the Progressives. But even when compared to the Alliance, the Progressives appear decidedly less environmentalist.

On three of the issue areas considered, there are some interesting differences between the urban Progressives of the South-West and the regional followers in other constituencies. Urban Progressives are much more likely to favour the market over the state and are much less nationalistic than those in the provinces. Moreover, with regard to foreign policy, the urban voters are near to the Alliance and Independence Party, whereas provincial voters more closely resemble the position of the Left Greens. Even more interestingly, there appear to be significant differences between urban and provincial Progressives on issues relating to the interests of the regions, on the one hand, and South-West, on the other. Thus, while provincial Progressives are generally the strongest advocates of regional interests, their urban counterparts are much less well disposed towards the regions. Among the five groups of voters shown in Table 5.6, in fact, the urban Progressives are second only to the Independence Party in their lack of support for regional concerns, although of course voters for the other parties are not broken down by residence.

In respect of foreign policy, the state-market dimension and regional development, there is potential for division within the Progressive Party. On average, the urban Progressives are further to the right than the provincial ones. When asked to position themselves on a scale running from 0 (furthest to the left) to 10 (furthest to right), the mean self-placement of provincial Progressives was 5.03 compared with 5.62 for those in Reykjavik and Reykjanes.[10] Although each group of Progressives is closer to the other than to voters of any other party, their divergence is still a factor of potential political significance. This is especially the case when it is kept in mind that there exist considerable differences on other political dimensions, apart from the left-right one, such as foreign policy and regional development. From a strategic viewpoint, the increasing weight of the urban Progressives may make the return of radical nationalist policies increasingly unlikely, while the party may develop a greater taste for the market economy (albeit counter-balanced by a moderate welfare state), globalism and right wing governments. But it also seems quite possible that the party will simply lose its pivotal position on account of electoral decline.

**Conclusion**

The Progressive Party was formed during the first world war as a consequence of the inability of the established parties to deal with the emergency food crisis and the conflict it generated between town and country. In part, the established parties were weak structures, ill prepared to deal with rapid change. But the exigencies of war threw up new kinds of challenges which were difficult to reconcile with the previously established lines of conflict in Icelandic politics. In contrast to nascent farmers' parties elsewhere, the Progressive Party was not indebted to a lowering of the threshold for representation to secure its parliamentary breakthrough. The electoral system was conducive to the emergence of a farmers' party and the fragmentation of the established parties facilitated the Progressives' task, despite the plurality system in operation.

    Apart from political factors, the social structural conditions in Iceland were also relatively favourable to the development of a farmers' party. The agrarian sector still numbered 40 per cent of the population at the time of the party's formation and its interests were unusually homogenous. There were no ethnic, linguistic or religious cleavages and the Catholic Church was virtually non-existent. The agrarian population comprised mainly independent farmers and their families who worked holdings based on cattle and sheep. Issues such as land reform and/or grain tariffs created no divisions among the Icelandic farmers.

    In order to understand why the Progressive Party began to seek urban support before its Scandinavian sister parties, it is necessary to consider the nature of the party organisation. The Progressive Party was originally a loose-knit alliance of parliamentarians with little means of enforcing decisive policies or party discipline. This allowed a group of radicals to attach themselves to the party and declare their loyalty to the cause of the farmers. In 1925 Jonsson characterised the situation as follows.

> 'The task of the Progressive Party is to galvanise the farmers of this country behind the protection and promotion of the interests and culture of the rural areas. Working together with the farmers there are a few middle class men from the towns. These are men who believe that, in the interests of the nation's physical and spiritual health, the centre of gravity of the nation's life must always be in the sparsely populated countryside' (Timinn, 31 October, 1925).

The political ambitions of the radicals, however, turned out to be broader than merely maintaining a sectional farmers' party. With a view to fighting the conservatives in the Independence Party, they began organising Progressives in urban areas and eventually became engaged in conflict over strategy with the party's farmer-dominated parliamentary group. There ensued a power struggle which ultimately resulted in a split.

The Progressive Party's attempts to compete for the urban vote have not in general been preceded by careful deliberation or an elaborate consultation process in the party. The radical tradition has tended to create internal strife and even splits when its adherents have felt that government co-operation with the Independence Party should be ruled out. The regional development focus, on the other hand, grew more naturally from the concerns of the party's parliamentarians and has not thus far generated serious internal friction. The emphasis on regional development has been closely interwoven with the party's clientelistic practices and fits easily with an office-seeking strategy and a centre position in the coalition system.

The major tactical problem for the Progressives has been that the most effective office-seeking strategy, namely maintaining an effective centre position, has not always been very effective at the polls. Put simply, right-wing governments have tended to harm the party electorally, whereas staying in opposition seems to deliver the best electoral results. The party has reacted to this in the last quarter of the twentieth century by playing down its radical and left-wing predilections. But this has been accompanied by a smaller share of votes than before. The real challenge facing the party, if it is to maintain its position as a major player in Icelandic politics, is to build a clearer profile in the urban centres of the country without alienating its former clientele in the regions.

Despite the inevitable problems faced by a former farmers' party in an urbanised society, the Icelandic Progressive Party has been immensely successful. It is still a major contender for governmental leadership, despite the fact that its core class of agriculturalists has declined sharply in electoral significance. Its approach to party strategy can be criticised as being unsystematic and opportunistic, but it cannot be denied that it has secured an enormous amount of financial (and other) support for its clientele in agriculture and the regions. Thus, although it may leave something to be desired from the viewpoint of participatory democracy, it has none the less been a rational and efficient party with regard to vote-getting, office-seeking and policy making.[11]

## Notes

1  In the 1920s, the farmers' party of Switzerland emerged in the protestant cantons, while the only predominantly Catholic country to produce a farmers' party was Ireland, the only Catholic country as Rokkan points out without a distinctive Catholic party.
2  Consider by contrast the struggle of Canadian prairie farmers who were unable under the Canadian system to form a sectional party and looked instead for broader alliances, e.g. in the Liberal Party, the CCF and Social Credit.
3  A union with Denmark (primarily including a joint crown) was maintained until 1944, when Iceland became a republic.
4  Kristinsson 1991, ch. 10.
5  Iceland has had the following minority governments in the post war era: a minority government of the Independence Party was ousted after a few months in office in 1950; a minority government of the Social Democrats was formed in 1958 to bring about reform of the electoral system the following year (after which it left office); and a minority government of the Social Democrats in 1979-1980 covered the period from the fall of the left wing government in 1979 until a new government was formed early in 1980.
6  Kristinsson 1999, ch. 3.
7  The technique used is described in Langbein and Lichtman (1978).
8  Kristinsson 1991, ch. 11.
9  Keman 1994, p. 146.
10  The mean, by comparison, for the Left Greens was 3.15, Alliance voters 3.76 and Independence Party voters 7.38.
11  On the contrast between party democracy and rational-efficiency, see Wright 1971.

## References

Arter, D. (1984), 'The Nordic Parliaments', London: C. Hurst.
Berger, S. (1972), 'Peasants against Politics,' (Cambridge, Mass.: Harvard University Press).

Browne, E. (1973), 'Coalitions Theories: A Logical and Empirical Critique', Beverly Hills: Sage.
*Dagsbrun* (Reykjavik working-class paper).
Downs, A. (1957), 'An Economic Theory of Democracy', New York: Harper & Row.
*Framsokn* (Farmers' Party organ).
Graham, B. (1963), 'The Country Party Idea in New Zealand Politics', in Chapman & Sinclair (eds), *Studies of a Small Democracy* (Paul's Book Arcade – for the University of Auckland).
Grimsson, O. (1978), 'Network Parties', paper presented at ECPR Workshop on Mass Political Organisation, Grenoble 1978 (Mimeo: Reykjavik, 1979).
Hardarson, O. (1995), 'Parties and Voters in Iceland', Reykjavik: Social Science Research Institute.
Hardarson, O. (1996), 'Iceland', *European Journal of Political Research*, 30/3-4 (Dec. 1996).
Jonsson, J. (1952), 'Komandi ar', Reykjavik: Isafoldarprentsmidja.
Keman, H. (1994), 'The Search for the Centre: Pivot Parties in West European Party Systems', *West European Politics*, Vol. 17, No. 4, 124-148.
Kirchheimer (1966), 'The Transformation of Western European Party Systems', in Lapalombara & Weiner (eds), *Political Parties and Political Development*, Princeton: Princeton University Press.
Kristinsson, G.H. (1991), 'Farmers' Parties. A Study in Electoral Adaptation', Reykjavik: Social Science Research Institute.
Kristinsson, G.H. (1999), 'Ur digrum sjodi', Reykjavik: Felagsvisindastofnun.
Langbein, L. & A. Lichtman (1978), 'Ecological Inference', Beverly Hills: Sage Publications.
Lipset, S. & S. Rokkan 1967. 'Cleavage Structures, Party Systems and Voter Alignments,' in Lipset & Rokkan (eds), *Party Systems and Voter Alignments*, New York: The Free Press.
*Logrjetta* (Reykjavik paper).
Moore, B. (1966), 'Social Origins of Dictatorship and Democracy', Boston: Beacon Press.
Rokkan, S. (1970), 'Citizens, Elections, Parties', Oslo: Universitetsforlaget.
Strom, K. (1986), 'Deferred Gratification And Minority Governments In Scandinavia', *Legislative Studies Quarterly*, XI, 4, 583-605.
*Timinn* (Progressive Party paper, published in Reykjavik).
Urwin, D. (1980), 'From Ploughshare to Ballotbox', Oslo-Bergen-Tromsø: Universitetsforlaget.
Wright, W. (1971), 'Comparative Party Models: Rational-Efficient and Party-Democracy', in W. Wright (ed.), *A Comparative Study of Party Organizations*, Columbus, Ohio: Charles E. Merrill.

# Conclusion
DAVID ARTER

Whilst there is a voluminous comparative literature on the other main European party families, especially the class-based Social Democrats, surprisingly little attention has been paid to another, and in many ways purer genus of class party - the *farmers' party*. This book has sought to remedy matters by providing case-studies of the 'life cycle' of five agrarian parties in the Nordic countries which, founded early in the twentieth century, have survived into the twenty-first. They are the three parties with a capital 'A', the Agrarian Parties in Finland, Norway and Sweden, along with Venstre in Denmark and the Icelandic Progressive Party, both of which emerged as farmers' parties in all but name. All five have necessarily had to adapt to a changing political environment and, as part of the modernisation process, the Finnish, Swedish and Norwegian parties changed their names to become Centre Parties between 1957 and 1965 with a view to developing an urban support base. What general conclusions, if any, can be drawn from the country chapters about the success of former farmers' parties in extending their support into the towns? Have a group of class parties successfully transformed themselves into catchall parties? Above all, what does the attempt at electoral adaptation indicate about the process of *party change*? This concluding chapter will attempt to draw the main threads together without repeating the main arguments of the country authors.

## The Origins and Emergence of Agrarian-Centre Parties

It was not so much the emergence of farmers' parties in the Nordic region – agrarian parties formed widely in Europe before and after the first world war – or, indeed, their subsequent electoral strength – outside Finland they were generally small parties – that was distinctive. Rather, it was their persistence until the late 1950s and 1960s. The peculiarity of the Agrarian parties of Finland, Norway and Sweden in short lay in their durability and their survival into predominantly industrialised societies.

Agrarian parties were not an exclusively Nordic phenomenon. They emerged from Ireland to Estonia. Some, like the Bulgarian party under Stamboliiski, had radical credos. The numerical supremacy of the peasantry, it was asserted, entitled that class to control of political society. Others represented the interests of the larger commercial farmers and were close to agricultural interest groups. There have been few attempts to classify the inter-war agrarian-peasant parties that met in the Green Internationals in Prague. In his study *The Politics of Agrarian Defence*, however, Derek Urwin distinguishes the interest-oriented agrarian parties of western Europe, which were primarily concerned with the *economic* position of the farmer from the peasantist parties of eastern Europe which were mainly concerned with the *social* and *political* position of the cultivator. He concludes that the Scandinavian parties 'were not peasantist in any real sense; rather they can be described as farmer's parties or interest-group parties' (Urwin 1973: 447). Yet at the rhetorical level at least, the Finnish and, to a lesser extent Swedish party, argued the moral as well as economic case for small farming. Indeed, in defending a vision of rural society based on the spirit of peasant *gemeinschaft* against the contamination of urban *gesellschaft*, they possessed at least some of the characteristics of the east European peasant parties. It is important not to draw too hard and fast a distinction.

Many of the first 'green wave' of parties became victims of the collapse of democracy and the rise of rightist authoritarianism by the 1930s and their subsequent re-emergence a decade later was snuffed out by the tightening grip of Communist rule. The Nordic agrarian parties in contrast operated in stable democracies only briefly disrupted (outside Finland and Sweden) by the Second World War. Unlike, say, Estonia, there was no need for the elite to decamp and form parties in exile, although in the Norwegian case at least the Agrarian leadership was to an extent tarred with the brush of collaboration with the occupying Nazis. A miniscule Farmers' Party (*Bondepartiet*) in Denmark – it gained its best result of 3.2 per cent and 5 parliamentary seats in 1935 – also became increasingly fascist and collaborationist in orientation (Fitzmaurice 1981: 18).

The conditions for the *emergence of strong agrarian parties* were set out in Lipset and Rokkan's seminal introduction to *Party Systems and Voter Alignments* in 1967. Strong agrarian parties emerged, it is claimed, when the following four conditions were met.

1. The cities and industrial centres were still numerically weak at the time of the decisive extensions of the suffrage.

2. The bulk of the agricultural population was active in family-sized farming and either owned farms or comprised legally protected leaseholders largely independent of socially superior landowners.

3. There were important cultural barriers between the countryside and the cities and much resistance to the incorporation of farm production into the capitalist economy of the cities.

4. The Catholic Church was without significant influence (Lipset and Rokkan 1967: 45).

The first condition relates to the extent of urbanisation and industrialisation at the point of mass democratisation and is easily measured. So, too, is the second, which concerns the social structure of the farm population and the extent of structural differentiation between its strata. The final condition presupposes the absence of other salient cleavages and, in particular, the absence of Catholicism as a factor mobilising the farm population. The third condition is more problematical. The existence of rural-urban cultural antagonisms – town and country were worlds apart and mutual suspicion rife – need not imply a reluctance to modernise agricultural production and become market-oriented producers.

The Nordic countries at the time the agrarian parties emerged were characterised by numerically significant primary sectors employing between about a third (Denmark), two-fifths (Norway, Iceland and Sweden) and four-fifths (Finland) of the economically active population (see Table 6:1). Moreover, the agricultural population comprised predominantly independent farmers rather than crofters and agricultural labourers. The extent of structural differentiation was smallest in Iceland and greatest in Norway and Sweden where there were significant economic disparities between the larger commercial producers in eastern and central Norway and Götaland in Sweden respectively and the poorer small farming areas elsewhere. The large farmers in turn invariably favoured protection. True, in Denmark the extent of socio-economic division within the agricultural population militated against a single class-based farmers' party and in fact two farm-based parties emerged. Thus, in 1885 28.2 per cent of landed proprietors – the large and middle-sized farmers – owned 89.2 per cent of the land whereas the 71.8 per cent of farmers who were smallholders owned only 10.8 per cent. The smallholders' association, which the latter formed, ultimately forged close ties with the Radicals. But nowhere in the Nordic region was there a situation comparable to say Austrian Bohemia at the turn of the century. There, 43 per cent of all farms comprised less than half an acre, whilst 0.1 per cent of the total number of proprietors owned no less than 35.6 per cent of the surface area of the province (Arter 1978: 23). The Schwartzenburg family alone owned one-third of the land (Drage 1909: 64). In Scandinavia in short there was a sizeable core class of middle-sized farm owners and this it was that largely provided the basis of agrarian party mobilisation. Throughout the region, moreover, the emergence of class-based farmers' parties was also facilitated by the absence of other major social cleavages such as religion or language. None the less, the Norwegian party made least headway in the so-called 'Bible Belt' area in south-west Norway – where the farmers tended to remain with the Liberals (*Venstre*) – whilst the Finnish party eschewed any attempt to appeal to farmers among the Swedish-language minority.

**Table 6.1  The Proportion of the Economically Active Population Employed in Agriculture in the Nordic Countries in 1920 (%)**

| | |
|---|---|
| Denmark | 33.0 |
| Finland | 81.5 |
| Iceland | 42.9 |
| Norway | 37.0 |
| Sweden | 40.0 |

The Finnish party was the only one of the agrarian parties with a capital 'A' to emerge before the first world war. It was a by-product of the superimposition at a stroke of mass democracy – universal suffrage, including women, and a proportional electoral system – on the predominantly rural society in the Grand Duchy of Finland. The abolition of the antiquated quadricameral Diet of Estates and the introduction of a single-chamber Eduskunta comprising two-hundred delegates were facilitated by Czar Nicholas II's October Manifesto in 1905. Until the achievement of independence in 1917, however, the Finnish Agrarians were a small party, their support concentrated on the medium-sized farmers in the north-west and south-east of the country. The party gained 5.8 per cent at the first fully democratic election in 1907 and averaged 7.9 per cent in the eight general elections between 1907 and 1917. Interestingly, the early Agrarian leadership was influenced to a degree by the populist

People's Party of America and insisted, in line with the latter, that the needs of small producers should be taken into greater account (Alanen 1976:717).

The Finnish, Swedish and Norwegian Agrarians all emerged as *mass membership parties*. In the Finnish and Swedish cases, this involved direct membership and there were no formal ties to interest organisations. They antedated the emergence of agricultural producers' organisations – although in the Swedish case the German agricultural lobby group *Bund der Landwirte* was an influence – and rested on a loose base formed by agricultural and co-operative societies and youth clubs (the latter non-partisan in character). The Norwegian party was also a mass organisation although, until the 1930s, its membership was indirect and through the agricultural producers' organisation. Indeed, the Norwegian party emerged as the political arm of *Landmandsforbundet* - which had been founded in 1896 – and represented a clear case of an *externally created party* in Duverger's terms. As Christensen has written in his chapter: 'the Agrarian Party was founded as nothing more than a branch of the Norwegian Union of Farmers'. In fact, the latter did not become politically neutral (officially at least) until 1946.

Of the two half sisters, Venstre in Denmark was originally a nineteenth century proto-party that split into two in 1905, the original party becoming de facto a party of family-sized farmers and acquiring a more functional character. Venstre's predecessor, The United Left, emerged as an internally created grouping in the 1870s with ties to the Society of Friends of the Peasants (*Bondevennesskabet*). There was a parallel in Sweden, since a Farmers' Party (*Lantmannapartiet*) emerged in the bicameral Riksdag in the 1860s. Venstre was not the political arm of an agricultural producers' organisation, although it did rest on a loose, albeit highly mobilised pre-existing base outside the legislature comprising co-operatives, farmers' associations and folk high schools. The high level of local associationalism in the countryside was reflected in the fact that Venstre did not create a national party organisation until 1929.

For nearly a quarter of a century after the acquisition of a Folketing (lower chamber) majority, The United Left worked to gain acceptance of the parliamentary principle. After the Radical split in 1905, Venstre became more exclusively a farmers' party and lost its urban support. Thus, whereas in 1903 Venstre gained 18 per cent of the Copenhagen vote, this had declined to a mere 1 per cent by 1918, although in the last mentioned year it was the second largest party with 30 per cent of the national vote. In 1918 Venstre polled 11 per cent in the large provincial towns and 18 per cent in the smaller provincial towns. Significantly, however, it was the largest party in Zealand and the other islands with 39 per cent and claimed no less than two-thirds of the vote in rural Jutland. Although becoming more of a single interest party after 1905, Venstre also became more liberal since the promotion of the class interests of the farmers (agrarianism) and liberalism went hand in hand. Put another way, the export needs of the farmers dictated a strong preference for free trade and competition, especially the removal of trade barriers.

In Iceland, as in Finland, the emergence of a farmers' party preceded the resolution of the national question when the existing parties proved incapable of accommodating the increased salience of economic cleavage lines. The Progressive Party brought together the two farmers' parties that had contested the 1916 elections – a Farmers' Party formed in the Althingi in 1912 and a loose grouping of Independent Farmers that emerged three years later. Together they won 20 per cent of the forty Althingi seats. As Kristinsson has emphasised, the conditions for the emergence of a class-specific farmers' party were thoroughly conducive. There was an absence of countervaling religious and ethnic cleavages. Icelandic society was predominantly rural and there was a sizeable primary sector. Before the first world war, 40 per cent of the economically active population was engaged in agriculture (excluding fishing) and 60 per cent lived in rural areas. There was an absence of accentuated structural differentiation between the agricultural strata and the farming population was relatively homogenous. Accordingly, there were no strains over the issue of protection, as in Denmark and Norway. Finally, the (plurality) electoral system was favourable to the emergence of a farmers' party in so far as it involved the overrepresentation of the rural constituencies. Yet importantly, politics was dominated by the independence issue and attitudes to Denmark and there was nothing inevitable about the emergence of a class-based farmers' party in Iceland. The conditions created by war provided the catalyst, since they exacerbated urban-rural antagonisms and made demands of the existing political forces that they were unable to cope with. Indeed, whilst the Farmers' Party was a grouping of existing parliamentarians, the Independent Farmers were fuelled by the mood of farm protest generated by a proposal to levy a tax on the extra profits going to agriculture and fisheries on account of war. That the Progressive Party tapped a rich electoral seam can be seen in the way it had gained 26.5 per cent of the vote by 1923.

Unlike the Agrarian parties with a capital 'A', the Progressive Party in Iceland is best regarded as a *cadre party* rather than a mass party and was based on a network of local personalities. It was a 'network party' in Grímsson's phrase (Kristinsson 1991:113). True, a national organisation was created in 1931. But prior to the second world war in particular, informal contacts between the party and the co-operatives served in many respects as an effective substitute for an effective membership organisation (Kristinsson 1991:118). The co-operative movement gave its financial backing to various party projects, especially the party organ, *Tíminn*, although there is no evidence of direct financial support to the national party organisation.

The *electoral breakthrough* of farmers' parties was tied to the emergence of issues that heightened the perceived differences between rural producers and urban consumers and thereby served to mobilise a wider body of farmers. Of particular importance, as Gunnar Helgi Kristinsson has noted, was the food crisis during the first world war. Thus, the decisive condition for the electoral breakthrough of the Farmers' League (*Bondeförbundet*) and Agrarian League (*Jordbrukarnas Riksförbund*) in Sweden in 1917 was the food situation during the war (Kristinsson 1991: 34). In Norway, too, during the war, there was a growing feeling among farmers that government policies favoured industry at the expense of agriculture, consumers at the expense of producers and part-time smallholders at the expense of full-time farmers. In addition, compulsory cultivation was unpopular and the government was thought to give in too easily to the demands for state intervention and social reforms (Kristinsson 1991:48). Rising prices in Iceland following the outbreak of war in Europe prompted calls for governmental intervention to improve the situation of the town population. Proposals to that end split parliament broadly speaking into farmers and non-farmers and created the groundswell of agrarian protest that formed the basis of class-specific mobilisation (Kristinsson 1991: 83).

The introduction of PR facilitated the parliamentary breakthrough of farmers' parties in Finland, Norway and Sweden. In Norway and Iceland, moreover, the electoral system institutionalised the rural-urban divide and led to the over-representation of rural areas. In Norway, two-thirds of all seats were allocated to rural areas. In contrast, the Danish Venstre, officially founded in 1910, antedated the introduction of PR in 1915 and this affected it deleteriously.

The *electoral consolidation* of the Nordic farmers' parties varied in scale from one country to the next. In the Finnish case there was a period of steep electoral growth in the late 1920s and the Agrarians became the largest party in 1929. Several factors might explain this. First, there was the Agrarians' role in the state-building process, since the form of government question mobilised the pro-republican bumpkins against the bigwigs in the towns, most of whom favoured a constitutional monarchy. Put another way, the Agrarians' emergence as a national (rather than regionally based) party in 1919 (with 19.7 per cent of the vote) was integrally linked to its stance on a question of 'high politics' (the nature of the new constitution) and not to an essentially economic class issue. Thereafter, land reforms over the first decade of independence, designed in the Jeffersonian tradition as measures of social engineering, significantly bolstered the class base of agrarianism. According to Jefferson, small farmers are the most valuable citizens, tied to their country, wedded to its liberty and a guarantee of its vigorous health (Malone 1948:383-384). Finally, the economic crisis in agriculture pointed up the contrasting interests of town and country and enabled the Agrarian Party to achieve its best-ever poll of 27.3 per cent in 1930.

## The Political Impact of the Nordic Farmers' Parties

In the foregoing chapters, the political impact of the individual agrarian parties tends to be viewed in terms of 1) the extent of their participation in government and/or 2) their involvement as opposition parties in legislative coalitions. In relation to their participation in government, the Finnish Agrarians and Icelandic Progressives stand apart from the rest. The size and ruling status of the Finnish party was striking. It was the largest party with 23 per cent of the electorate when, the last of the Nordic Agrarians, it changed its name in 1965. Its average poll at general elections between 1919 and 1962 was more than double that of the Norwegian party and nearly double that of the Swedish Agrarians. Moreover, it was a 'genuine pivot party' in Hans Keman's term or a 'hinge group' in that it was *the* dominant governing party (Arter 1979). As such it played a significant role in the completion of state building in 1917-1919, an extensive land reform programme in the 1920s and the resettlement of the displaced Karelian population following two wars with the Soviet Union between 1939 and 44. Until 1966, it was the Agrarians, not the Social Democrats, that were the natural governing party in Finland. Indeed, an historic paradox need emphasis. The Finnish party emerged as an anti-Establishment grouping opposed to the political power of the socio-economic elites in the towns and the capital city in particular. By the time it changed its name in 1965, however, the Agrarian Party had become *the* Establishment party in Finland. It controlled governments, had a special relationship with

President Kekkonen – and, accordingly, a special rapport with Moscow – and its nominees were strategically placed at the head of central boards and agencies.

The Icelandic Progressive Party has also been a regular governing party that has occupied a pivotal position in coalition building. Between 1927 – when it brought down the Conservative government and formed a minority cabinet with the support of the Social Democrats – and 2000, the Progressives have been in opposition less than one-third of the time and have held the post of Prime Minister for thirty years. In general, majority coalitions (the norm) in Iceland have involved the participation of the Progressive Party. Above all, the Progressive Party has pursued a line of 'pragmatic centrism' (see Kristinsson's chapter) keeping its options open to left and right. Almost inevitably perhaps, there have been occasions when real differences have surfaced in its ranks regarding the appropriate direction of the party. In 1956, the Progressives and Social Democrats entered an electoral alliance with a view to winning a parliamentary majority and, thereafter, possibly merging the two parties. Whilst the attempt failed, nearly two decades elapsed before the Progressives entered another coalition with the Independence Party. In 1974 the radicals in the Youth Organisation broke with the mother party and many joined the short-lived Union of Liberals and Leftists. The leadership line was that the Progressive Party was a centre party, a position from which it could promote its core interests by working with either left or right. On the point of pragmatic centrism, Kristinsson notes that although the Progressives at times spoke as though the Independence Party was the main enemy, when it came to the crunch, they were unwilling to sacrifice the advantages of a centre position on the altar of radicalism.

In Sweden, the merger of the two farmers' groups did not signify any attempt to broaden the class base of *Bondeförbundet* and the 'class option' was pursued until 1943. The refurbishment of the party's name in 1943 to 'The Rural Party Farmers' League' signified the adoption of the 'rural party option' in Christensen's terms. The period before the adoption of the title 'Centre Party' in 1958 was what Widfeldt describes as the 'limited strategy' phase. It was based on protectionism in terms of subsidies to farm products and an improvement in the infrastructure (health care and schools) in rural areas. Yet the 'limited strategy' phase was not unsuccessful in respect of political influence. The historic class compromise between the ruling Social Democrats and the opposition-based Agrarians in 1933 – the so-called 'cow trade deal' – laid the foundations in a period of deep recession for the development of the post-war welfare state. Moreover, although the Swedish party enjoyed nothing like the perennial ruling status of its Finnish counterpart, and was very much the junior coalition partner, it was in fact out of government for only six years between 1936 and 1957.

Although the last of the agrarian parties by name to emerge, the Norwegian party made the greatest initial electoral impact, polling 13.1 per cent at its first general election in 1921 and gaining seventeen Storting seats. The Norwegian Agrarians proceeded to form a troubled minority cabinet between 1931and 1933 (it had the backing of only 25 out of the 150 parliamentary seats) and entered into a similar type of deal with the ruling Labour Party in 1935 as its sister party in Sweden. The farmers were granted measures of protection in return for social policy measures of benefit to the blue-collar workers. However, unlike Finland and Sweden, the Norwegian Agrarians never entered a 'red-green' coalition with the Labour Party and the political impact of the party must be regarded as rather marginal.

Finally, Venstre enjoyed its heyday and started to decline before the farmers' parties elsewhere in the Nordic region were really formed. It was the leading party until being overtaken by the Social Democrats at the 1924 general election. Boasting a lower chamber majority for much of the period 1870-1910, Venstre, like the British Liberals at broadly the same time, was instrumental in the passage of all major social policy legislation before the first world war. It was also party to an historic package on social reform with the Social Democrats in 1933. However, from the completion of mass democracy and the introduction of PR in 1915 to the so-called 'earthquake election' in 1973, which rocked the traditional four-party system in Denmark, Venstre enjoyed only limited participation in government. In fact between 1924 and 1973 it took part in only four governments – 1926-1929, 1945-1947, 1950-1953 and 1968-1971.

The Scandinavian farmers' parties were 'relevant' in forming legislative coalitions with the Social Democratic Labour parties in the 1930s and these historic 'red-green' class compromises laid the foundations for the celebrated post-war welfare state. But an accelerated decline in the size of the core class of farmers, coupled with deep-seated economic change, dictated the need for consideration to be given to a strategy for *electoral adaptation* in the post-war period.

## The Modernisation of the Nordic Agrarian Parties

In the case of farmers' parties, modernisation involved responding to the twin processes of industrialisation and urbanisation by taking steps – a new name, programme or electoral strategy – designed to move the party in a catchall direction. In particular there was a concern to penetrate the increasingly urban electorate. Moves to broaden their class base usually emanated from the youth wing of the agrarian parties and met with variable resistance from the main body of the rank-and-file. The Swedish party had a genuine modernisation strategy, the Norwegian party was in no hurry to change its ways, whilst Venstre in Denmark, despite its long-term electoral decline, never engaged in a debate about a fundamental modernisation at all. The Finnish party was the last to change its name in 1965, but a new programme antedated this by four years. In the context of modernisation, Iceland is the deviant case, since the Progressive Party sought to attract the urban vote much earlier than its sister parties elsewhere in the Nordic region. However, this was never part of a pre-conceived or concerted strategy.

The Progressives' attempt to win urban support came in two stages. They were both facilitated by the fact that the party's name provided no barrier to broadening its support base. Also relevant was the fact that the Progressive Party possessed a very loose organisation which allowed [if only by default] internal groupings considerable freedom to operate. As noted, there was no national party organisation until 1931. The previous year, a group of middle class radicals ran a list at the local elections in Reykjavik. It was headed by the newly appointed chief of police, Hermann Jónasson, gained 12 per cent of the vote and returned two of the fifteen members on the Reykjavik city council. It was marketed as a centre party list directed against the big financial capital which, it was claimed, controlled the capital city. The radicals won a similar proportion of the vote (12.7 per cent) at the constituency election in 1931. The radicals' activity in Reykjavik, and their leader, Jonas Jonsson's opposition to co-operation with the Independence Party, however, split the Progressives' ranks – they were seen to be hijacking the party by capturing its central committee – and a splinter Farmers' Party, led by Tryggvi Thorhallsson, gained 6.4 per cent in 1934.

By the late 1940s, in response to increasing urbanisation, the Progressive Party again sought to attract town voters. Symbolically, it gained its first Reykjavik MP in 1949 and, more importantly, began to make inroads into the small rural towns. Especially in the 1960s and 1970s, nationalism was a major component of the Progressive Party's modernisation strategy. The party in short took a leftist stance on such issues as the US military base in Iceland, the fisheries dispute with Britain and the question of foreign economic influence in Iceland. Such a strategy was designed to attract support from moderately left-wing but non-communist nationalists who were critical of Iceland's political, military and economic position in the Western bloc (Kristinsson 1991:189). The tactic was successful (at least before the exodus to the Union of Liberals and Leftists) and, in the 1960s, the Progressive Party was the second largest party in the towns, surpassing the People's Alliance and Social Democrats.

In Denmark, the broad electoral trend for Venstre was one of decline following the election of 1929 when it polled almost 30 per cent of the votes. The decline was accentuated in the 1930s and, whilst the party's fortunes revived in the 1950s, the support curve from 1960 to the late 1980s was again downwards. By 1981 Venstre's vote had fallen to 11.3 per cent and in 1987 to 10.5 per cent. Despite the long-term decline in its support, there was no debate in Venstre about a fundamentally new approach. Indeed, in 1963 it emphasised its traditional liberal credentials by adding the suffix 'Denmark's Liberal Party'. True, with a view to presenting a credible challenge to the Social Democrats, Venstre, as the largest non-socialist party until 1968, engaged in extended discussion about the possibility of a merger between itself and the Conservatives. But this ultimately came to nothing. One possible reason for the absence of a modernisation debate was the relatively frequent achievement (at least from the late 1970s) of its primary objective of participation in government. It is worth noting, too, that in 1957, the year the Swedish Agrarians changed their name, Venstre polled 25.1 per cent, its best result for decades. In the 1970s, when the Swedish Centre made its greatest inroads into the towns, Venstre's performance in the urban areas reflected the overall volatility of the electorate. It gained a creditable 12.3 per cent in Copenhagen in 1975, but only 2.9 per cent in the capital city two years later.

When the three Nordic Agrarian parties with a capital 'A' changed their names to become Centre parties, they did so when their fortunes at the polls were sharply contrasting. The Swedish party did so from a position of electoral weakness. It was both a small party and, at the general election the previous year, had contrived its worst-ever result of 9.4 per cent. For some in the party electoral necessity was the mother of party modernisation. As Gunnar Hedlund, the party leader since 1948, put it: 'The number of real farmers is about 15 per cent of the population and is declining at the rate of about six thousand per year. The countryside, that is those communities (villages) with less than two-hundred inhabitants, comprises no more than 30 per cent of the total population. Should we abandon the 70 per cent and compete with four other parties for the remaining 30 per cent?' (Jonnergård 1985:20). The modernisers, particularly in the party's Youth Organisation, favoured a strategy of targeting small firms. In contrast, opponents of a change of name argued that the party had the potential to become more of a class party. In the words of Axel Rubbestad, 'not much more than half the farmers support the Agrarian Party and it is crucial to try and attract more (Jonnergård 1985: 20).The change of name in 1957 was not the first in the party's history. At its national conference in Västerås, the Swedish party had complemented the 'class option' with the 'rural option' and adopted the title 'Rural Party-Farmers' League' (*Landsbygdspartiet bondeförbundet*). Under pressure from the Youth Organisation SLU, and its secretary, Lars Eliasson, a greater emphasis was given to rural questions. Indeed there was a group in the party that wanted exclusively to use the name 'Rural Party'. At Karlstad in 1957 the hybrid Centre Party-Farmers' League was adopted by a relatively narrow margin of 118-71 against Rural Party. The party conference the following year at Ronneby confirmed the name Centre Party.

In addition to changing its name, the Swedish party developed a wider modernisation strategy. A new programme was adopted in 1959 – targetting small businesses in particular – and by the 1970s the party appealed on the basis of the holy trinity of 'decentralism, environmentalism and market liberalism'. Moreover, with a view to winning urban support, the Swedish Centre distanced itself from the Social Democrats and assumed an unambiguously non-socialist alignment. There was at very least symbolic importance in the election of its first MP in Stockholm in 1964.

Unlike the Swedish party, electoral support for the Norwegian Agrarians showed an upward trend when the modernisation of the party began in the late 1950s. Consequently, the incentives for a fundamental recasting of party policy were less obvious than in the Swedish case. Furthermore, the greater competition for the farm vote in Norway made radical change too risky. Hence the strategy adopted was of trying to attract the smaller farmers that had traditionally supported the Labour Party. Indeed, the tendency was for the Norwegian Centre Party to gain a stronger electoral hold on the farmers in the 1960s and 1970s. The new catchall name led ironically to the party developing a more accentuated class identity. All in all, the Norwegian Agrarians were reluctant to modernise, divided over the change of name and did not engage in significant programmatic renewal.

Their reluctance was reflected in the extraordinary conference in June 1959 when the hybrid 'Centre Party-Agrarian Party' defeated the mongrel combination 'Centre Party-Rural Party' by 103 votes to 33, although in practice the Agrarian Party suffix was quickly forgotten. A new statement of principles was not formulated until 1965 (and then it was taken virtually wholesale from the Swedish party's 1959 programme) whilst urbanisation was scarcely acknowledged until the 1970s and the first action programme for the cities did not see the light of day until 1977. Christensen identifies three alternatives available to the Norwegian Agrarians in the late 1950s – the 'class party option', the 'rural party option' and the 'catchall party option' He notes that in the 1960s, after the change of name, the Centre Party pursued the rural party option. Curiously, the Oslo Agrarian Party, an independent section within the party, fought elections in the capital city in 1930 and 1933, albeit on a more radical rightist platform than the mother party (Kristinsson 1991:137). However, it was not until 1993 that the Norwegian Agrarian-Centre elected its first MP in the national capital when Arne Haukvik was returned to the Storting with 4.4 per cent of the vote.

The Finnish Agrarian Party changed its name from a position of notable electoral strength as it was the largest single party in 1965. This was slightly deceptive as the 1962 election was held in the immediate wake of [the former Agrarian] President Kekkonen's successful resolution of the Finno-Soviet 'Note Crisis'. In fact, there had been ephemeral discussion of modernising the party from 1950 onwards and this gained momentum following the Agrarians' setbacks in the 1958 general election. As in Norway, there were elements of institutional diffusion in the decision to rename the party. The Swedish party's new title had led to electoral gains, it was noted, whilst Virolainen, the party chairman, cited Venstre in Denmark as a model of how an agrarian-rural party could develop into a nationally based party.

Unlike the Norwegian Agrarians, there was little opposition to the Finnish party's change of name at an extraordinary party conference in Kuopio in October 1965. Earlier a grassroots questionnaire of members revealed that only in one of the party's organisational districts – Varsinais-Suomi in south-west Finland – was there a narrow majority of 50.6 per cent of local branches in favour of retaining the old name. In Kuopio, the chairman of the Varsinais-Suomi district organisation, Einari Karvetti from Naantali, condemned the unseemly haste in jettisoning the old name and argued that a small Agrarian Party would be better equipped to make its voice heard than a large and disparate Centre Party. He continued that a change of name would open the door to those young men – presently gaining space in the party's capital city organ – who want to alter the party programme so as to gain power for themselves. He concluded that: 'In twenty or thirty years time, there will be nothing left of the Agrarians' ideological foundation' (*Suomenmaa* 18.1.1965).

It needs emphasis that, prior to the pursuit of strategies designed to facilitate the adaptation of the parties to an increasingly urbanised electorate, the Finnish, Norwegian and Swedish Agrarians consolidated their class base by overhauling their organisations and promoting their positions as mass membership parties. Put another way, there was a period of intensive organisation-building after the Second World War. In the Finnish case, this was not least to meet the threat posed by re-legalised Communism in its northern strongholds. In the Norwegian case, it was part of the process of reconstructing the party and working to erase memories of the unhappy associations with the occupying Nazis. It will be recalled that some Agrarian leaders considered it advisable for the party not to contest the 1945 election and to wait until 1949 when, it was hoped, memories of the war would have faded. In the last-mentioned year, a separate Youth Organisation was founded and this was followed in 1953 by a Women's Organisation. Membership grew from 29,000 in 1947 to 64,000 ten years later. In the Swedish case, the organisational drive was designed to complement its refurbished name, adopted in 1943, and subsequent concern to mobilise support in the countryside generally and not simply among farmers. The Swedish party's membership virtually doubled between 1940 and 1950. It remains the second largest membership party although its membership is ageing and it contrived a significantly lower degree of organisation among non-agrarian voters during its expansionist years in the late 1960s and early 1970s.

## The Electoral Profile of the Agrarian-Centre Parties since their Change of Name

In the case of the Swedish Agrarian-Centre, the re-named party developed rapidly in a catchall direction. Its support grew from 13.4 per cent in 1964 to 25.1 per cent in 1973, the best result (thus far) of any of the re-designated Nordic farmers' parties. Between 1968 and 1979, the Centre overtook the Liberals to become the second largest party and headed three different coalitions between 1976 and 1982. It led the challenge to the Social Democrats' governmental dominance, promoted a judicious mix of regionalism (decentralisation) and environmentalism, broadened its support base and penetrated the towns. It appealed in particular to small firms and white-collar workers. The proportion of the party's vote comprising salaried employees virtually trebled between 1960 and 1968, whilst no less than 38 per cent of small entrepreneurs voted for the Centre in 1973. This was the 'successful adaptation' phase. However, the significant amounts of extra support it built up in the late 1960s and first half of the 1970s, though impressive, proved unstable. The growth appeared 'hot house growth' largely contingent on a *single issue association*.

In the late 1950s, the issue was the supplementary pensions' question. Thus, in 1957, the Centre Party's alternative in the supplementary pensions' referendum was supported by 15 per cent of voters and was part of a strategy directed at small businesses. The party opposed any scheme that would jeopardise the small entrepreneur's chance of accumulating capital and was rewarded with the support of one quarter of the small business vote and 6.1 per cent of the urban electorate. The success for the Centre at the 1958 general election created the backdrop for extensive changes in the new party programme, which was adopted without dispute. Ironically, when in 1976 the Centre claimed the post of Prime Minister for the first time in forty years, its percentage support had already fallen back on three years earlier and there began a process of what turned out to be radical decline. Widfeldt identifies two particular factors in the 'decline phase'. First, there was the final collapse of the merger talks with the Liberals in 1973. More crucially, there was Fälldin's 'betrayal' of his commitment, made during the 1976 election campaign, not to commission any more nuclear power reactors and to phase out nuclear power by 1985. Single-issue association in short proved a double-edged sword for the Swedish Centre. The pensions' issue benefited the newly renamed party. The commitment to winding down nuclear power contributed to the surging growth in the early 1970s, but disillusion quickly set in once it became apparent that the Centre in government was unable to deliver on its promises.

By the 1990s, the Swedish Centre Party had shrunk dramatically to a mere 5.1 per cent at the last general election in 1998. In that year, only 37 per cent of farmers voted for the party compared with 55 per cent four years earlier (Allmänna valen 1994:155). There was somewhat greater support among the larger farmers (with between 21-100 hectares of arable and 101-400 hectares of forest land) than the smaller farmers (Partisympatiundersökninger maj 1998). As in Finland, the EU issue had been a divisive one for the Swedish party. Although the final decision of the Swedish Centre was to recommend EU membership, about 75 per cent of its members were against accession and those areas such as Dalarna, Jämtland and Västernorrland – where the farmers were dependent on forestry – were particularly opposed. In an exit poll held in conjunction with the EU referendum in November 1994, it emerged that 55 per cent of Centre voters had voted against the EU compared with 45 per cent who were in favour (Interview with Kjell Andersson 17.8.1998). Plainly, the Swedish party did not have the platform for the type of *single issue growth* its Norwegian sister party derived (however briefly) from its unequivocal opposition to 'Europe'.

The Finnish party has remained by far the strongest of the Nordic Agrarian-Centre Parties. It was the largest single party at the 1991 general election with virtually one-quarter of the vote and was the largest non-socialist party at all three general elections in the 1990s. At the local government elections of October 2000 the Centre again emerged as the largest single party with 28.8 per cent of the poll. Particularly in the rural towns in its stronghold areas in northern and eastern Finland, the Centre has succeeded in increasing its support significantly since the 1960s. The towns of Vaasa and Seinäjoki are cases in point. In its core areas up country the Finnish party is a catchall party. However, in the capital city Helsinki it has never exceeded 6.1 per cent of the vote and there is a strong regional bias in its support.

Unlike the greenhouse growth of the Swedish party in the late 1960s and early 1970s, the Finnish party's change of name was followed by a series of election defeats. By 1972 it had plunged to 16.4 per cent and remained at 16-17 per cent in the late 1970s and throughout the 1980s. Certainly the phenomenon of rural depopulation did not (initially at least) benefit the Centre and there was no wave of 'imported centrism' to parallel the 'imported agrarianism' that gave the Agrarians a base in areas of the south in the late 1940s after the loss of much of Karelia. In contrast to the displaced Karelians who mostly remained farmers, those who moved south in the 1970s mainly took blue-collar jobs where a 'leftist climate' prevailed and they were quickly unionised. They were also disillusioned with, and blamed the Centre for the agricultural rationalisation programme (packaging smallholdings) which displaced them from the land. Indeed, in contrast to the short-lived breakaway Farmers' Party in Iceland in the 1930s, the populist Finnish Rural Party, led by the former Agrarian Veikko Vennamo, which capitalised on the disgruntlement of the smallholders in 'forgotten Finland', hit the Centre Party hard for two decades. This can be seen in the fact that, whereas in the early 1970s 63 per cent of farmers in

Denmark voted for Venstre and 65 per cent and 83 per cent of farmers voted for the Norwegian and Swedish Centre parties, the figure for Finland was only 52 per cent (Worre 1980:302). During the 1970s, moreover, according to Paavo Väyrynen, the Centre also lacked a clear ideological identity. There was a widespread perception of a close association between the Centre Party and the agricultural producers' organisation MTK. Not least, the party suffered from an 'anti-Kekkonen effect' for the long-serving president contrived to keep the Centre in government almost irrespective of the election result and at times the inclinations of the party itself.

A merger (short-lived) with the Liberals in 1982 (cf. the failure of merger talks in Sweden) enabled the Finnish party to elect its first MP in Helsinki in 1983, about twenty years after the Swedish party, and this election marked something of a turning point for the Centre. When asked to identify the watershed years in the history of the Agrarian-Centre Party, the present chairman, Esko Aho, identified three. 1964 saw the advent as chair of the arch-moderniser, Virolainen; the 1983 election saw the Centre emerge from Kekkonen's shadow (he retired through ill health in 1981); and 1994 witnessed the Centre vote in favour of EU membership. According to Aho this last development meant that the Centre was no longer a class party dominated by the farmers' interests (Interview with Esko Aho 15.8.1998). Finally, unlike its Swedish sister under Fälldin, the Finnish Centre Party has never nailed its colours to the non-socialist mast; rather it has sought to bargain with the parties to both left and right.

The Norwegian Centre Party, like its Swedish counterpart, has experienced steady electoral decline, arrested only when it has been able to present itself as the leading opponent of EU integration. Put another way, the Norwegian Agrarian Party was founded as a single issue party and its successor, the Centre Party, flourished electorally as a single issue (anti-EC/EU) party at the polls in 1972 and 1993. In the first-mentioned year it gained 11.1 per cent and in the latter 16.8 per cent, compared with an all-time low of 6.5 per cent four years earlier. In 1993 it became the second largest party and recorded the best vote in the Agrarian-Centre's history. Indeed, vigorously led by Anne Inger Lahnstein, the Centre was the only party other than Labour to gain representation in all twenty constituencies. It profited in particular from the fact that in northern Norway anti-EU opinion was running at 68 per cent compared with only 18 per cent of the electorate who were in favour of Norwegian membership of the EU (Madeley 1994:197-203).

However, the Norwegian party did not succeed, either after 1972 or 1993, in integrating the anti-EU interests into a broad, lasting coalition.

Neither did it attract new members as a result of its dogmatically anti-European stance. Membership fell from 61,726-56,542 between 1971 and 1976 and from 48,503 to 46,627 between 1989 and 1995. Indeed, as Christensen has noted, the EC/EU issue reactivated two deep-seated historical cleavages -- the centre-periphery axis and the rural-urban axis. Although the anti-European stance yielded a substantial electoral dividend, it projected the party as very much a class party of the farmers and rendered more difficult the task of penetrating the urban centre. True, by 1997, the preponderant share of the [modest] Centre vote derived from 'the new middle class'. None the less, it still appears mainly a party of and for the rural periphery, holding on to an extremely loyal but dwindling clientele.

As Andersen and Jensen note in their chapter, Venstre, despite its name, was traditionally a farmers' party based on a strong core group of medium-sized farmers that were extremely loyal to the party. It was not, to be sure, the only farmers' party in Denmark, but it was the dominant one at the polls. At general elections between 1964 and 1998, an average of 63 per cent of farmers voted Venstre compared with 9.2 per cent for the Conservatives and 7.5 per cent for the Radical Liberals. Yet whereas in the 1960s over half the Venstre vote derived from farmers, by 1998 only 7 per cent did so. Venstre is no longer a class party. Rather, the contributors argue that it has become a catchall party in the limited sense of piecing together an unusual coalition of farmers, blue-collar workers and the urban middle class. Venstre has developed particular strengths among senior private sector employees (managers and executives), two fifths of whom voted for the party in the 1994 and 1998 general elections. As in the case of the Finnish Centre, Venstre, from the mid-1990s, has also been the largest Danish party in terms of its membership.

Like Venstre, the Icelandic Progressive Party's support was initially almost exclusively confined to farmers. It was a class party *de facto* even though just under half the farmers supported the Independence Party and the political cohesion of the farmers was bifurcated. As Svanur Kristjánsson has observed about the period 1929-1944: 'In general, the Progressive Party did not try to appeal to manual workers; the party defined itself as a party of farmers' (Kristjánsson 1979:41). The Progressives, moreover, received less support in those districts where a high proportion of the economically active population was engaged in fishing, the only exception being S-Múlasýsla in the east of the country. In short, in the *rural party system* there was competition between the Independence Party and the Progressive Party, with the latter faring best in the north and east of the country where the co-operative movement was strongest (Kristjánsson

1979:37). The co-operative connection was particularly important in explaining the strength of the Progressives in the northern town of Akureyri.

With the name not acting as a barrier, the Progressives also picked up significant support in the towns from the 1930s onwards. They gained 12.5 per cent in the urban south-west in 1959 and approximately the same level forty years later. In the elections of 1963 and 1967, the Progressives polled over 28 per cent, significantly in excess of the support of any of the other farmers' parties in the Nordic region. Since then there has been an overall decline in support for the party and in 1978 – following a four-year coalition with the Independence Party – it plummeted to 16.9 per cent. Excluding the 1956 election, when the Progressives ran in an electoral alliance with the Social Democrats – and did not put up candidates in many constituencies – this was their worst result since 1919. At the last general election in 1999, the Progressives polled 18.4 per cent at a time when 60 per cent of voters were resident in the urban centre of Reykjavik and its hinterland. Clearly the Progressive Party is no longer a class party. Equally, as Kristinsson observes, its rather amorphous occupational profile outside agriculture may be used to characterise the Progressives as a catchall party, although, he adds, they are no different from the other Icelandic parties in this respect.

## Conclusions

Agrarian parties cannot easily be dismissed as relics of a bygone era – that is, as 'period pieces' of little interest and importance in the present post-industrial age of electronic politics. Across the 'Iron Curtain' countries, the collapse of Communism paved the way for the resurgence of agrarian-peasant parties, *inter alia* the Smallholders' Party in Hungary, the Peasant Parties in Poland and Croatia, the Agrarian Union in Bulgaria and the Rural Centre in Estonia. The Swedish Centre took the initiative in organising this grouping into an international network of centre parties that also included the Lithuanian Centre Union and Edgar Savisaar's Centre Party (modelled directly on the Swedish example) in Estonia (Arter 1996). Democratisation in short has spawned a revival of agrarian parties, some new, but some with a history dating back to the inter-war years.

Nor can the Nordic agrarian parties be consigned to the dustbin of history. Either as Centre parties, or still with their original names, all five parties dealt with in this collection remain highly 'relevant' in the Sartorian sense of having participated in governing coalitions in the last decade. As an opposition party, the Swedish party also formed part of a *legislative coalition* with the ruling Social Democrats between 1995 and 1997. Outside Iceland, moreover, all retain real organisational strength and in the Finnish and Danish cases are currently the largest membership parties. In three of the countries in the region, Denmark, Finland and Iceland, the parties attract the backing of about one-fifth of the electorate and it is clear that whilst most farmers still vote for the former farmers' parties, most of their voters are no longer farmers. Indeed, as Gunnar Helgi Kristinsson has noted in his volume on *Farmers' Parties*, 'the [Nordic] farmers' parties have shown a remarkable ability to maintain the support of the old groups, whilst increasing their support among new ones,' (Kristinsson 1991:229). But what do the five chapters in the present book indicate about the electoral adaptation of agrarian parties and, by extension, what does their performance suggest about the phenomenon of party change?

Originally class parties for the agrarian population, all five Nordic farmers' parties have *at varying times* developed in a catchall direction and attracted significant urban support. The Icelandic and Swedish parties did so in the 1960s and 1970s and the Danish, Finnish and, to a much lesser extent, Norwegian parties did so in the 1990s. Urban growth has been associated *inter alia* with new ideological directions – left nationalism in Iceland, nationalism (opposition to European integration) in Norway, environmentalism in Sweden and Thatcher-style neo-liberalism in Denmark. Only in Finland has the Agrarian-Centre party's progress in the rural towns not clearly been linked to a period of accentuated 'ideologisation'.

In his chapter, Christensen notes that political parties seldom go out of business. Yet in Norway and Sweden the parties are on the 'critical list' and could well lose their parliamentary footing at the next general elections. The Norwegian Centre averaged 5.7 per cent in the polls over summer 2000 whilst the Swedish party is presently (September 2000) below the four per cent qualifying threshold for Riksdag representation. Elsewhere – in Finland in the 1970s and 1980s and Denmark until the late 1980s – there have been periods of electoral decline – for the time being reversed – whilst in Iceland it is concluded that the Progressive Party's pivotal centrist position may be threatened by diminishing support. In short, at a time when the farm population is in irreversible decline and constitutes only a tiny fraction of voters, the former farmers' parties have struggled to stabilise non-agrarian support and to build durable alliances with significant sections of the predominantly urban electorate. They have attracted at times considerable support outside the *classe gardée,* but, importantly, not on a regularised basis. Clearly, the relative weakness of their organisations in the towns, has not assisted their cause. Nor has the heightened volatility of urban voters. Clearly too, the support Venstre currently attracts from the senior echelons of the private sector suggests at least the possibility of replacing, or at least complementing the original core class with another. But in this last case, judgement should be reserved. Two or three successful elections do not make a thesis. Rather, a longer perspective is necessary, and this would suggest that the way to successful electoral adaptation is long and hard. Parties, like leopards, find it difficult to change their spots and, in the case of the Nordic agrarian parties, lasting party change in the electoral arena has not (yet) been achieved. In sum, the parties remain strong in the farmyards but have not enough loyal supporters in the city squares.

## References

Alanen, A. (1976), 'Santeri Alkio', WSOY: Porvoo.
*Allmänna valen 1994* Del 3 Special undersökningar Statistiska Centralbyrån: Stockholm 1995.
Arter, D. (1978), 'Bumpkin Against Bigwig', *The Emergence of a Green Movement in Finnish Politics*, Tampere University: Tampere.
Arter, D., 'The Finnish Centre Party: Profile of a "Hinge Group"', *West European Politics* 2, 1:108-127.
Arter, D. (1996), 'Parties and Democracy in the Post-Soviet Republics, *The Case of Estonia*', Dartmouth: Aldershot.
Drage, G. (1909), 'Austria-Hungary', London.
Fitzmaurice, J (1981), 'Politics in Denmark', Hurst: London.
Jonnergård, G (1984), *Så blev det Centerpartiet* LTs förlag: Stockholm.
Kristjánsson, S. (1979), 'The Electoral Bases of the Icelandic Independence Party 1929-1944', *Scandinavian Political Studies* 2, 1, 1979: 31-52.
Kristinsson, G.H. (1991), *'Farmers' Parties:* A study in electoral adaptation', Félagsvísindastofnun Háskóla Íslands.
Madeley, J. (1994), 'Norway's 1993 Election: The Road to Europe Blocked?', *West European Politics* 17, 2: 197-203.
*Partisympatiundersökningen maj* (1998), Statistiska centralbyrån: Stockholm 1998, pp. 31-32.
Urwin, D. (1973), *'From Ploughshare to Ballotbox'*, Universitetsforlaget: Oslo-Bergen-Tromsø.
Worre, T. (1980), 'Class Parties and Class Voting in the Scandinavian Countries', *Scandinavian Political Studies* 3, 4: 299-320.

9781138258297